While reading this book, be  *will start to supernaturally (..., ... bag, bank account, house, car and other unexpected places. Strikingly, you will find some of it slipped within the pages of this book - Apostle Gabriel Coke*

Unveiling
The mystery
of
MIRACLE
MONEY

A DIVINE REVELATION OF HOW TO RECEIVE MIRACLE MONEY AND MANIFEST IT IN THE NATURAL REALM

APOSTLE FREQUENCY REVELATOR

Global Destiny
Publishing House

Copyright © 2017 Apostle Frequency Revelator.

All rights reserved. No part of this book may be reproduced, stored in a retrieval system or transmitted in any form or by any means, electronic or mechanical, photographic (photocopying), recording or otherwise, without the written permission of the copyright holder.

ISBN: 9781521723500

The author has made every effort to trace and acknowledge sources, resources and individuals. In the event that any images or information has been incorrectly attributed or credited, the author will be pleased to rectify these omissions at the earliest opportunity.

Scripture quotations are all taken from the Holy Bible, the New King James Version (Authorized Version). First published in 1611. Quoted from the KJV Classic Reference Bible, Copyright © 1983 by The Zondervan Corporation

Published by the Author © Global Destiny Publishing House,
No. 128 Peter Road, Greystone Office Park, Sandton, 2031, South Africa

Website: www.globaldestinypublishers.co.za

Email: frequency.revelator@gmail.com

Phone: 0027622436745 * 0027785416006 * 0027797921646

Book layout and cover designed by Godwin T. Mupakairi for Global Destiny Publishing House

OTHER BOOKS PUBLISHED BY APOSTLE FREQUENCY REVELATOR

How to Become a Kingdom Millionaire

Deeper Revelations of the Anointing

How to Operate in the Realm of the Miraculous

The Realm of Power To raise The Dead

The Realm of Glory

New Revelations of Faith

A Divine Revelation of the Realm of The Spirit

The Prophetic Move of the Holy Spirit

The Ministry of Angels in the World Today

The Power of Praying in the Throne Room

Divine Rights and Privileges of a Believer

The Prophetic Dimension

The Dynamics of God's Word

The Practice of God's Presence

The End Time Revelation of Jesus Christ

Rain of Revelations Daily Devotional Concordance

A CATALOGUE OF MIRACLE MONEY TESTIMONIES

AN EPITOME OF WHAT WILL HAPPEN TO YOU AS YOU INUNDATE YOUR SPIRIT WITH THRONE ROOM REVELATIONS ON MIRACLE MONEY ENCAPSULATED IN THIS BOOK:

1. *I recall vividly the day I made a supernatural withdrawal of Heaven's wealth in the form of Miracle money from an ATM. I initially inserted my bank card and received a receipt indicating that I did not have any money. In other words, I did not have even a cent in my bank account as reflected by a negative balance. However, even though I had a negative balance in my natural account, I knew that I had a positive balance in my Heavenly account, hence I had to make a decision to choose which account to believe. Being determined to change my status quo, I then released my faith by inserting the debit card back into the ATM and this time, I supernaturally transferred the money from my spiritual account into my natural account by faith and believed that the transfer had gone through successfully. I then commanded the ATM to release Four Thousand Rands which I urgently needed. Instantly, I heard the sound of the ATM machine rolling paper notes indicating that money was being processed and as the machine ejected the full amount, I grabbed it with both hands and started declaring Miracle Money and shouting praises to God. Since then, my faith to function in the arena of divine exploits in the demonstration of Miracle money skyrocketed and it is my daily consciousness to seek for new avenues of power and opportunities to demonstrate it, to the glory of God. With that being said, continue reading this book to learn more divine principles of how you can follow suit and command Miracle Money into manifestation in the natural realm.*

-Apostle Frequency Revelator

A Catalogue of Miracle Money Testimonies

2. I thank God for the money multiplication miracle which took place right in front of my own eyes. After failing to pay my monthly rent, collectively church members dug into their pockets and blessed me with R1 700. I was then asked to count the money before I leave, hence I double checked and confirmed that I had the exact amount needed. When I got home, I recounted the money, only to realise that there was an extra R200 note. Baffled by this, I counted the money again and was still left with an extra R200. I thought that it was fake money, so, I rubbed the brown R200 note together and, miraculously, the R200 note split into two R200 notes, hence I had an additional R400. Overwhelmed by what I had just witnessed, I checked the money once again and verified it by recounting it carefully. This time around, there was an additional R300 notes. It was as if the money multiplied just like Jesus multiplied two fish and five loaves to feed the thousands!. In total, I had now been blessed by the Lord with an additional R700. I sat there in a daze holding the extra R700 in my hand and the rent money in my other hand and the Lord spoke to me saying: "depend not on your flesh but on Me." The Lord had superseded my expectations of what He can do for me. Through this, He showed me that He is capable of doing even greater things, glory to Jesus!

- Melissa Simon, South Africa

3. I asked God for a financial breakthrough in 7 days and the following week, I received a FedEx package containing a letter from the bank confirming that I was approved for a full principal debt cancellation of my home equity line of credit on my investment property for $136,937.15, including all fees and interest. The debt was completely cancelled! This was the same property that I gave the tithes on. I didn't apply for this relief, so I know that it was miracle from God. My husband and I had used this money to do restoration work on our home a few years ago, so by cancelling this debt, God paid for the work that was done, glory to Jesus!

- Carole Coleman-Florestal, Briarcliff Manor, NY, USA

4. Me and my husband were struggling in our finances and we were praying for a financial breakthrough. We were 3 weeks late on our rent and I was working cleaning houses but I hardly had any income. We were faithfully tithing and giving and stood on the promises of God's word for this financial breakthrough and yesterday unexpectantly, we received a Miracle cheque of $14,000! We are now able to get caught up on our

rent and we are tithing and using the money with wisdom. God's timing is amazing. I was also blessed with 2 jobs from interviews I went on yesterday!! God is moving and operating in our lives in an amazing way. This is just a small part of what God's doing in my life. He's rewriting my story and turning my life into His story. He's changing me from the inside out and has set me free from bondages and from so much. I give Him all the glory and Praise. He's is a faithful and Loving God.

- Christine Benson, Brookhaven, NY, USA

5. Dear Man of God, Praise The Lord! Allelua! Please allow me to give a bold testimony. Yesterday I called the 24 hour Prayer line and was talking to one of the Pastors on the phone and the Pastor was strongly talking to me about the importance of tithing. I would always use the excuse and say that as soon as I get paid I am left with nothing to pay my tithes. The Pastor prayed for me over the phone and at that time in my bank account I only had 6 dollars. The following morning I felt led to check my bank account something which I do not usually do and I found that there was $206.51 in my bank account! Praise God! God is doing so many wonders in my life. I sowed the seed and paid my Tithes. I am just so excited that I received Miracle Money! I've made a vow that I will continue to sow $43 every fortnight in Jesus name!

– Mr V.M Sydney, Australia

6. We have received an $11,000.00 debt cancellation notice from a credit card company. I have been sowing supernatural seed toward debt cancellation and declaring it for our lives, but it completely unraveled me when it actually happened. The Lord directed me to John 16:27, and then had me scroll up to verses 23-24. Hallelujah! He is so good and worthy!

- Pam Taupin, USA

7. I owed the IRS (Tax Office) $10,000 and they were about to garnish my paycheck. I went to the tax office and God sent an angel to help me. The agent found numerous errors on my taxes. She offered to review my taxes and told me to come back the following day. When I returned, she said that I did not owe $10,000 but $980 and stopped the garnishment. To God be the Glory!

- Crystal Barclay- Brooklyn, NY, USA

PRELUDE

Welcome to the World of Miracle Money!

The Reserve Bank of Heaven (BOH) holds funds adequate to every need in your life. The treasures of Heaven are unreservedly open to be tapped and drained into natural avenues of your bank account in this season. Your account has accrued the dividends of the promise of God's Word coupled with your Prophetic declarations, hence the clouds of Heaven have been saturated. The atmosphere is now reverberating with the sound of the flapping of wings by angel tellers coming on feet in your direction. The torrential downpour of the heavy rain of Miracle Money is ready to precipitate directly from the Throne Room of Heaven upon you. Likewise, the angel tellers stand ready to respond to every demand you make at the window of faith and all forces of divinity are postured to act on the Word you speak. The confidence of the currency of the Kingdom is backing your confessions of faith today as all Heaven's attention is directed towards you. The deposits of hope that you have held in your heart are ready to be tendered in your life. There is no hold on the reserves of Heaven on your behalf as the flood gates, doors and windows of Heaven are wide open over you. God is not reluctant to cash out the economy of Heaven to meet your need, hence a divine arrangement of circumstances in the realm of the spirit have been prearranged for you. Now, get ready for the rain of Miracle Money, in all currencies of the world is precipitating through every facet of human existence and accentuating an avenue to infiltrate right into your bank account.

The Reserve Bank of Heaven (BOH) is being shaken to its core by the authoritative voice of God. Angel tellers have received authorisation from the Master Himself, certified with a stamp of His approval and authenticated by the signature of His own handwriting, endorsing that billions in Miracle money should be dispatched, propagated and rained over the masses in this season. Accounts are being supernaturally debited, debts are cancelled and money transfers authorised. Angel tellers are therefore ready to dispatch Miracle Money and make angelic deposits. Bank account numbers of recipients on earth have been generated and your name has been enlisted. You have been enlisted in God's prosperity agenda in this season. You have been singled out to be a recipient of Wealth transfer, hence you are in line to receive thousands and millions in Miracle Money in this season. Therefore, as you step into the realm of the undefinable, uncharted and unrecorded miracles, signs and wonders in this season, welcome to the world in which it's naturally supernatural to receive and release Miracle Money. A world in which waking up in the morning and receiving thousands supernaturally deposited in your bank account and hundreds stacked in your bags, wallets and houses is a normal occurrence, glory to God! Let the divine spectacular begin!

DEDICATION

In retrospect of my first book on Kingdom Finance titled, "***How to Become a Kingdom Millionaire***," I have unpacked Throne Room revelations of how believers in the Body of Christ across the globe could be catapulted from the convictions of ordinary life of complacency and mediocrity to the realm of Kingdom Millionaires. The book has helped thousands across the globe to amass humongous wealth in millions and billions on behalf of the Kingdom. In this new book, I have therefore decoded the divinely coded mysteries on Miracle Money, which for ages have remained an inexplicable, implausible and unfathomable phenomenon. This book will usher you into a consistent stream flow of copious, torrential and perennial rain of Miracle Money, precipitating upon your life from unexpected sources. This spectacular display of God's power in the invisible arena is what will culminate in a catalogue of Miracle Money testimonies as humanity in the extreme quarters of life unreservedly partake of this fresh manna which God is unfolding from the Throne Room of Heaven. This book is therefore dedicated to millions of believers across the globe who shall receive Miracle money and demonstrate it's grace by striding at the frontline of a global Miracle money revival. With the advent of the new manifestations of the Spirit, it is unequivocally evident in this spectacular season that Christianity doesn't have to be a mundane routine anymore. There are enthralling and thrilling divine experiences such as Miracle Money manifestations which God is now using to draw multitudes to faith in Him. God has gone beyond natural provision to divinely orchestrate Miracle money in the supernatural realm, so that His divine plans and purpose on earth is expedited with a sense of urgency. Therefore, it is important in this "God moment" that you determine to grow your faith in line with God's purpose as you move away from impossibility thinking and its limitations and be open to Heavenly resource thinking.

In view of this Heavenly mandate, as an Apostle in the Kingdom, I have therefore been inspired by the Holy Spirit and used as a vessel of divine truth to demystify every misconception, confusion and scepticism concerning the doctrine of Miracle money and to put this concept into its correct divine perspective. The central theme of this book is therefore to enlighten you on the subject of Miracle money with intent to show you how to experience God's promised super abundance in your life so that you can unreservedly reap the things God has already prepared for you even before the world began. The divinely coded mysteries on Miracle money which for ages have been considered as an inexplicable phenomenon, have been decoded in this book such that Miracle money is no longer an impossibility. The consistent stream flow of Throne Room revelations encapsulated in this book are set to revolutionize your life forever. There is a new type of man to which this book is dedicated, who is emerging on the horizon and rising beyond the confines and limitations of the realm of senses to perambulate in an arena of divine exploits. Those who are comfortable with the status quo and have drowned themselves in the valley of religion and tradition will be dazzled in this critical hour as you are about to explode in the demonstration of Miracle money like the scattering of foliage under the influence of a storm. I see you mightily demonstrating Miracle money in this season like the splattering of piles of paper in the direction of the wind. I see you partnering with angel tellers, like a man working with his own friends. God will open your spiritual eyes so that you will see battalions of angels carrying piles of paper money, ready to dispatch it through the natural avenues into your account. You shall be catapulted into a ripe atmosphere of glory that is reverberating with the sound of the flapping of wings by angel tellers, coming on feet in your direction. What a spectacular moment God has ushered us into in this season!

Dedication

However, the recent controversial debate that has surfaced across the Body of Christ with regard to the credibility and authenticity of Miracle money is ample evidence that multitudes of believers are still sailing their boats through shallow streams of spiritual understanding, where Miracle money is concerned. Hence, this publication is a means to dispel any misconceptions which have been engraved in the microscopic mind of humanity concerning Miracle money and to present a correct picture and accurate perspective of how Miracle money manifests in the natural realm. As you step into the realm of the undefinable, uncharted and unrecorded miracles in this season, God is about to do something so brand new that you won't yet have the language to describe it, nor will you have any vocabulary to speak about it. It would be like what Paul described as *"Something inexpressible for man to tell"*. What God is about to do for you and through you in this *kairos* moment is something unfamiliar to your status quo. You will run to your dictionary and not find its meaning because it is not part of the vocabulary of man. You will make an attempt to google it and not find its source because it is not yet uploaded on the internet. You will even try and peruse through your Bible and not find it because it falls within the realm of unrecorded miracles. This is what Prophet Elijah described in prophetic language as a *"new thing"*. The reason why God calls it a *"new thing"* is because it doesn't have a name as yet. It's a brand new phenomenon unfolding from the Throne Room of Heaven such that even the angels are still trying to comprehend it. You too will not be able to look at it or recognise it because it will be completely brand new. You will not call it by the name you used in the past, hence you would need a new vocabulary to describe it. That is why in this season, you will call it *"Miracle Money"*. In the same way the children of Israel looked at the food of angels that was rained down from Heaven and explained, *"manna!"* meaning *"what is this!,"* in this season, you will wake up to find piles of paper money littering the floor of your house like morning dew and you will exclaim, *"Miracle Money!"* which is a new vocabulary and buzz word in the realm of God's prosperity in this new season. With that being said, sit on the edge of your seat and fasten your seatbelt as the author takes you through an adventurous journey, to usher you into a catalogue of supernatural acts that will dazzle your mind and thrill you to the last degree.

ACKNOWLEDGEMENTS

First and foremost, I would like to ascribe to God the Almighty, all the glory and honour due to His name, for granting me through His grace, the divine opportunity to decode the divinely coded mysteries on Miracle money and to function in an arena of divine exploits through the practical demonstration of Miracle Money in this generation. This writing appears in its current form due to the influence of several people, hence as a token of appreciation, I would like to offer my sincere gratitude to all of them: Apostle-Prophet Maphosa the President of the Manifest Sons of God Movement (MSG), Apostle Ron Tramell of Elijah Miracle International Ministries (USA), Apostle Guillermo Maldonado of King Jesus International Ministry (USA), Pastor Benny Hinn of the World Healing Centre, Pastor Chris the President of Believers' LoveWorld International Ministry, Bishop D.J Comfort of Favours Cathedral Church, Apostle Chris Lord Hills of the Supernatural Church, David Zuzig (USA), Apostle (Dr) Renny G. McLean of Global Glory International Ministries, Prophet Eubert Angel of Spirit Embassy, Prophet Mathew B. Nuek (Malaysia) the founder of the Prophet's Mail Box and Dr. David Herzog of David Herzog Ministries, for their deeper insights into the realities of the Glory Realm and for enlightening me in the integral matters of operating in God's glory. It is through their tutelage that I was awakened into the reality of living in the Glory Realm and the need to propagate the *creative miracles of glory* to the furthest extremes of the world, of which Miracle money is a part. These men of God truly made such a tremendous impact in my life, for it was through their influence that I developed an insatiable appetite, unquenchable thirst and perennial hunger to practically demonstrate Miracle money in the natural realm.

I would like to extend a hand of appreciation to Maryna De Canha (my Manager), for her relentless inspiration and professional guidance in my writing career. Further appreciation goes to Moses Vhikey my Director for Resurrection Embassy, Nicole Campher my Marketing Director for Kingdom Millionaires Global Investments (KMGI) (Pty) Ltd, Pastor Gabriel Coke my Director for Global Power Ministries, Pastor Patson May, Lana Holmes, Pastor Victor of Faith Life Ministries International, Prophet Ron, Dr. Franklin (SA), Dr. Ira Marshal (USA), Tolu Somolu (UK), Prophetess Staphanie Menezes (USA), Deborah Maria Tromp (Holland), Prophetess Emelda and my dear friends Chris and Godwin, for being instrumental in creating a conducive spiritual climate for the birthing forth of the revelations which God has laid in my spirit. I owe special gratitude specifically to one of my best spiritual sons, Paramjeet Singh Makani from the nation of India, who inspires me a lot through the demonstration of the undefinable, uncharted and unrecorded miracles, signs and wonders in this very hour.

Further tribute goes to my siblings: Kaizer, Target, Keeper, Colleter and Presence Nkomo for their love and support in every way. Thanks be to the men and women of God all around the world from whom we are receiving donations, Ministry partners, Television viewers, members of *Resurrection Embassy* (REM), Associates of *Christ Resurrection Movement* (CRM), Trainees at our *Global School of Resurrection* (GSR) and staff at our *Global Destiny Publishing House* (GDP House), for being at the frontline of the Miracle Money revival through the global distribution of this Holy Ghost-breathed publication. Further thanks goes to my best college students who have now become part of my family namely, Clarissa Strachan, Chantel Dickson, Precious Akapelwa, Phylicia Green, Felicia Roopram and Jessica Venter. To Author House (UK), I recognize that this project would not have been possible without your initiative. Thanks for heeding God's call to have these Throne Room revelations propagated from the United Kingdom (UK) to the extreme ends of the world. To God be the glory!

-Apostle Frequency Revelator

CONTENT

Prelude...vii

Dedication...ix

Acknowledgements...xiii

Introduction...xvii

1. The End Time Prophetic Revelation Of Miracle Money

    ▶ *What Is Miracle Money?*..1

2. The Theology Behind The Manifestation Of Miracle Money

    ▶ *What Is The Scriptural Basis Of Miracle Money?*..............................28

3. The Seven Supernatural Dimensions Of Manifestation Of Miracle Money

    ▶ *In What Forms Does Miracle Money Manifest In The Physical Realm?*..............84

4. Spiritual Laws And Principles That Provoke Miracle Money Into Manifestation In The Natural Realm

    ▶ *What Spiritual Principles Can I Tap Into In Order To Release Miracle Money?*..152

5. A Divine Revelation Of Higher Laws Of Financial Prosperity

    ▶ *What Higher Spiritual Precepts Can I Take Advantage Of In Order To Partake Of The Grace For Miracle Money?*...............................185

6. The Secrets Behind The Practical Release Of Miracle Money From The Spirit Realm Into The Natural Realm

    ▶ *How Do I Release Miracle Money Into Visible And Tangible Manifestation In The Natural Realm?*..204

7. The Role Of Angels In The Supernatural Manifestation Of Miracle Money

- *What Role Do Angels Play In The Manifestation Of Miracle Money?* **235**

8. A Divine Prophetic Revelation Of God's End Time Kingdom Financial Prosperity Plan

- *What Role Do I Play in Releasing Miracle Money In This Season?*.................**246**

9. The Practical Demonstrations Of Miracle Money In The Natural Realm

- *How Do I Practically Demonstrate Miracle Money In The Natural Realm?* **259**

About The Author..**271**

INTRODUCTION

DISPELLING THE MYTHS AND MISCONCEPTIONS ABOUT MIRACLE MONEY

Have you ever imagined going to sleep with your bank account empty and waking up the following day with a fat bank account of half a million dollars? Have you ever thought of how you would feel if ever you found an extra ten thousand dollars supernaturally deposited in your bag, pockets or wallet? Have you ever envisaged what difference it would make in your life if all your debts worth hundreds of thousands were supernaturally cancelled in a twinkling of an eye? This spectacular demonstration of God's power is happening live, right across the Body of Christ in what seems to be a divinely thrilling and enthralling move of the Spirit, as God manifests His last wave of prosperity revival on earth. We are beginning to feel the sprinkles of this massive global revival sweeping across the Body of Christ as we await His second coming. Metaphorically speaking, we are beginning to experience a whirl of extraordinary divine aura invading the natural realm, leaving the masses dazzled to the last degree. God is exploding in the demonstration of power as the mass are witnessing a factory of mind-blowing signs and wonders, coupled with a warehouse of jaw-dropping miracles, which are culminating in an inventory of breath-taking testimonies, across the globe. This new move of God, which marks the greatest prosperity revival ever witnessed in the history of humanity, is characterized by the supernatural manifestation of the wealth of Heaven though Miracle money, instantaneous debt cancellation, wealth transfer, financial and food multiplication, a heightened degree of visible angelic manifestations as well as the stirring of a pool of creative miracles in which the original blue print of body parts emerge in bodily territories where they previously did not exist. This third wave of prosperity revival is also coupled with what we call *"the Golden Rain,"* which is the supernatural appearance of Heavenly precious stones such as gold dust, diamonds, silver and supernatural oil on the surface of buildings and in some cases, raining down through the hands and other body parts of believers during worship sessions, where they gather to honor the Lord. It is for this reason that Miracle money has become a household name, a buzz word and the most overworked Christian vocabulary in this end time season. This spectacular divine phenomenon has attracted global attention as it has dominated international news headlines, invaded every space on social media and became a hotly contested topic of discussion in many Christian forums worldwide.

However, it is of paramount significance to unveil right from the onset the divine truth that the subject of Miracle money as it relates to the end time church still remains a contentious topic and an inexplicable phenomenon to many folks. This is highly attributable to lack of revelation and understanding of God's million ways of supernatural provision as well as insensitivity to His times and seasons in this present hour. The other inhibiting factor that has derailed the receptivity of Miracle money is it's perpetration and misappropriation by some religious charlatans masquerading as agents of God. Owing to it's heightened abuse by these clergy religious men, people now have a tendency to throw the baby out with the bathwater. This is what has culminated in severe criticism of Miracle money, not only perpetuated by some ill-informed believers but in some cases by government officials, in the name of protecting the economy. The truth is that God cannot be put in a box where He is expected to gravitate to the level of man's thinking. Taking into account the nature of the season into which we have been ushered, money is such an integral and crucial tool in the proliferation

Introduction

and propagation of the gospel of Christ Jesus across the globe. As much as the gospel is rendered free of charge, however, the means to take it to the extreme ends of the world requires humongous financial sacrifices and this is the reason why God says *money answers all things* (Ecclesiastes 10:19). This means that contrary to what multitudes of people presume, money is a crucial tool in pursuit of the agenda of the Kingdom in this end time season, hence without it, we would be hamstrung and inhibited to fully achieve what God has assigned us to do. It is for this reason that God has gone beyond natural provision to divinely orchestrate Miracle money in the supernatural realm, so that His divine plans and purpose on earth is accomplished with a sense of urgency. Therefore, it is important in this "God moment" that you determine to grow your faith in line with God's purpose as you move away from impossibility thinking and its limitation and be open to Heavenly resource thinking. Spiritually speaking, if God were to rely on the natural processes of money making for His divine plans to be accomplished, it would certainly take a considerable amount of time due to limitations of the realm of senses in which the masses have been held hostage. This is one of the reasons why He uses Miracle Money to expedite His plans and purposes on earth.

However, despite its significance as a key blessing in the acceleration of God's divine plans in this end time season, so many negative things have been said about Miracle Money. Owing to people's ignorance and lack of revelation of the times and seasons of God and of His sovereign supremacy as the Most High God, Miracle money has suffered severe criticism, not only from the general unsaved community but in some Christian cycles, with some folks citing that God cannot violate natural laws by raining money from Heaven. Others are still gleaned to the natural principles that money can only be economically produced by the Reserve Bank or Economic harbour of a country, hence they have always relegated the manifestation of Miracle money to an inexplicable phenomenon. This is gross ignorance of God's Word because God cannot be put in a box as He has millions of ways through which He provides for His children. He is a Supreme God who has a title-deed of the whole Universe, hence has an exclusive right to rain Miracle money upon His elect, whenever He wants to. Therefore, the fact that some folks do not understand the dynamics of the realm of the spirit as birthed by the new move of God in this last wave of prosperity, does not make it wrong. Moreover, the fact that you don't understand something from God does not mean that you should contradict or oppose it. It's only a pity that those who do that are setting up themselves for extreme disadvantage and ignorantly limiting themselves from partaking of the grace which God is freely ushering in the Body of Christ at this final chapter of human history.

To cement this divine truth with reference to a quintessential example, the Bible records an incident whereby Prophet Elisha declared a 24 hour turnaround financial miracle of economic revival in Syria, saying, *"Tomorrow about this time a seah of fine flour shall be sold for a shekel, and two seahs of barley for a shekel, at the gate of Samaria"* (2 Kings 17:1). To the sceptics and those sailing their boats through the shallow streams of spiritual understanding, He then declared, *"You shall only see it but not partake of it"*. And in accordance with the Word of the Prophet, those who doubted and opposed the new move of God surely did not partake of it as God birthed a turnaround financial miracle which ruffled the feathers of the critics and dazzled the minds of religious charlatans. This is how many people have ignorantly missed the blessings from God. However, those who shall catch the revelation of this amazing divine phenomenon of Miracle money will continue to walk in the light of it and benefit from its manifestation in divergent ways, while those who are still sceptical should seek God for a revelation so that they are not left behind. It is spiritually dangerous for a believer to be left clinging on the shoreline and standing at the bus stop when God has already moved from there. The believer in question is still holding on to the old manna yet God is now unfolding new mantles, new waves of provision and new anointings. The church must therefore be conscious of the new move of God in the arena of prosperity and be highly sensitive to God's new ways of doing things so that they are not left behind or gravitate lower than the standard of grace which God is raising for the end time church.

In view of the above, it is worth highlighting that life is made up of things that we are aware of and those things that we are not aware of. The fact that

Introduction

we are ignorant of some laws or facts of life doesn't mean that they will not affect us. Even if you were never told about the existence of gravity, that doesn't stop it from affecting you. It is true that the earth is revolving around the sun, but who among the mortal is able to tell us where the driving force is coming from? The fact that in your community people don't know whatever is happening to the earth, does not stop it from revolving. Your knowledge of some things does not validate or authenticate them. Even without your knowledge, some things are authentic and are of great value. In the book of John, Jesus told one Pharisee that *the wind blows where it wishes and you hear its sound, but you do not know where it comes from or where it goes* (John 3:8). What Jesus was contextually saying is that if a spiritual man sent from God comes to town, no natural man is able to define him. From the beginning of the beginnings, no natural man is able to understand the things of the spirit for they are spiritually discerned. The cognitive capacity of a human mind is too microscopic to fathom all that God is doing in the supernatural realm. This is why even today, some folks critically comment on the prophetic move of God, yet they do not exactly know what they are saying or claiming to know. Just like wind, the natural man does not know where Miracle money comes from and where it goes. Miracle money does not become what it is because it is defined by you. As long as it is a spiritual substance, it is like wind blowing from one unknown corner going to another unknown destination. Therefore, your duty is not to try and decode the divinely coded mysteries of Heaven using your microscopic human mind but to rightly position your spirit so that you are able to flow with what God is brewing in the invisible arena. It's not your duty to try and explain the chemical composition of a miracle. Instead, your duty is simply to receive it and manifest it's results in the physical realm. This is how matters are settled in the natural realm where arguments, controversies and debates are bound to surface because the natural man does not understand the things of the spirit.

With that being said, when God intervenes and provides a solution bypassing the natural laws, it becomes a miracle. Miracles do not become miracles because they are endorsed by ministers of religions, other clergymen or what. They are just miracles because they are divinely orchestrated by God.

In the first place the miracle did not happen because you were consulted or because you will deny or accept them. They do happen because God is meeting a need or He is managing a crisis in the natural realm. As a matter of fact, God has never required man's understanding or approval of the ways He chooses to accomplish His design in creation, or to reveal His glory among men. Instead, God has simply spoken, acted, and moved, hence He requires you to just believe and in tandem with what He is doing in the invisible arena, you do exactly that in the natural realm. You must realize that God's ways are different from human ways and understanding (Sense and reason). God even punctuated in Isaiah 55:8-9 that *"For my thoughts are not your thoughts, neither are your ways my ways. As the Heavens are higher than the earth, so are My ways higher than your ways and My thoughts than your thoughts."* This must tell you that your lack of understanding of Miracle money as a key blessing from Heaven will not in any way stop it from manifesting. Instead, your ignorance might culminate in a debilitating scenario in which the blessing eludes you and others from partaking of it. It is for this reason that many are still trapped in a morass of debilitating poverty and entangled in a web of debt.

Despite the sovereign display of God's power in the fabric of His creation, it is disheartening to note that in some Christian cycles across the world, some folks ignorantly criticize Miracle money, citing that it is from the devil. But why would you want to relegate such a good gift from God to the devil's provision? Why should you take the glory that you are supposed to ascribe to God and attribute it to the devil? The truth is that Satan does not provide anything because he doesn't have or own anything. Instead, he can only counterfeit what God has already made available. Contrary to what some folks have been lied to believe, the devil cannot give anybody money because he doesn't have it. If it happens that he has some, it's because he would have stolen it. The devil is financially broke, spiritually bankrupt and ideologically empty. Therefore, he cannot stop the torrential flow of God's blessings from raining on us but uses the power of lies and deception to keep God's people in dark so that they doubt God's supernatural provision and miss it. This is how he whispers in the ears of some so that they won't

Introduction

believe that Miracle money is from God. To cement this divine truth with reference to scriptural evidence, the Bible says, *"Every good and perfect gift is from above, coming down from the Father of the Heavenly lights, who does not change like shifting shadows"* (James 1:17). This is to tell you that Miracle money is one of the good and perfect gifts which God is raining down from the Heaven's Store House upon His children in the same manner in which He rained manna from Heaven for the children of Israel to partake of. The truth is that as an unchanging God, if He did it in the past, He can still do it now because to Him, the past, present and the future are all in past tense.

Did you know that raining down Miracle money from Heaven is the easiest miracle which God can ever perform in a generation? The Lord Himself said it when He promised to cause water to supernaturally appear in a desert even without a sign of a cloud. He asserted that *performing this miracle is an easy thing for the Lord to do* (2 Kings 3:17-18). To Him, raining down Miacle moeny from Heaven is akin to someone spilling a tank full of water onto the ground. That's exactly how easy it is for God to unreservedly precipitates or rain down Miracle money upon the masses who are connected to His Word. To the unwavering Sarah, God said, *"Is anythig too hard for the Lord to do?"* (Genesis 18:14). In essence, it is actually easier for God to release Miracle money from Heaven than it is for the inhabitants of the earth, who dwell so much in the lower plane of life, to receive and embrace it. The apostle Paul tells us how eager God is to abundantly bless you financially. In Romans 8:32, he contends that if *He (God) spared not His own son but delivered him up for us all, how shall he not with Him also freely give us all things?* Miracle money is one of these blessings which God is freely and liberally lavishing upon His children, before He closes the curtain at the end of this age. For those who still doubt that God cannot give us Miracle money, are you not aware that Jesus taught us how much God cares for each of us, even for the smallest things?. Consider what He specifically said: *Aren't five sparrows sold for two pennies? But God does not forget even one of them. In fact, He even counts every hair on your head! You are worth more than many sparrows* (Luke 12:6-7). If God could take care of the smallest bird in the sky, why would it be difficult for you to think that God can give you Miracle money? Without a shadow of doubt,

He will certainly give you Miracle money so that you can take care of your needs and have your faith in Him strengthened. Therefore, if it happens that you receive Miracle money either in your bank account, wallet or any other unexpected places, give God glory for you are more valuable than the birds of the sky.

On the basis of the above scriptural evidence, it could be deduced that those who doubt, criticize or question the credibility and authenticity of miracle money as a means of God's supernatural provision in these end times, in a way question God's sovereignty, wisdom and creativity which is more superior than the microscopic mind of man. If you still doubt that God can rain Miracle money from Heaven, let me ask you some few interrogative questions? Who would have ever thought that God could rain manna, the Heavenly food of angels, for His people to freely and sumptuously indulge? Who would have ever thought that God could cause water to supernaturally appear in a desert without a sign of a cloud? Who would have ever thought that God could cause quails to blow in the direction of His children so that they could have meet to eat on a daily basis? Who would have ever thought that God could cause water to come out of a rock in order for millions of His children to drink in the wilderness? And since the above scenarios typify how Miracle money manifests in the natural realm, this is to tell you that the human mind is too microscopic to fully comprehend the depths of God's supernatural provision. This is the reason why Miracle money has been subjected under heavy criticism. As far as God is concerned, all the above-mentioned supernatural acts represents the former rains, of which the Bible states clearly that *the glory of the latter house shall exceeds that of the former house* (Hagai 2:9). This implies that in this end time season, God can do more than what He did in the former days. And if God did it in the past, what can stop Him from doing it now? This is because God is the same yesterday, today and forever. His methodological operations might have changed in line with His times and seasons but His principles remain the same. If He gave people Miracle money but in the form of food, fish and water, it follows that in this summation of ages, it is possible for Him to rain Miracle money directly upon the masses in their bank accounts, bags, cars

Introduction

and houses. It is therefore imperative that you get rid of any misconstrued Christian traditional teachings that are against the new move of God if ever you want to abundantly partake of this enormous grace. Colloquially speaking, any attempt to resist the Miracle money grace is tantamount to biting the very hand of God that is trying to feed you. Believers must therefore be circumspect and relook into their theology so as not to put God in a box because He is not a man who can be manipulated but rather, a sovereign God who has infinite ways through which He supernaturally provides for His children.

Contrary to what multitudes of people presume, Miracle money is not a new Biblical phenomenon although the gravity, magnitude and intensity of its manifestation has heightened in this end times. Instead, Miracle money coupled with supernatural debt cancellation and wealth transfer has always manifested even during the Old Testament dispensation. To make it explicitly clear, its manifestation actually dates back to an era before the foundations of the world when God completed everything perfect in Him. In a similar fashion in which we were born in the glory realm, where our origin and identity is and then brought to the earth for a purpose at an appointed time, Miracle money is also a product of God's glory, given birth to in the glory realm and now dispatched to planet earth at an appointed time. To cement this revelation with reference to scriptural evidence, the Bible unveils the divine truth that *God's works were finished from the foundation of the world* (Hebrews 4:3). On the basis of this finished Work of God, we therefore, have to embrace the spiritual reality that *God has blessed us with all spiritual blessings (resources) located in the Heavenly places,* (Ephesus 1:3). As a spiritual Heavenly substance, Miracle money is one of those spiritual blessings which God has freely lavished or deposited for us in the Heavenly places. Hence, it is our duty to step up in faith to translate this blessing from the Heavenly realm into visible and tangible manifestation in the physical realm. This explains the mechanics behind the divine orchestration of Miracle money in the invisible arena. This is akin to the disposition of the *riches in Christ glory* in the Heavenly realm, which Paul talks about in Philippians 4:19, which allude to God's abundant provision which can be tapped and drained from the spirit realm and manifested in a visible and tangible form in the natural realm. As a product of God's glory released in the deepest territories of the glory realm, Miracle money is one of *the riches in Christ glory* which God is unreservedly unleashing in these end times. It is evident that the challenge or failure to demonstrate Miracle money is not a consequence of lack of faith but a glory problem. Did you know that poverty is not a money problem but a glory problem? Poverty is not a case of lack of money per se but a lack of perceived access to the glory of God because everything, including Miracle money flows from the glory realm. In the Greek Hendrin, the rendering of the word *"glory"* in it's original context is the same word for *"wealth"*. This tells me that a man who is rich in the glory of God is also rich in material wealth because the latter is a product of the former. Paul concurs in Philippians 4:2 that *My Lord shall supply all my needs* **according to the riches in glory by Christ Jesus.** This tells me that as long as you are born again and you are still in lack, you don't have a money problem. Instead, you have a glory problem. This is because every need or provision is supplied in commensurate with the measure of the glory of God in your life. Miracle money is accessed in the same manner. Therefore, the solution to poverty is to tap into the higher realms of glory where everything is made available and access His glory and poverty will disappear.

Furthermore, the supernatural acts of God's provision which are chronicled in the Bible are not just fallacies. The Bible is not just a book full of stories and historical events. Instead, it is an action-packed catalogue of supernatural acts performed by God in specific times and seasons. As a thrilling and enthralling divine spectacle, Miracle money shows that God is in action and is directly involved in the daily affairs of His children. God is current and He moves with times and seasons. If He were to rain down *manna* today, some people would run away from it. That is why He blesses you with Miracle money, something that is current, which everybody can easily relate to. The Bible is a live catalogue of supernatural acts, showing you that there is no special *day of miracles* somewhere in the distant past because God is a *God of miracles*. Wherever He is, *miracles happen!* It is naturally supernatural for

Introduction

Him to perform miracles. To the unwavering Sarah, He asked, *"Is anything too hard for the Lord to do?"* (Genesis 18:14). And several generations later, to the doubting Zachariah, He echoed the same voice saying, *"Is anything too difficult for the LORD?"* (Luke 18:27). And to the sceptics in this present time, He is still asking, **"Is Miracle money too difficult thing for the Lord to do?"** This is indeed such an invigorating and provocative question that must challenge your faith *to do the impossible,* knowing that nothing is implausible to God, because it is naturally supernatural for God to perform miracles, of which Miracle money is a part. The word, *"Miracle money"* itself is derived from the word *"Miracle,"* which alludes to the fact that it is a miracle demonstrated in the arena of finances. It's still natural money which humanity uses as a medium of exchange, but for it to manifest in unexpected places in the natural realm, a miracle has to take place. It brings to mind what Moses said of God: *"You are the God who performs miracles"* (Psalm 77:14). This means that it is God's nature to perform miracles. In other words, it is naturally supernatural for God to precipitate Miracle money. Just as it is the nature of a carpenter to work on wood, just as it is the nature of a mechanic to work with machines, so it is with God. It is His nature to work miracles. Miracles are as natural to God as breathing is to us. Raining down Miracle money from Heaven therefore falls within the domain of the realm in which He exists, functions and operates. This is to tell you that demonstrating Miracle money is not a big deal since it is within our genetic make-up and DNA as sons of God.

In view of this Heavenly mandate, as an Apostle in the Kingdom, I was therefore inspired by the Holy Spirit and used as a vessel of divine truth to demystify every misconception, confusion and scepticism concerning the doctrine of Miracle money and to put the concept of *Miracle money* into its correct divine perspective with reference to God's word so that the believers in the Body of Christ across the globe could freely partake of this grace because you cannot receive something that you don't understand. The central theme of this book is therefore to enlighten you on the subject of Miracle money with intent to show you how to experience God's promised super abundance in your life so that you can unreservedly reap the things God has already prepared for you even before the world was created. The divinely coded mysteries on Miracle money which for ages have been considered as an inexplicable phenomenon, have been decoded in this book such that Miracle money is no longer an impossibility. The consistent stream flow of Throne Room revelations encapsulated in this book are set to revolutionize your life forever. Those who are comfortable with the status quo and have drowned themselves in the valley of religion and tradition will be dazzled in this critical hour as you are about to explode in the demonstration of Miracle money like the scattering of foliage under the influence of a storm. I see you mightily demonstrating Miracle money in this season like the splattering of piles of paper in the direction of the wind. I see you partnering with angels of finances, like a man working with his own friends. God will open your spiritual eyes so that you will see battalions of angels carrying piles of paper money, ready to dispatch it through the natural avenues into your account. What a spectacular moment God has ushered us into in this season! What a thrilling moment to be alive and witness only what humanity could possible dream of, glory to God!

After reading only this far, you have already begun your journey out of financial instability of this world's system of chance and insufficiency, into the financial stability God has for you. Don't let anything stop you, for your **Miracle money** release is nearer now than it's ever been. Proceed to the passages below to learn more about the secrets of how to unlock the divine phenomenon of Miracle money and thus secure a revelation of what Miracle money is, where it comes from, how it operates and how you can receive it in your bank account as well as how you can practically demonstrate it and cause it to manifest in a specific territory in the natural realm, to the glory of Jesus!

CHAPTER ONE

THE ENDTIME PROPHETIC REVELATION OF MIRACLE MONEY

What is Miracle money? Where does it come from? How do I become a recipient of this treasure? How do I practically demonstrate or manifest it in my life and upon others in ministry? How do I qualify to partake of this grace? And what is the scriptural basis of this spectacular divine phenomenon? These are provocative questions which multitudes of believers and dazzled spectators, all around the world are still asking themselves with regard to the supernatural manifestation of the phenomenon of Miracle Money. While others might have experienced or partook of this end time grace, dozens of folks still do not understand the dynamics of this supernatural manifestation. As aforementioned, the recent controversial debate that has surfaced across the Body of Christ with regard to the origin of Miracle money, is ample evidence that multitudes of believers are still sailing their boats through shallow streams of spiritual understanding, where Miracle money is concerned. Hence, this publication is a means to dispel any myths which multitudes of people have engraved in their minds concerning Miracle money and to present a correct picture and accurate perspective of how Miracle money manifests in the natural realm. The greater truth is that many of God's miracles of provision have never been revealed in the previous generations but are a brand new package unfolding directly from the Throne Room of God as He manifest His last wave of signs and wonders. I know that I'm about to step on some religious toes but the truth is that the Bible only tells us a little of what Jesus did while He was on earth. If every miracle He performed were to be recorded, this world would not have enough capacity to contain the books. John concurs with this divine truth when he says,

"And there are also many other things which Jesus did, which, if they should be written every one, I suppose that even the world itself could not contain the books that should be written" (John 21:25).

In view of this divine truth, there is a level or dimension in the realm of God's power called, *"The realm of the unrecorded miracles,"* which unfolds new manifestations of the Spirit from deeper territories of the glory realm, which are unfamiliar to the status quo. It is evident that in this season that as we walk in the footsteps of our role model, Jesus Christ, we are stepping into the realm of the undefinable, uncharted and unrecorded miracles, signs and wonders. This alludes to miracles which humanity has never seen or heard of before. They are not recorded, not talked about and not even known. They are alien to the natural mind and foreign to man's thinking. In actual fact, when Jesus made a public declaration that *greater things than these shall you do* (John 14:12), He spoke in the context of these unusual brand new miracles which shall become a major characteristic feature of the end times. Although some might feature in the Bible, yet others might not have been recorded but reserved as a spectacle of the end time dispensation. With regard to the unveiling of these new dispensational manifestations, God declared through the voice of Prophet Isaiah saying, *"Behold, I'm doing a new thing! They are created now, and not so long ago, you have not heard of them before today, so you cannot say, "Yes, I knew them"* (Isaiah 48:7). Why is He telling you? Because there are certain things that God is brewing the spirit realm which man in his natural senses does not perceive. He is also telling you so that in tandem with what He is doing in the realm of the spirit, you can also do the same in the natural realm. God is about to do something so brand new that you won't yet have the language to describe it, neither will you have any vocabulary to speak about it. It would be like what Paul penned as *"Something inexpressible for man to tell"* (2 Corinthians 12:14). What God is about to do in this *kairos* moment is something unfamiliar to your status quo. You will run to your dictionary and not find its meaning. You will even try and peruse through your Bible and not find it because it falls in the realm of unrecorded miracles. The reason why God calls it a *"new thing"* is because it doesn't have a name as yet. It's a brand new phenomenon unfolding from the Throne Room of Heaven such that even the angels are still trying to comprehend it. You too will not be able to look at it or recognise it because it will be completely brand new. You will not call it by the name you used in the past, hence you would need a new vocabulary to describe it. That is why in this season, you will call it *"Miracle Money"*.

It therefore suffices to adjudicate that believers in this end time season shall be elevated into a dimension of unrecorded miracles to the extent of raining down Miracle money in a similar fashion in which Elijah rained down fire from Heaven. This is unequivocally a time and season for the proliferation of *"new things"* as Prophet Isaiah described in prophetic language. When manna was rained down from Heaven for the first time, to the children of Israel, it was something brand new, which they had never heard of, nor did they have a reference point as it never manifested in the previous generations. In a similar vein, there are certain special miracles which God has reserved for this end time season, which marks the conclusion of God's eternal plan on earth. Such a torrential rain of miracles will dumb found the sceptics and ruffle the feathers of those comfortable with the status quo because it will not be possible for anybody to trace them, research about them or even predict their occurrence. Metaphorically speaking, you are about to witness a warehouse of miracles and a factory of signs and wonders that will dazzle the minds of the masses and leave the critics dumbfounded to the last degree. As you step into the arena of divine exploits, to demonstrate the undefinable, unchartered and unrecorded miracles, the masses are about to witness a catalogue of supernatural acts that will culminate in an unprecedented avalanche of the rain of Miracle money from Heaven, in what we describe in spiritual terms as *"Money Rain"*.

Unveiling The Mystery of Miracle Money

In this last wave of signs and wonders, many people around the world are beginning to experience money supernaturally appearing in their purses, pockets, bank accounts and other unexpected places. Moreover, instant debt cancellation, coupled with the supernatural wealth transfer are increasingly becoming commonplace as this wave of generosity swells with Kingdom wealth. The viscosity of the glory of God is evidently being released in this day with a flow of financial blessing! In this season of established prosperity, scriptures are being fulfilled right in front of our very own eyes as Paul penned: *"I pray that you may prosper in every way and that your body may keep well, even as I know your soul keeps well and prospers"* (3 John 1:2). It is interesting to note that Paul's prayer is being unresevedly answered in this end time season of boundless prosperity. Heaven is expediently responding to this prayer through the dispatch of humongous financial wealth from its Store Houses upon the masses, in the form of Miracle money. This is to tell you that God has an end-time transfer of wealth available for you as He is releasing the rain of Miracle Money in abundance.

This is undeniably an hour of the global demonstration of Miracle Money and the season is rife for the worldwide precipitation of the rain of money, to expedite God's purpose on earth. We have already felt the first sprinkles of the waves of Miracle money revival sweeping across the Body of Christ. As one enlisted in God's agenda for prosperity in this season, I can literally sense it in the very atmosphere. Heavens are pregnant with the possibilities of God as the spiritual clouds are raging and winds are billowing, depicting their readiness to birth forth new manifestations. The skies are shifting and the waves are changing, heralding the dawn of a new season of Miracle Money. There has never been a season when Heaven is so aligned with the earth like the present time. This is unequivocally the "God moment", a ripe season for God to act and usher a new move of the Spirit, which will give birth to new manifestations of the Spirit. Pertaining to the seasons as chronicled in the calender of God, the Bible speaks of the Sons of Issachar who had an acute understanding of times and seasons of God, hence they knew what Israel ought to do at a time. It specifically says, *"From Issachar, men who understood the times and knew what Israel should do—200 chiefs, with all their relatives under their command* (1 Chronicles 12:32). In other words, they were gifted by God in a special way as they were catapulted into the realm of *prophetic perception*. This is a spiritual sight necessary to see what God is doing in the invisible arena and in tandem with Him, you do exactly the same in the visible realm. It incorporates the ability to see the unseen, hear the unheard and then speak the unspeakable. This means that your imagination was intended by God to be the lens through which you apprehend the realms of spiritual realities and in terms of the current times and seasons as stipulated in God's calendar, all scriptural evidence seem to align with the divine truth that this is indeed the most ripe season for Miracle money! In other words, the season of the global precipitation of the rain of Miracle money has just exploded. Therefore, the most integral question that we should ask ourselves in this critical season is:

In what direction is the Wind of the Spirit blowing and are we navigating the high seas of adventure by setting our sails to catch the Wind?

This is because quails are being blown in our direction, so to speak, in this end time season as God is calling men and women to step into deeper territories of the Glory Realm, to unravel the fullness of His loving grace on behalf of His children. Only if you could step into the Wind with a sense of urgency when it begins to blow, then you will hear where you need to go. God says, *"The sound of the blessing is reverberating in the Wind. I have put the name of the blessing in the Wind because this is an hour that My people will begin to direct the Wind. Therefore, call forth provision from the North, West, South and East and as you begin to loose your breath, the blessing in the Wind will begin to settle on My people and they will be blasted into the new territories of their manifested destiny"*. Metaphorically speaking, the clouds are saturated, the skies are changing and the winds are billowing in the direction where lack, poverty and insufficiency has enthroned itself in the fabric of humanity. This is why it is expedient in this Kairos moment that you flow in the current of the river of Miracle money because you may know your season but if you don't know your time (God-moment), you might act after God has passed by. And it is spiritually dangerous for a believer to be standing at a bus stop, waiting for God yet He has long passed by. Evident in this last wave of prosperity is the realization that both the times (*Kairos*) and seasons (*Kronos*) are coming together, culminating in the highest concentration of God's power on the earthly realm. It is for this reason that Miracle money is a key characteristic feature of this last wave of prosperity because it is a product of the rain of God's glory. This is the vision which Prophet Habakkuk saw in the olden days when he prophesied by the Spirit saying,

> *"Write down the vision and make it plain on tablets so that the one who reads it, may run with it. For the vision awaits an appointed time; it speaks of the end and will not prove false. Though it linger, wait for it; it will certainly come and will not delay"* (Habakkuk 2:2-3).

This portion of the scripture prophetically speaks of the end time season whereby believers shall be catapulted into the greater depths of the miraculous, to an arena of divine exploits in which they practically demonstrate the uncharted and unrecorded miracles, one of which is the rain of Miracle Money. Do you notice that it says a vision awaits an appointed time, but at the end, it shall speak? The appointed time has come, hence Miracle money speaks and cries out for men or women of faith to tap into the spirit realm and command it to manifest in the natural realm. It cries out in the hands of the wicked man of this world and its desiring for the righteous to possess it and use it for Kingdom purposes. David prophetically declared in Psalm 102:13, *"Thou shall arise and have compassion on Zion, for it is time to show favor to her; the appointed time has come."* It is undeniably evident that the time for a greater manifestation of Miracle money grace has come. This is indeed the set time to walk in the revelation of the fullness of sonship in Christ by practically demonstrating the Miracle money grace which God has unreservedly poured upon the Body of Christ in this end time season.

DEFINING THE PHENOMENON OF MIRACLE MONEY

What is Miracle Money?

It is of paramount significance in our analysis of the phenomenon of Miracle money that we define it from a holistic perspective. In order to fully understand what Miracle money is, you need to understand first what a miracle is. By definition, *a miracle is a phenomenal or supernatural occurence in the natural world that surpasses all known human understanding, and more often than not, cannot be explained by the laws of nature.* It is worth exploring the divine truth that God sovereignly governs the Universe with laws and He never operates contrary to His Word or to the laws of nature which He has established, but He has the prerogative to override them. Likewise, Miracle Money is a supernatural intervention in which God bypasses natural laws to freely precipitate the rain of money upon His children. Money itself is never a miracle because it is a unit of exchange used to facilitate economic transactions but when its manifestation in the natural realm can only be traced to divinity, and is beyond human comprehension, it is said to be *Miracle money*. It is of paramount importance in our understanding of the divine phenomenon of Miracle Money that we clarify the difference between a *blessing* and a *miracle*. As aforementioned, a miracle is a supernatural intervention of God in a crisis situation, bypassing the natural laws in the physical realm. On the other side of the coin, a blessing is a supernatural influence, metred by God's favour and benediction that causes all things to work out for you and aligh with God's purpose in your life. A blessing is still God's power divinely orchestrated in the spirit realm, but it flows through natural channels. Blessings supersede miracles in that a miracle can be a blessing. If you live your life from one miracle to the next, you will live from crisis to crisis. It's better to be blessed with good health than to always need divine healing because God's will is for us to walk in the blessing. However, we all need a miracle at some time to simply jump-start our faith. If it weren't for miracles, we wouldn't grow to the point where we could walk in the blessings of God. So, miracles introduces us into the realm of walking in the fullness of God's blessings in a similar fashion in which a river ushers it's waters into a Lake. This is because it's manifestation in the natural realm always points us to the Blesser, who is God. Miracle money is one of those reserved miracles which God is using to bless His children in the end times, hence we need to catch a revelation of how to receive it and also demonstrate it upon others. As much as there *are greater truths* and *lesser truths* as unveiled in the word of God (Genesis 1:16), there are also *greater spiritual laws* and *lesser spiritual laws*. Miracle Money is a result of the operation of the greater law of God, which is the principle of grace by which He intervenes in an unusual way to freely provide money and other resources to His children in the natural realm.

In the natural realm, there are divergent forms of money and the kind of money one receives is determined by the source it came from. Philosophically speaking, money that comes from working is called *"wages" or "earned money."* Money that comes about when a relative or loved one dies and money is left to the survivors is called *"Inherited Money."* Money that comes after winning by chance in a contest, draw or lottery is called *"Chance money"*. By the same token, the kind of Money that comes from Heaven through supernatural means can only be described as *"Miracle money"*. Miracle Money is a special kind of money that God Himself supernaturally releases upon His children who trust Him and believe His Word for its supernatural manifestation. The term *"Miracle money"* is not in the Bible because it is a new manifestation of the Spirit which God is unfolding from the Throne Room of Heaven, in what Prophet Isaiah described in prophetic language as a *new thing*. Throughout ages, the wealth of Heaven as mirrored by God's supernatural provision has been manifested in divergent ways, through Miracle money and gold dust manifestations. However, the gravity and intensity of its manifestation has heightened in these last days, in what I have coined a *"Miracle Money Revolution"* as God concludes His eternal plan on earth. The truth of the matter is that the unparalleled degree of manifestation of Miracle money coupled with gold dust in this end time season is not intended to be just a *Church phenomenon*, but a *Church revelation*.

The End Time Prophetic Revelation Of Miracle Money

> *Firstly, Miracle Money is the supernatural manifestation or appearance of money in unexpected places such as people's bank accounts, wallets, bags, pockets or houses, without any trace of how it got there in the natural realm and whose manifestation cannot be explained by natural laws.*

Taking centre stage recently in packed churches is a new phenomenon that really is not that new. It is the supernatural appearance of *"Miracle Money"*, a thrilling divine spectacle that have been hailed as a new move of God that is sweeping across the charismatic churches worldwide. A supernatural phenomenon in the realm of God's prosperity that has been happening for quite some time in the Body of Christ is Money supernaturally appearing in unexpected places such as people's bags, wallets, pockets, bank accounts, cars and houses, as a sign of the manifestation of the wealth of Heaven on earth and the unveiling of higher realms of God's glory. This divine phenomenon is usually coupled with the supernatural appearance of gold dust, silver and diamond stones and supernatural oil soaked on people's bodies, littering the floor or clinging on buildings where saints gather to worship the Lord. The truth is that while paper notes are widely accepted as a measure of wealth, Miracle money doesn't always have to manifest in the form of paper notes and coins. In some instances, it can manifest in the form of gold dust, diamonds, silver stones and other precious stones, which represent the wealth of Heaven. This is what we call the *Golden rain*. These precious stones have the same monetary value just like any other currency in the world, hence could easily be sold and converted to liquid money.

The greater truth is that Miracle money is a product of God's glory. It's given birth to in the deepest territories of the Glory Realm. That is why its manifestation is aggravated where the viscosity of the glory of God is demonstrated to a heightened degree in the natural realm. It is no doubt that we have been ushered right into the very special divine moments in the calendar of God whereby we are feeling the first sprinkles of the greatest revival of miracles, signs and wonders ever recorded since the Book of Acts. This is the result of the highest level of concentration of the glory of God being manifested upon the Earth. This wave of revival shall be greater than any other because we are entering the culmination of time, whereby we will experience the former rains and the latter rains of revival glory combined. A season of heightened exploration of the Glory Realm has begun as great mysteries are being unveiled, that will unleash the greatest outpouring of God's glory and harvest since the early Church, even since the beginning of time. While some of these things we are experiencing in this golden age are familiar, many of them are actually a brand new phenomenon unfolding directly from the Throne Room of Heaven. Therefore, Miracle money is one of the new manifestations of God's glory whose precipitation alludes to the combination of the *former glory* and the *latter glory*.

> **Secondly, Miracle money is a supernatural or divine transference of the original blue print of money from the spirit realm into direct visible and tangible manifestation in the physical realm under the ministration of angel tellers and the current of the financial anointing.**

It is worth exploring the divine truth that in the spirit realm, there is an original blue print of everything that exists in the natural realm. In a similar vein, as much as we have money stacked up in Banks or circulating in the economy, there is an original blue print of money in the spirit. When this money is supernaturally translated, transferred and transmuted from the realm of the spirit into the natural realm as a visible and tangible substance, it is called *Miracle Money*. It is a portrait of God's divine intervention in the light of man's everyday life and need. The greater truth is that as much as money is manifested in a physical form, in the natural realm it is also spiritual. This means that there is an original blue print of money in the spirit and when this money is manifested in the physical realm where it is transmuted into a form that is visible and tangible, it becomes what we call *Miracle Money*. It's manifestation denotes a level in which the spiritual materialises or chrystalises itself into the natural realm. The vehicle for the divine transportation of this unusual money from the spirit realm into the physical realm is the work of *angel tellers* but the pipeline for its practical demonstration and visible manifestation in the natural realm is through the *anointing* of the Holy Spirit. Notable is the realisation that Miracle money gravitates in the direction in which the anointing is flowing. Therefore, the anointing is a divine magnetic substance that releases a supernatural influence for Miracle money to move from the spirit realm into visible and tangible manifestation in the natural realm. That is why there is such a thing called *Miracle money anointing,* which is an impartation of God's supernatural ability upon a yielded human vessel, to enable him to practically manifest Miracle money in unexpected places in the natural realm. Miracle money is therefore a tangible, direct transference of money from the realm of the spirit into the physical realm under the current of the financial anointing.

It is worth exploring the divine truth that the manifestation of Miracle money in the natural realm depicts the reality of two types of economies, that is, the *Heavenly economy* and the *Worldly economy* and its precipitation in the natural realm denotes the pre-eminence and supremacy of the Heavenly economy over the Worldly economy. Miracle Money depicts God's sovereign reign and intervention in the lives of His own people where natural means have failed to make a way. In other words, the river of Miracle Money oftenly flows when the natural outflow of blessings are stopped or hindered, especially at such a time when it is a daunting task for God's people to prosper financially through the natural processes of money making. Notable is the realisation that the financial system of this fallen world is unjust as it creates opportunities for hustling wicked man to prosper while God's people are still yoked in poverty. Therefore, the precipitation of Miracle money in the natural realm is an indication that God, in the face of impossibilities will prove Himself strong on behalf of those who will trust Him and obey His word. To cement this divine truth with reference to scriptural evidence, the Bible records a thrilling scenario in which *Isaac planted crops in that land and the same year reaped a hundredfold, because the Lord blessed him. The man became rich, and his wealth continued to grow until he became very wealthy. He had so many flocks and herds and servants that the Philistines envied him* (Genesis 26:13). Bear in mind that Isaac's blessing was released in a time of highly unfavorable economic conditions characterized by a great famine and recession and when his enemies had stopped all methods to assure continued blessings. In other words, Isaac's hundred fold release came to him at a time when the devil's crowd had blocked all his methods of increase. By the same token, Miracle money usually comes when things are hindered in the natural realm, at such a time when wicked man are amassing humungous wealth at the expense of God's children. This is exemplified in the plight of Isaac. The Bible says *the wells that his father's servants had dug in the time of his father Abraham, the Philistines stopped up, filling them with earth and [Isaac] built an altar there and called on the name of the Lord and pitched his tent there, and there Isaac's servants were digging a well* (Genesis 26:25). In this portion of scripture, we learn that your situation is not determined by your environment or the state of the economy of the country in which you live. Instead, your situation is really determined by the availability of the abundance of wealth in the Heavens' Store Houses, which the apostle Paul penned as, *"the riches in Christ' Glory"*. It is determined by your ability to depend on the Heavenly economy, which does not run short of any supplies., even though provision in the natural realm has run dry. But how possible is it that a man can sow in dry ground and yet reap a hundred-fold increase? It's a miracle that is inexplicable to the natural mind. This tells me that what dozens of pastors customarily rant and rave behind the pulpit as a hundred-fold increase is actually a manifestation of Miracle money! Imbued with this Heavenly understanding, your ability to practically demonstrate Miracle money in this economically dry season will make you a personal witness to the fact that a hundred-fold release was not a one-time event that happened only to Isaac in the distant past but a progressive and continuous grace which God unreservedly lavishes upon His children right across generations.

> *Thirdly, Miracle money is a divine orchestration of a special end time grace to dispatch, distribute and propagate Heaven's wealth and financial resources to the earth, for the purpose of expediting God's divine plans and purpose. It is an outworking of God's grace that is released upon humanity in this end time season to amass humungous wealth, where natural processes of money making would have failed to accentuate an avenue for such wealth to be accumulated.*

The End Time Prophetic Revelation Of Miracle Money

Miracle money depicts a scenario in which God freely cashes out the economy of Heaven to meet the financial needs of humanity in the natural realm. In this regard, an open invitation has been made by Heaven, through angel tellers, calling for men and women to step up in faith to freely access the grace which God has reserved for His children. Miracle money is one of those free gifts which God wants His children to partake of in these end times. One key characteristic of a gift is that you don't have to do anything spectacular in order for you to qualify to be a recipient of it. This is what the Bible describes as *"Buying without Money"*. Consider what Jesus said:

"Hey there! All who are thirsty, come to the water! Are you penniless? Come anyway—buy and eat! Come, buy your drinks, buy wine and milk. Buy without money—everything's free! Why do you spend your money on junk food, your hard-earned cash on cotton candy? Listen to me, listen well. Eat only the best, fill yourself with only the finest. Pay attention, come close now, listen carefully to my life-giving, life-nourishing words (Isaiah 55:1).

Isn't it interesting to note that Jesus is using the language of money to invite the masses to His Kingdom? This is the same voice which Jesus echoes across generations for humanity to step into the unlimited possibilities of God's grace and receive the abundance of supernatural wealth directly from God's hand. In view of the above scripture, people tend to ask a question, *"Can God give anybody money without working for it?"* Emphatically, Yes! He can because He is revealing to us His integral role as the father who cares for His children. Did you do anything to qualify for God to send Jesus to come and die for your sins? If no, then why would you think of qualifying or doing something notable in order for you to receive Miracle money? Both scenarios above depict a manifestation of God's grace on behalf of His own people who bore an inscription of His very own image. Did you know that there are certain blessings that can manifest abundantly in your life even without fasting and praying? While I'm careful not to mess up with your theology, the greater truth is that Miracle money is given by God free of charge, even without working for it or paying for it or doing anything spectacular. It's God's boundless grace unreservedly bestowed upon humanity as a way of exhibiting deep love and care for His very own people.

THE RATIONALE BEHIND THE SUPERNATURAL MANIFESTATION OF MIRACLE MONEY

Why is Miracle Money such an important Divine Phenomenon in God's agenda in this End Time season?

From a financial point of view, there is no way we can get to a dimension or level where we comprehensively address the subject of Kingdom prosperity without talking about money because one becomes a Millionaire or prosperous by the measure of the amount of money that he has. The greater truth is that money is such a central tool in the Kingdom of God. It is for this reason that God declared that a *feast is made for laughter, and wine makes one merry but money answers all things* (Ecclesiastics 10:19). There are people who desire to demonstrate Miracle money but they are still bound by misconstrued denominational teachings in which they erroneously believe that not having enough is a sign of humility and a mark of holiness. Unless you change your pattern of thinking about money and view it as a golden substance, you might be inhibited and humstrung in your ability to demonstrate Miracle money as you should. Contrary to what multitudes of people across the globe presume, money is not evil but good. The pursuit of money for its own sake is usually evil and destructive but the pursuit of money to have financial resources to accomplish a greater cause can be quite rewarding and beneficial. To cement this affirmation with reference to scriptural evidence, the Bible declares in Timothy 6:10 that, *"For the love of money is the root of all evil."* In other words, it is the love of money that is evil, not money itself. If money is evil as it were, then the lack of it is evil too, because it's not of God. In actual fact, it is more evil *not* to have money than to have it, because having it is God's plan and purpose for us to spread the gospel and propagate His End Time plans on earth. It is evident that money itself is neutral, how it is used determines whether is evil or good.

The End Time Prophetic Revelation Of Miracle Money

Taking into account the nature of the wealth transfer season into which we have been ushered, it is absolutely possible for the rain of Miracle money to appear supernaturally from Heaven, anywhere, anytime and anyplace in the same way God rained manna fell from Heaven when the children of Israel needed food to eat (Exodus 16:4). However, there are certain misconstrued traditional teachings in some Christian cycles whereby people are taught that they need to toil from dusk till dawn because God will not let money fall down from Heaven into people's hands. While such teachings seem to be reasonable from a logical perspective, however, the realm of the spirit does not operate on the basis of logic, because God's principles of supernatural financial provision operates antagonistically to the crooked monetary systems and policies of this fallen world. This is exemplified in Dr. Leroy Thompson's encounter in which he testifies that one day he was shopping at the grocery store and while in the checkout line, the person ahead of him turned to him and said, *"Money goes."* Dr. Thompson then answered, *"Money goes."* But while in his way to his car, the Lord precauteously corrected him and said, *"Money comes!"* The Lord then told him that this was meant to be a prophetic word for the Body of Christ. As far as God is concerned, Money is not going. Instead, it is coming on feet in your direction. Therefore, the Lord said we are to declare, *"Money cometh to me, now!"* The word *'money cometh'* obligates Jesus the Apostle and the High Priest of our confession to oversee that word. It releases a supernatural influence in the realm of the spirit which compels all forces of divinity to work for you and all Heavens'attention to be directed towards you. In other words, at the mention of that word, angels are bumping into one another because they are going to get your Miracle Money and bring it to you, glory to Jesus!

Notable is the realisation that as anointed vessels, we have a divine mandate to attract or magnetise money so that we can use it for Kingdom purposes, specifically for the furtherance of the gospel. In other words, we are a *Money magnet,* designed to make a pulling on the supernatural realm by manifesting the abundance of Miracle money in the natural realm as though it were gold paving the streets of Heaven. Since money always gravitates in the direction in which the anointing is flowing, it is highly imperative that we persue the substance of the anointing in this season. According to the law of attraction, every spiritual substance is drawn, magnetised or attracted to you if you call it by name. By the same token, the substance of money hears and therefore comes when you call it. That is why the Bible declares in Romans 4:17 that *God calls things that be not as though they were*. In other words, He calls into existence the things that are not visible in the natural realm as though they are a tangible reality in that realm. The Greek word for call is *Kaleo* which means to summon or give an authoritative command, demanding that someone should appear. Therefore, spiritually speaking, when you say *"Money cometh to me, now,"* you are actually saying, "Money — you are hereby notified to appear and it will appear speedily according to your instruction. This is what I call *authority over money*.

UNVEILING THE SECRET OF MIRACLE MONEY AS A SPIRITUAL SUBSTANCE

How does the divine phenomenon of Miracle Money operate and in what form does it manifest?

In order for us to have an in-depth understanding of what Miracle money is, where it comes from and how it is manifested from the spirit realm into the physical realm, it is of paramount significance that we first understand money as a *spiritual substance*. Understanding money as a spiritual substance means understanding the original blue print of money in its spiritual form and how it is transmuted from the spirit realm into the natural realm. In our endeavour to comprehend any natural phenomena, it is always important that we understand spiritual things because the Bible says that *the things which are seen are made from the things which are not seen* (Hebrews 11:3). Owing to lack of revelation, many at times people don't view money as a spiritual substance, hence they are limited in their understanding of the dynamics of the supernatural manifestation of Miracle money. The greatest challenge that multitudes of believers across Christian cycles are facing is not because the phenomenon of Miracle money is difficult or too spiritual to understand, but it's simply because they lack a revelation and an acute understanding of the mechanics behind its manifestation. To unpack and uncover this divine truth, the Bible says in Hebrews 11:1 that *Now, faith is the substance of things hoped for, the conviction of things not seen*. We need to get a divine revelation engraved into our heart and mind that there is such a thing as a *spiritual substance*. From a scientific point of view, the word *substance* connotes to matter; something that is heavy, tangible and visible such that it bears the properties of weight, mass and density, hence can be touched., felt and seen. By the same token, faith is a tangible spiritual substance. The truth is that as much as there are natural substances, there are also spiritual substances which are more real than what is seen (2 Corinthians 8:18). The greater truth is that as aforementioned, there is an original blue print of everything that exists in the natural in the spirit. For example, there are houses, trees, people, and money in the spirit. And if only you could decide to live by this Heavenly understanding, you won't struggle to understand the dynamics of Miracle money, thus positioning yourself to be used as a vehicle or instrument to propagate its manifestation in the physical realm.

Notable is the realisation that the spirit world has its own material form which is different from that of the natural world. For example, God, Jesus and angels have a form. In 2 Corinthians 8:18, the Bible speaks of these two different realms of existence, that is, the realm of the spirit and the realm of the natural. These two worlds don't contact each other directly. Sometimes people in their visions make contact with the spirit world. It's because the spirit world would have chosen to materialize into the realm of the natural for us to feel its tangibility. On the other hand, the natural cannot move into the spiritual and go backwards because when the natural becomes spiritualized, there is no return path. It is for this reason that when Enoch walked with God, he walked Heavenward and stepped into the deepest and most scacred territories of the Glory Realm realm until he couldn't reverse back (Genesis 5:24). His being just got transformed into the spiritual realm to the level where he was translated into the spirit dimension to take a permanent abode in the spirit world.

Unveiling The Mystery of Miracle Money

The spiritual realm can affect and transmute itself into the physical for the inhabitants of the physical realm to touch and contact it. That is why it is possible for money in the spiritual form to manifest into the physical realm as Miracle Money.

Notable is the divine truth that during the Angelic era when God made angels, He took spiritual substances and brought them together. When God made man, He made him in a different realm with a spiritual ability, hence there is a substance that is very real. The Bible also speaks of the existence of angels' food in the spirit world called *manna*. In the book of Psalms, it says that the manna which the Children of Israel ate in the wilderness was actually angels' food (Exodus 16:31). It was transformed into a physical world so that natural man could eat it and survive for 40 years. It is breath-taking, to note that for 40 years, the whole nation of Israel survived on manna from Heaven. And that manna provided all the protein, carbohydrates, vitamins and minerals that they needed. It is remarkable to note that the spiritual substance can become a physical substance and provide everything that the physical world could have provided. They had everything in a manna form. Did the angels eat this manna too? Yes they did. It is called in the book of Psalms *angels' food* (Exodus 16:32). In view of the above revelation based on scriptural evidence, it is therefore evident that faith is not the only spiritual substance. Instead, *Grace is a spiritual substance, Glory is a spiritual substance and by the same token, Miracle money is also a spiritual substance.* As a matter of fact, a lot of the gifting of God comes as impartation of spiritual substance, hence it suffices to adjudicate that everything is a spiritual substance from the spirit world. One peculiar characteristic of the spirit world affecting our lives is not just by believing something. There must be some real impartation that comes into our life.

It could therefore be deduced that everything in the spirit world is a spiritual substance. By the same token, Miracle money comes from the spirit world and is transmuted into the physical realm, hence it is a spiritual substance.

Notable is the realisation that everything that we receive from God comes in the form of spiritual substances. If you receive wisdom from God, God imparts some real substances into your spirit although He could give these spiritual substances in measures. And the spirit of God's presence in our life is also a sort of spiritual substance coming into our life. Moreover, you have to embrace the divine truth that the anointing of God is a spiritual substance. The Holy Spirit is a person but the anointing of God, which comes from the Holy Spirit, and the *dunamis* of God is a spiritual substance. The spiritual attributes of wisdom, knowledge, power, authority, love, peace, joy, self-control, meekness, can be viewed as spiritual substances. The anointing of God is a substance of God. The power of the Holy Spirit is a substance of God and likewise Miracle money is a visible and tangible spiritual substance manifesting in the natural realm. Let me redefine the whole system. *Practically everything in the spirit world is a spiritual substance.* You may have never viewed these attributes as substances before, but I want you to know that they are substances. It's a different question when you talk about how the substance is imparted and what actually happens. You have never thought of humility or meekness as a substance, yet we know that there are different degrees of humility.

Sadly, many believers don't perceive Miracle Money as a spiritual substance yet it is a spiritual substance which is produced in the natural realm but proliferated from the spirit realm into the physical realm. It is for this reason that many of God's people are inhibited or humstrung from manifesting the reality of this unlimited grace in their sphere of contact.

If only you could live by Heavenly understanding and secure the divine revelation of Miracle money as a spiritual substance, you will be catapulted into a realm in which you will easily understand where it comes from, how it manifest and how it is transmuted from the spirit realm into the natural realm. It is worth exploring the divine truth that the realm of the spirit (supernatural) is a precursor of the natural realm; meaning that things happen first in the spiritual realm before they could manifest in the physical realm. The Bible concurs with this divine truth in 2 Corinthians 4:16-18, that *the things in the natural realm are a shadow or foretaste of the things which are in the spirit.* Therefore, before there could be any manifestation of Money in people's bank accounts, bags, houses or other unexpected places in the natural realm, it first exists in the spirit in a spiritual form. Such an understanding will make it easy for you to command Miracle money to manifest anywhere as a recipient of God's end time supernatural financial provision. The absence of revelation is what confines multitudes to a place of average thinking. That is why many are hamstrung and inhibited to manifest this grace. Since revelation preceeds manifestation, this divine revelation will unlock destiny codes and jettison you into an arena of your manifested destiny such that you will demonstrate Miracle money like a farmer sent out to the ripe fields for a bumper harvest, glory to God!

UNVEILING THE DIVINE REVELATION OF MIRACLE MONEY AS A "NEW THING"

Do you know that in every generation, God unfolds new manifestations of the Spirit to His elect so that they are able to freely partake of what God is doing in the invisible realm? Although many of the miracles that were performed in the Bible right across generations are now considered to be old *manna,* during the days when they transpired, they were actually regarded by the masses as a *new thing.* God operates according to the times (*Kairos*) and seasons (*Chronos*), hence there is something specific and *new* that He always does in a generation. In this end time season, the most overworked vocabulary in the realm of God's prosperity is the word *Miracle money* because it denotes the specifics of what God is currently brewing in the invisible arena. The greater truth is that in every generation, God unravels His hidden wisdom through the revelation of *new things.* These are divine substances which are unreservedly released from Heaven to earth, which unveils the reality of God's tangible Throne Room presence. It seems that the Lord is now doing very unusual things which simply don't have any physical explanation. There are realms of God's personality being revealed now that were not known five minutes ago. The angels are parading around the Throne, revealing the new realms of glory that they haven't seen before. The glory of God at the Throne Room is constantly evolving, with each change reflected through the radiation of different colours. Like birth pangs signalling the time of delivery, things are being released from the Heaven's Throne Room that have been preserved through the ages for this particular hour. The glory realm is becoming more real than the reality we are living in the natural realm. Therefore, the time has come for us to align ourselves with the blueprints of Heaven as it is undeniably evident that this is indeed a season of new things.

Prophetically speaking, a new day in the spirit is dawning. There is a new dimension of glory surfacing on the horizon. The skies are changing and the waves are shifting, heralding the times of refreshing that are dawning in the Body of Christ in this season. Tremendous manifestations of new realms of glory are surfacing on the horizon as the Body of Christ is catapulted right to pinnacle of God's glory on earth. As we step into the deepest territories of the Glory Realm in this season, God is ushering us into an era of rebirth of spiritual knowledge and a renaissance of new revelations. The Lord is echoing the same words which He spoke through the voice of Isaiah and He is saying, "*I'm doing a new thing! They are created now, and not so long ago, you have not heard of them before today*" (Isaiah 48:7). God is about to explode in the demonstration of signs and wonders by doing something so brand new that you won't yet have the language to describe it, neither will you have any vocabulary to speak about it. It would be like what Paul penned as, "*Something inexpressible for man to tell*" because there won't be any vernacular, jargon or vocabulary good enough to define it. The reason why God calls it a "*new thing*" is because it doesn't have a name as yet. It's a brand new phenomenon unfolding from the *Throne Room* of Heaven such that even the angels are still trying to comprehend it. It doesn't exist in your dictionary nor does it have a reference point. Hence, you will not call it by the name you used in the past because then, you would need a new vocabulary to describe it. You will not be able to reference it because it is not recorded; it cannot be photocopied, counterfeit or plagiarised. You will not be able to research about it because it is not written about. It cannot be googled but revealed.

Miracle money is therefore a "*new thing*" which God is unfolding from the Throne Room of Heaven for His people to freely and unreservedly indulge in this end time season. The term, *"Miracle money'* though you won't find it in the Bible, is a new terminology that we use to describe this brand new phenomenon that God is raining down from Heaven in this season. Money itself is never a miracle because it is a unit of exchange used to facilitate economic transactions but when its manifestation in the natural realm can only be traced to divinity, and is beyond human comprehension, it is said to be Miracle money. Prophetically speaking, God said, *"Down through the ages, I have given every man and woman a foretaste of my glory but what is coming now, it's never been seen"*. There is a rebirth of new manifestations in these end times such that humanity will not be able to look at it or recognise it because it will be completely fresh and brand new just like when *manna*, the food of angels was rained down on earth for the first time from Heaven. You cannot call it by the name you used in the past, hence you would need a new vocabulary to describe it in the same way the children of Israel looked at the food of angels that was rained down from Heaven and explained, *"manna,"* meaning *"what is this"* because they had not seen such a thing before. Therefore, in this season of the *glory invasion,* you need to break loose from the old and step into the new realms of glory, to impact the nations with the fresh spark of God's glory by demonstrating Miracle money everywhere you go.

Have you ever asked yourself how Jesus multiplied five loaves and two fish? It's because the glory realm is a realm of *new things*, hence natural substances are multiplied and new processes are continually given birth to in the deeper territories of the Glory Realm. This also explains how Jesus converted water into wine because in the Glory Realm, any substance can be changed into another form without altering its natural properties. Do you notice that God announces to the masses saying, *"Behold, I'm doing a new thing!* (Isaiah 48:7). Why is He telling you? Because there are certain things which God is unfolding in the spirit realm which man in his natural senses does not perceive. He is also telling you so that in tandem with what He is brewing in the realm of the spirit, you can also do the same in the natural realm. The greater truth is that as a Master of Creativity and Divine Orchestrator of new things, God is in the business of creating and proliferating *new things*. Although many of them might be brand new to the inhabitants of the natural realm, they are actually common place to the subjects in the spirit realm. The truth is that subjects in the natural realm are constantly being transformed and made anew so that they can conform to the original blueprint of how things are in the spirit realm. Although our physical bodies do not change at new birth, there is a regeneration, transformation and newness of life that gets imparted into our spirit as it is made anew by the Spirit of God. However, there are deeper realms of the Spirit in which the whole body of a believer gets to be transformed or metamorphosed as it enters the deeper and unexplored territories of the glory realm, a similar case to Jesus Christ's transfiguration on the Mount. These deeper realms of the Spirit are akin to inside-the-body and outside-the-body experiences which Paul testifies about when he was caught up to God's Throne Room in Heaven.

UNVEILING THE MECHANICS BEHIND THE DIVINE ORCHESTRATION OF MIRACLE MONEY IN THE INVISIBLE REALM

WHERE DOES MIRACLE MONEY COME FROM? IS IT MANUFACTURED IN HEAVEN OR IS IT DIVINELY TRANSFERRED FROM ONE SECTION OF THE ECONOMY TO THE OTHER?

In retrospect of the controversial views aired by those who question the credibility of Miracle money from an economic point of view, especially citing the issue of whether or not it is created in the spirit realm, this publication will put all your arguments and controversies to rest. I thank God that as one conferred with a Post Graduate Degree in Business Economics, I'm in a position to shade a greater light on this issue both from an economic point of view and from a theological perspective. To clear the air, there is no re-invention or re-creation of money involved in the divine orchestration of Miracle money. In His manifold wisdom, God does not need to tamper with the natural monetary system of this fallen world in order to transfer money for His intended purpose. Instead, God sovereignly works with the system which He created for man in the physical realm, bypassing natural laws and processes, to transfer money that is already in circulation in the economy and that is already laid down as financial reserves in the bank systems of nations and world renowned financial institutions such as the World Bank, IMF and other global financial institutions. It is for this reason that high ranking angels (*Angel Tellers*) are granted a Heavenly mandate to sit in the forums of the IMF and Global monetary institutions, in order to determine the direction in which money should be channelled. Miracle money is an end-product of what in the realm of God's prosperity I have coined as *"Divine income distribution"*. This is based on the following promise that God made to His people in the Old Testament and by extension, in the New Testament despensation: *"I will give you treasures of darkness and the riches in secret places, that you may know that it is I, the Lord, the God of Israel who call you by name"* (Isaiah 45:3). The phrase, *"treasures of darkness"* in the context of the above-mentioned scripture does not connote to evil as perpetuated by the devil but it alludes to the unexplored reserves of the wealth of Heaven, as mirrored by new manifestations of supernatural provision which God is unfolding from the deepest and most sacred territories of the Glory Realm. This is what God described in metaphoric language as *"secret places"*. This tells me that there is a divine equitable distribution of wealth that is divinely orchestrated by God, by which wealth is transferred from the secret places (unexpected places) into the hands of believers via the banking systems and other avenues in the natural realm.

To cement this revelation with reference to scriptural evidence, Proverbs concurs with this divine truth that *God transfers wealth from the hands of the wicked to believers.* And since both the wicked and the righteous don't live in Heaven but are inhabitants of this fallen world, it means that Miracle money is being supernaturally transferred from one section of the economy to the other through the natural avenues of monetary and banking systems. Owing to lack of revelation, some people presume that when you loose money on the earth, the Lord looses money in Heaven. No! The Lord in Heaven looses the money which is already here on the earth. Nowhere does it say that God transfers the money from Heaven, although Heaven is the central decision making point for it's global distribution. Alluding to the supernatural release of our finances, Jesus said, *"Whatever you loose on earth, I will loose it in Heaven."* Note that He is not talking about loosing something in Heaven. Yes, Jesus is in Heaven, but He is "loosing" *from* Heaven, not *in* Heaven. In the context of this revelation, He is speaking of releasing Miracle money from a Heavenly realm where you are seated with Him at the right hand of God. In Heaven, Miracle money won't need to be loosed, because it is not bound! So, Jesus was talking about loosing something on the earth because the Miracle money you need is already in the earthly realm although it might be in the hands of wicked people. Therefore, when you release it using your Heavenly authority, it is loosed from the hands of the wicked and starts to gravitate like a current, streaming in your direction. When you loose money, using your authority on the earth, the Lord looses the ability (anointing) to cause that which you declared to come to pass. In other words, when you command Miracle money to manifest in the natural realm, Heavens releases a supernatural influence that causes all forces of diinity to partner with you and angel tellers to be postured to act on the word you speak.

It is scripturally evident that Miracle money is not created *in* Heaven per se but *from* Heaven. Although it is divinely orchestrated in the Heavenly realm, it is not created in Heaven. If it was created in Heaven, do you think it would be in the condition in which people are receiving it? No! It would definitely be brand new paper notes, scented with a fresh smell of Heaven, mingled with an aroma of God's glory. It would be aromatised with a tantalising divine aura emanating directly from the Throne Room of Heaven. Besides, if it was manufactured in Heaven, do you think it would be having the images and inscription of man engraved on it? Definitely not! It would definitely have the image or inscription of the Lord Jesus, authenticated by the signature of God's own hand writing on it, and not those of Governors and politicians of this fallen world. This should tell you that God has a sovereign authority over all things and has an exclusive right and prerogative to manoeuvre human circumstances. Don't you know that money is created by the Reserve Bank of a country but the highest decisions pertaining to its dispacth in the economy come from the office of the Presidency? By the same token, money is created by the Reserve Banks of nations in the natural realm but the ultimate decisions governing it's propagation are made in the Heavenly meetings and angelic forums. This is to tell you that God owns everything and owes nothing, hence He can sovereignly dispatch Miracle money to which ever bank account He desires without any reservations.

Don't you find it interesting that God said, *"I own a thousand cattle on a thousand hills,"* yet referring to cattle owned by man. Do you think He was referring to wild animals? No! He was referring to cattle owned by people in this world but He brands them as His own. This shows you that as one with a title deed of the Universe, everything, including money belongs to God. Consider what God had to succinctly say concerning this divine truth: *Silver and gold is mine* (Hagai 2:7-8). Do you think God was referring to Silver and Gold in Heaven? No! The one in Heaven is used to pave the streets, hence there would not be any need for God to re-enforce the reality of its ownership because it is not subject to any corruption, wickedness and manipulation. So, He was referring to the money that is already in this world and this is the same Miracle money that He is supernaturally dispatching upon the masses in the Body of Christ, to expedite His purpose on earth shortly before He closes the curtain at the end of this age. If God could own silver and gold, which is a measurement of wealth and a portrait of the best monetary currencies of the world, it means that every money in this word, whether in the Banks, in circulation in the economy or in possession of human beings, belongs to God. Hence, He has a sovereign say as to who should have it, how it should be dispatched and for what purpose it should be used. Since the main business of Heaven is the propagation of the Gospel of Jesus Christ and the subsequent salvation of billions of souls across the globe, a large portion of God's money on the earth is being chanelled and allocated towards advancing the preaching of the gospel to the extreme ends of the word. In the same way Banks have Bank tellers who are responsible for the administration, processing and transaction of money in the natural realm, God has entrusted the responsibility for angel tellers to administer, transact and dispatch Miracle money to those whom He has given a mandate to propagate the gospel. In veiw of the above, it is therefore evident that Miracle money is the financial reserves that is tied up somewhere in the economy which requires the finacial anointing to loose it so that it can stream in your direction. So, it is more of a restoration principle than a re-invention concept which dozens of folks have erreneously presumed it to be.

CHAPTER TWO

THE THEOLOGY BEHIND THE MANIFESTATION OF MIRACLE MONEY

Unveiling The Secret Behind The Supernatural Manifestation of Miracle Money In The Natural Realm.

Where Does Miracle Money Come From And How Does It Manifest In The Natural Realm? And What Is The Scriptural Basis of This Divine Phenomenon?

It is of paramount importance to highlight in this regard the fact that there are dozens of scriptural references in the Bible which alludes to the mechanics behind the manifestation of the divine phenomenon of *Miracle Money*. Although many folks presume that this is a new Biblical concept, it is actually not. It might be demonstrated to a heightened degree in this end time season yet it has always been a notable supernatural act in the Christian fraternity by which God cashes out His Heavenly economy to meet a human need in the natural realm. God's supernatural provision has always grossly manifested in the Old Testament era although it's viscosity and degree of manifestation has skyrocketed in the New Testament dispensation, following the Holy Ghost invasion in the natural realm. It is important to note that as a generational phenomenon in the Bible, Elijah, Elisha, Jesus, Peter and the apostles demonstrated Miracle money although in different ways and in divergent forms. Have you ever wondered why Jesus commanded His disciples not to carry any money and shoes as they were sent out on a commission, yet they never lacked anything? (Luke 22:35). It's because finances were miraculously provided. In other words, the disciples of Jesus survived on Miracle money as they ministered the Word of God in various regions. I'm conscious of the fact that I might be stepping on religious toes of someone who might be asking, *"Can I really make a living on Miracle money?"* Emphatically yes! Miracle money is not something that is provided once a year when there is a church conference or a special religious gathering but a daily provision just like manna. Did God provide manna once a year for His children? Definately No! It was rained down from Heaven like dew every morning for God's people to feast sumptuously. In a like manner, Miracle money is designed to be a daily provision for God's people who trust and depend on Him for their daily bread. Manna is a Miracle money equivalent because it was supernaturally provided on the basis of the same divine principle as Miracle money.

Note that the term *"Miracle money"* as used in this publication, does not only refer to money expressed in financial terms but also connotes to any form of wealth that has monetary value and that could be readily converted to liquid cash. While coin and paper money is a widely used medium of exchange, the one who finds a diamond stone in his bag is also a recipient of Miracle money for upon selling it, he can receive actual paper money. Similarly, the one whose debts are supernaturally cancelled is in a way a recipient of Miracle money just like the one who finds money slipped through his wallet. In a similar vein, the one who finds quails blown to his feet, a ram caught by its horns or receives food from a raven is in a way a recipient of Miracle money. All these are divergent forms of Miracle money but their commonality is that they all carry the same monetary value. This is what defines the distinction between wealth and riches. Unfortunately, what most people are looking for is not wealth but riches. There is a world of difference here. The Webster dictionary defines wealth as *the abundance of valuable material possessions and resources.* On the other side of the coin, being rich is the state of your wallet; when it's full, you are rich but when it's empty, you are broke. It's about how much you have in your bank account. Most rich people make a lot of money but the minute it stops flowing, they are no longer rich but wealthy people build sustainable wealth that can last for years through consistent streams of incone. It is for this reason that gold, silver and diamond stones which are manifested supernaturally, though not available in monetary form, also represents the wealth of Heaven which is more sustainable than mere worldly riches.

To cement this divine revelation of the wealth of Heaven with reference to scriptural evidence, presented below are several Biblical scenarios and cases whereby Miracle money was practically demonstrated in the natural realm across generations. This wealth of scriptural knowledge is designed to deepen your level of faith in God's supernatural financial provision:

THE CASE OF PETER EXTRACTING MONEY FROM THE MOUTH OF A FISH

As an opening perspective to this revelation, the Bible gives a thrilling account in Matthew 17:27, of how Jesus demonstrated Miracle Money following a debate whether He should pay tax or not. Taxes, otherwise known as tribute money in the Bible, needed to be paid for Jesus and Peter but instead of going into the treasury, finances were miraculously provided. Jesus chose to solve the dilemma by performing a miracle that dazzled the minds of spectators and ruffled the feathers of the sceptics. Through the demonstration of this miracle, Jesus showed Peter His power as the Son of God, providing the tax money for both Peter and Himself in a symbolic way. The Bible records that when Jesus and His disciples needed money to pay for tax, He instructed Peter to go and get the money out of the mouth of a fish, saying,

The Theology Behind The Manifestation of Miracle Money

"Go, to the sea, and cast a hook, and take up the fish that shall come up first and when you have opened its mouth, you shall find a piece of money [Miracle money]: that take, and give it to them for me and you". **(Matthews 17:24-26).**

As per prophetic instruction, Peter then went and caught the fish with money in its mouth and brought the money back to Jesus so that they paid their tax. This is a manifestation of Miracle Money which is similar to the one which God is unfolding from the Throne Room and precipitating upon the masses right across the Body of Christ in this end time season. In the context of the above-mentioned scripture, the Greek word translated as piece of money is *statér*, a silver coin which was equivalent to one shekel, and therefore was the exact amount needed for two people (the temple tax was a half-shekel per person. In King James Version, it is called *Miracle Tribute Money*. The tribute part denotes the use of the money. If you remove the use of the money, what remains is *Miracle money*, which is the buzz word and the most overworked Christian vocabulary that is currently trending in the Christian fratenity. The question you are probably asking yourself is:

Where did the fish and the money come from and how did the Money enter the mouth of the fish?

It is very striking to note what the Lord used to get the money to Peter—a fish. Who would have ever thought that a fish can be used to bring forth money? Spectacular as it seems, that was a supernaturally *"called"* fish. It was called by the Lord, summoned by the supernatural power of God, to *"come up first"* with the money in its mouth! In this verse, the Lord Jesus demonstrated in practical terms that He can control the system on behalf of those who unwaveringly trust Him! As aforementioned, Peter had been a fisherman for a long time, but I bet he never caught a fish with money in its mouth! What happened to him in this case was an irrefutable miracle! In modern day language, Peter received Miracle money! This shows that God has sovercign control over all things. He is intricately interwoven in every fabric of His creation and uses His royal prerogative to manoeuvre the very things which He created. He is the God of the Reserve Bank, the one who holds the title deed of every currency in this world and a sole proprietor of the whole Universe. Silver and gold belongs to Him (Hagai 2:8). He is the God of money, and not the devil as some folks have ignorantly presumed it to be. Therefore, what we only have to realize today is that God has sovereign control over the monetary system of the world but He needs someone to give Him some faith to work with to be able to show Himself strong on his behalf, in the same way He needed Peter's faith to work with in order to produce results in the natural realm. Inevitably, another provocative question that arises is: If God put the money in the fish's mouth, why didn't He simply put it in Peter's hand instead? Firstly, it's because He needed Peter to exercise his faith and launch out into a deeper realm in the same way Jesus did not put the fish in Peter's hand in Luke 5:4, but commanded him to cast the nets into the deep waters. Secondly, it's because God uses natural phenomena which He created, as means to supernaturally provide for His children. It is for this reason that He is currently using the banks to provide Miracle money.

Now, at least we know where the fish came from, but what about the money? This is exactly a typical scenario of how God operates in the current times concerning the release of Miracle Money. In the same way Peter caught the fish but did not know where the money came from and how it got into the mouth of the fish, many people receive Miracle Money supernaturally deposited in their bank accounts and they know that the money has come from the bank yet they don't know how it got into the bank. The reality is that it's not every day or any day that someone catches a fish and takes a coin out of its mouth but Jesus used Heaven's supernatural provision to pay His taxes. In other words, He instructed the economy of Heaven to supply the reserves to the economy of the natural realm. The greater truth is that Jesus chose to use the fish as a means to bring the money in the same way He is using a bank as a means to dispatch Miracle Money in this end time season. Philosophically speaking, the *fish* is the bank and the *coin* is the Miracle Money supernaturally deposited into the bank. It is clear that God used a fish not to create new money per se, but to divinely transport the money that was already in circulation, to gravitate and stream in the direction where Peter was in the natural realm. In a similar fashion, God can also divinely send people or angels to deliver money or anything wherever He wants in the same way He used a fish to bring forth the money He needed. In the current times, God can compel forces of divinity to supernaturally deposit money in the bank as a means to bring the money into your hands. He can release a supernatural influence in the realm of the spirit that will trigger a divine arrangement of circumstances for Miracle money to stream in your direction.

An investigation into the background of this narrative unveils a notion that Peter was an experienced fisherman who had caught thousands of fish in his entire life. Out of all those thousands of fish he had caught before, Peter had never found a coin in the mouth of a fish until Jesus gave him that revelation, let alone the exact coin that would adequately pay the tax for both of them. This was a live demonstration of Miracle money at its highest degree! Notable is the realisation that the distance between Peter and the money in the mouth of the fish was in *revelation*. Likewise, the distance between you and the millions you require in this season, is in the depth of revelation you have received from Jesus. In the same way Jesus caught a revelation of demonstrating Miracle money in order to pay for His tax, if you could decide to live by Heavenly understanding, you will cash out Miracle money from the economy of Heaven, to cover your bills. It should be further noted that Jesus did not instruct Peter to catch the fish and then sell it in order to obtain money. Neither did He go to the bank to make a withdrawal. Instead, He commanded Peter to obtain the Miracle money from the fish itself. In other words, the fish was not the wealth, but a means to bring the money or wealth into physical manifestation. It must be further noted that Jesus did not tell Peter to go for *selling* at the market in order to get the money. Instead, He told him to go for *fishing*. In other words, He instructed Peter to go and do what he already knew how to do best because Peter was a fisherman by trade. In a similar vein, Miracle Money might not come from distant sources but right in the profession or occupation where you are as long as the right spiritual atmosphere or climate is well cultivated for the glory of God to be manifested. Therefore, if you are a teacher, you should demonstrate Miracle Money in the classroom; if you are a vendor, demonstrate Miracle Money in the streets and if you are an Accountant, demonstrate Miracle Money in your office but the principle is that whenever you are, Miracle Money can be demonstrated, to the glory of God. It is interesting to note that Miracle Money was demonstrated live without a church gathering, a preaching or a religious song. Therefore, you need not to put God in a box by thinking that Miracle Money can only be demonstrated within the vicinity of church bars and doors for the glory of God has gone forth beyond church boundaries.

It is strikingly remarkable in this Biblical account to note that Jesus told Peter to go fishing and take the *first fish*, reach inside it and extract a coin and use it to pay for their tax. This is akin to how the *first person* who happened to step into the pool of Bethsaida after the angel stired up the pool, received their healing (John 5:1-15). The principle demonstrated here that keeps the Windows of Heaven opened for one to receive miraculous provision is when you put God first in every sphere of human endevour. The Bible concurs in Proverbs 3:9 that *to honour the Lord with thy substance and with the first-fruits of all thine increase, so shall thy barns be filled with plenty and thy presses shall burst out with new wine.* This is simply talking about if we put God first in financial matters, He would be responsible for helping us to increase financially. As Peter opened the fish's mouth, he found financial provision and obeyed the Lord's command to pay Jesus taxes first and then his own taxes. This is Miracle Money in action and Jesus chose to use a fish as a means to bring forth the miracle into manifestation. Jesus was conscious of His position of sonship, that the son pays the tax levied for his Father's house, but He exercises His royal prerogative in the act, and takes the shekel out of the royal treasury. As a man, He pays tax but as God, He causes the fish to bring Him the shekel in its mouth. Yet He did pay for Peter, as a foreshadow of the work of redemption for all men. Jesus did not actually owe the price but paid it nevertheless – and at the same time, with the same price, paid for Peter. What a spectacular financial miracle! In the same way Jesus got exempted from paying tax by cashing out the economy of Heaven, in this season, you will supernaturally receive your salary in your bank account without any tax deductions. This is something to shout about!

The Theology Behind The Manifestation of Miracle Money

The demonstration of this financial miracle is akin to how Peter toiled throughout the night in an endeavour to catch fish but could not catch anything until Jesus stepped on the scene and gave him a revelation to cast into the deep waters and let down the nets for a catch (Luke 5:4). It depicts a typical scenario across a broad spectrum of Charismatic faith in this season. Just like Peter, multitudes of people have been toiling and hustling in certain careers or professions yet they never experience humongous financial breakthroughs. Until Jesus steps on the scene with a deeper revelation from the Throne Room, you might sweat from dusk till dawn, toiling to the bone, yet you are barely making any significant progress in life. Until Jesus steps on the scene to intervene with Miracle Money, you might never become a Millionaire or prosper financially in this season. Until you receive an impartation of the Miracle money anointing, demonstrating Miracle money in the natural realm might remain a dream in the distant horizon. This is because the anointing is what causes the money to come to you because money is like a current; it always gravitates in the direction in which the anointing is flowing.

It is also interesting to note that while it seemed as if the fish were previously refusing to enter Peter's nets, following the revelation of casting the nets into a deeper realm, it now appeared as if the fish themselves started competing to enter his nets. You see, the problem was not with the gifting per se, because Peter was an experienced fisherman. Instead, the problem was the depth, dimension or level of operation, that's why Jesus told him to shift his position and cast into the deeper realm. You see, you need to cast your faith into the deeper realm and push beyond the dictates and confines of your comfort zone to a realm that is unfamiliar to your status quo. It's when you step into that deeper realm that Miracle money will be greatly demonstrated and millions of Kingdom wealth will stream in your direction. When the Kingdom net is thrust out into the deeper realm of the miraculous, it pulls in fish of your ministry, business and the world at large. Just like Peter, begin to put your foot out of the boat and God will make the waters solid under your feet. Shift your position and launch into a deeper realm in the supernatural, then you will see the difference. God says,

Unveiling The Mystery of Miracle Money

"I'm stiring the wind of provision that will unravel and baffle you to the last degree in this very hour. What you have cast in the deep waters is ready to float and gravitate to the shoreline. I will stir a whirlwind that will cause what you have cast in the deep waters in the past to come forth in abundance."

Probably, you might have read the above-mentioned portion of scripture a thousand times but have you ever assumed a moment to think that this was Miracle money demonstrated here? How many times does it happen that the fishermen catches a lot of fish to the extent that the nets breaks, let alone in Peter's career as a fisherman? This was indeed a demonstration of Miracle money in the natural realm by the Lord Jesus! This time, it's not the fish that came out with money in their mouths per se, but it's the fish themselves that came out in extraordinarily large quantities. As a fishermen, it's logical to think that Peter probably sold the fish and obtained a lot of money since fishing was a lucrative business at that time. Whichever way it comes, Miracle money will always manifest supernaturally although the avenues in the natural realm might be diverse. Notable is the realisation that before Jesus stepped on the scene, there were no fish but as soon as He appeared and gave a revelation, the fish also came. Propheticaly speaking, the same anointing that caused the fish to come when Jesus instructed Peter to cast his nets into the deep, will cause money to supernaturally stream in your direction. Where there was no money in your life before, money is coming on feet in your direction by the anointing of the Holy Ghost. Those who despised you before and deserted you on account of your dibilitating circumstances, will come back in the same way the fish made their way back into Peter's nets, glory to Jesus!

It must be therefore understood that Jesus is the Lord yesterday, today and forever and even though times have changed and His divine methodological operations might have changed in line with times and seasons, His principle remains the same. In other words, it is the times and seasons that changes but His nature, character and virtue stays the same. Hence, if He performed Miracle money by extracting it from a fish, then it is absolutely possible for us believers in this present generation to also obtain Miracle money supernaturally. If God could put money in the mouth of a fish that was under the sea where there are no shops, boutiques and banks, how much more would He not put the same money in your wallet, bag or bank account? In the current times, money might not come through a fish per se but the principle is that money is spiritual and can be obtained supernaturally. Do you notice that Jesus did not extract the money Himself directly from the spirit realm. Instead, He used Peter as a pipeline to channel the money into manifestation in the natural realm? Peter was postured in the realm of the spirit as a conduit of God's power, to pioneer Miracle money in the earthly realm. In the like manner, Jesus is going to strategically position you at the frontline of the global explosion of the Miracle money revival in this season. Hence, your duty is to cast your faith into a deeper spirit realm in order to manifest Miracle money in the natural realm. As a matter of fact, the end time revival of wealth grossly manifested through the supernatural manifestation of Miracle money has just exploded. Prophetically speaking, during ministerial meetings where believers gather to worship the Lord, money will supernaturally appear in people's bank account, bags, wallets and houses as a result of angelic deposits by the *Angels of finances* or *Angel tellers*. This thrilling and spectacular move of the Spirit shall be coupled with the supernatural appearance of Heavenly precious stones such as gold dusts, silver stones, diamonds, jewels and supernatural oil which represents the wealth of Heaven manifested by the *Angel of precious stones*. And these shall supernaturally appear soaked on people's bodies, on the ground or on buildings where saints gather for worship. This is a fulfilment of the scripture in Isaiah 43:19, which God declared through the voice of Prophet Elijah saying,

> *"Behold, I'm doing a new thing, something that you have not seen before. Can't you see it as it spring forth?".*

Why is God asking a rhetoric question: *Can't you see it as it spring forth?"* It's because He knows that there are those who will not be able to see what He is doing in the invisible realm in the same way multitudes are not seeing the explosion of the Miracle money revival that has already begun in this season. This is critical because in the realm of the spirit, things are procured through vision; as you see it, you get it. Sadly, those who are not attuned to the realm of prophetic perception, to see what God is brewing in the unseen realm, are likely to be eluded by this blessing of Miracle money. Therefore, to corroborate the authenticity of this divine phenomenon of Miracle money with supernatural evidence, it is always accompanied by the rain of creative miracles such as the infilling of gold teeth, germination of hair on bald heads, weight loss or gain, instantaneous increase or reduction in the height of people as well as the supernatural appearance of the original blue print of body parts in bodily territories where they previously did not exist. This is often accompanied by the presence of *Angel feathers* floating in the atmosphere or resting on the ground where saints gather for worship, signifying the presence of angel tellers responsible for depositing Miracle money in unexpected places. This is meant to reinforce a spiritual understanding that this phenomenon is from God, hence humanity should not be sceptical or hesitant to partake in His glorious financial provision.

PROPHETIC DECLARATION OF MIRACLE MONEY

In the same way God caused money to come out of a fish, I declare and decree that money will come forth from unexpected places and stream in your direction. By the power of the Holy Ghost, I release the fish that is carrying your Miracle money to begin to move in the direction in which you have cast the hook in Jesus name. I release a supernatural influence in the realm of the spirit to channel Miracle money in your direction. I declare and decree that the fish in your job, business and ministry will release money to you in Jesus name. I command anything that is supposed to produce money in your life to release it in abundance. I command your business, projects and workplace to be productive in Jesus name. Your business shall make a profit, your salary shall increase and your projects shall flourish in Jesus name.

THE CASE OF RAINING DOWN OF MANNA FROM HEAVEN

Another enthralling spectacle of demonstration of Miracle money involves the raining down of manna, the food of angels upon the children of Israel as they journeyed through the wilderness of Nain. This spiritually provocative narrative records in Exodus 16:1-18 that,

> *God supernaturally caused manna to fall like dew from Heaven and the children of Israel had to collect every morning and evening and were abundantly satisfied.*

In view of this revelation, it is imperative that you catch an in-depth understanding of the dynamics of the spirit realm or how the realm of the spirit operates in relation to the natural realm. Spiritually speaking, manna was a spiritual substance used as food of angels but it transmuted itself into a physical substance that is tangible and visible in the physical realm for the people of God to partake of. This is what we describe in geographical language as the *condensation, crystallisation and solidification of God's power*. In a view to unpack the divine revelation of the condensation of God's power, it is worth exploring the divine truth that there is a level and dimension which a man can operate in the spirit realm whereby he encounters the power of God as a solid spiritual substance. However, although power is a spiritual substance, it can transmute or manifest itself in the natural realm in a solid, tangible and visible form just like manna. For example, in the natural, you cannot touch water vapour. You could sort of try to catch water vapour but you cannot because it is in a vaporized state. But when water is condensed or crystallised into a liquid or solid form, it becomes tangible. In the same manner, manna is invisible while it is in the spirit realm yet God can cause a condensation of His Heavenly provision to take place in the natural realm such that it materialises into a solid, crude and tangible form. In other words, God can cause a solidification of Heavenly substances upon humanity in the natural realm so that they can be consumed as substitute products which meets a human need in the natural realm.

It is evident in this narrative that when the realm of the natural has run out of supplies, the spirit realm is always readily available as an alternative source of income. By the same token, if the economic system of the world does not provide a lee way or accentuate an avenue for you to become a Millionaire or Billionaire, God can cash out the economy of Heaven and create an avenue for you to supernaturally receive millions of wealth and instantaneously become the World's Richest Man. This implies that there are two ways through which one can become a Millionaire, that is, through natural processes of applying worldly monetary principles of investing in the economy or through spiritual means of applying higher spiritual laws, one of which is the manifestation of Miracle money. This scripture brings to light two different economies, that is, the *Heavenly economy* from which manna was rained down in abundance and the *World economy* which was in lack as evidenced by the prevalence of drought in the wilderness. It is evident that when the natural realm failed to provide the much needed daily supplies for humanity to thrive, God cashed out the economy of Heaven by releasing its own supplies from the Heavens' Storehouse to address the crisis in the physical realm. This scenario completely debunks the scepticism of those who say that Miracle money cannot be rained directly from Heaven. If manna was rained down from Heaven on a daily basis upon the wilderness, why would it not be possible for God to use the same avenue to release Miracle money upon the wilderness of this World's failing economic system?

To quantify this divine truth, let's assume that the Israelites numbered about 3,000,000 people, which is what many Bible scholars estimate. In that case, do you know how much manna was needed to feed the children of Israel in the wilderness? One scholar has estimated that they needed 4,500 tons of manna every day! If this is true, and if you take into account that God fed His people every day for 40 years, this means 65,700,000 tons of manna supernaturally appeared on the ground over a period of forty years! This manna appeared so regularly, so faithfully, so *"day in and day out,"* that after a while, the children of Israel didn't even think too much of it anymore. Supernatural provision became so commonplace among them that they forgot how supernatural it was and began to accept it as a normal, regular occurrence. Do you know that there is a level that you can reach in the realm of the miraculous whereby you experience a catalogue of miracles such that it becomes naturally supernatural to encounter a miracle? During those forty years, young children were born and grew up thinking it was normal for 4,500 tons of manna to appear each morning out of thin air (Exodus 16)! Hypothetically speaking, what do you think would happen if your city woke up tomorrow to find 4,500 tons of beautiful, freshly baked, nourishing manna lying on the streets all over the city, free to anyone who wanted to go out, pick it up, and take it home? I'm sure it would dominate the breaking news headlines! Scientists would fly from around the world to see it, study it, and taste it. Journalists would write about it, and major news programs would cover the story. It would be a worldwide sensation. But for the children of Israel, this was an event that occurred every morning. It was naturally supernatural for them to find manna rained on the ground every morning. As I pondered on this reality, I began to see clearly why it is easy for God to rain Miracle money in this dry end time season.

Prophetically speaking, in these end times, God shall cause money to fall directly from Heaven into people houses, bags, wallets, hands or designated areas during prayer or ministerial sessions in the same manner in which manna was rained down like dew from Heaven and this shall be used for the furtherance of the gospel. This is what we call in prophetic language, *Money Rain*. This is contrary to the logical misconstrued notion held by dozens of Christians that God cannot rain down money directly from Heaven. Unfortunately, some Christians across certain charismatic cycles only believe that God provides for His children through touching the hearts of other people to give, which is partially true. Although pastors have been customarily preaching that in order for one to receive from God, he must give, it appears that we have entered a season in which we operate according to higher laws of finance whereby we receive Miracle money even without sowing anything. This is what Jesus described in prophetic language as *buying without money*. The greater truth is that God must not be put in a box. As a matter of fact, God does not have one formula or one method of doing things, that is why He declared in Isaiah 55:8-9 that, "*My ways are not your ways, neither are my thoughts your thoughts. As high as heaven is above the earth, so are my ways higher than your ways"*. It should be noted that in His dealings with the Children of Israel in the wilderness, God could have used His sovereign authority to send other nations to provide food for them but He chose to directly rain down manna, an act that dazzle natural minds and ruffle the feathers of those comfortable with the status quo.

Therefore, those who are only looking out to other people to bless them with something are likely to miss their blessings and a lot more of what God is doing in the present time. Those who are customarily used to the art of sowing in hope to receive a hundred fold return on their sowing should examine the times and re-look into their theology so that they don't limit themselves by confining their ability to receive from God to a hundred fold exchange for what they have given. It is therefore advisable that every believer operating in these critical times be circumspect, vigilant and open to a myriad of ways of God's supernatural provision. As evidenced by the above scripture, God can go beyond mere touching the hearts of people into directly causing money to fall from Heaven in the same way He rained manna and the word of God is unquestionable in this respect. It is a precarious move for a Christian to be left at the same spot yet God has moved forward and He is currently using Miracle money to bless His children. A time will come shortly whereby Miracle money shall become a common phenomenon, an *"in thing"* and a household name as a dependable source of income in the Body of Christ. Therefore, failure to partake of this end time grace would be an indication of gross ignorance and insensitivity to God's times and seasons. As matter of fact, *the season of precipitation of unusual or miracle money is ripe since its widespread manifestation has just begun*. Therefore, this is the best opportunity for believers to become Kingdom Millionaires and Billionaires.

PROPHETIC DECLARATION OF MIRACLE MONEY

In a similar manner in which God rained manna directly from Heaven, I release the rain of Miracle money over your life, your bank account and your house in Jesus name. I declare and decree that you will eat the food that you didn't cook, for angels will cook for you. You will feed on groceries that you did not pay for. You will earn a salary that you did not labour for. You will reap where you did not sow. By the power of the Holy Ghost, I catapult you to a higher supernatural dimension, whereby you will never depend on common money, ever again. Angel's food shall be your provision, for you are more than a man. By divine protocol, I elevate you to the angelic realm, whereby you will feed with angels, dine with angels and commune with Heavenly hosts just like a man talks to his friends.

THE CASE OF THE SUPERNATURAL APPEARANCE OF WATER IN A DESERT WITHOUT ANY SIGN OF A CLOUD OR RAIN.

The Bible records another thrilling incident in 2 Kings 3:16-18 which involved defying the laws of nature through the supernatural appearance of water in a desert. This was a clear demonstration of God's sovereignty in the light of His creation and a sign of the prevalence of the spiritual climate over the natural atmosphere as natural weather conditions were changed, even without giving any notice in the natural realm. According to this narrative,

God supernaturally caused a flood of water to appear in a desert, without even a sign of a cloud or rain in the natural realm.

To provide an introductory perspective to this narrative, immediately after Elijah was taken to Heaven, Elisha began to be used by God to perform unusual miracles as the recipient of the *"double portion"* anointing. The Bible records how Elisha was then used to win a military battle for the nation of Israel as the Head Prophet. After the death of Ahab the King of Israel, the King of Moab decided to rebel against Israel. Joram, the King of Israel asked Jehoshaphat the King of Judah to be on his side and the two Kings united their armies and travelled toward their enemy. But after marching for seven days, they were completely out of water. There was no water for the soldiers and their horses. King Jehoshaphat had to ask the prophet of God for advice and Elisha told King Joram that if it weren't for Jehoshaphat, he wouldn't even speak to Joram. However, since Jehoshaphat was a King who respected the Lord, Elisha was willing to help them. Then Elisha heard a message from the Lord, and told it to the Kings. The Lord told them to dig ditches all over the land. The Lord said,

"You will not see wind or rain. But this valley will be filled with water. Then you, your cattle and your other animals will have water to drink. That's an easy thing for the Lord to do. He will also hand Moab over to you." (2 Kings 3:17-18)

Acting on God's prophetic word, the soldiers dug the ditches, and the next morning water came flooding in! It didn't come from a rainstorm but it came flooding in from the country that the soldiers had just travelled through. What a miracle! With the ditches full of water, the soldiers and their horses had plenty to drink. Note that the act of soldiers digging the ditches was registered in the realm of the spirit as a prophetic action of faith which enlarged their capacity to receive from God. It's akin to the action of faith exhibited by the widow of Zeraphath whom upon receiving a prophetic instruction from prophet Elijah, unwaveringly acted on the Word by gathering empty jars from her neighbours in order to contain the oil. The narrative records a sudden dramatic turn of events that when the Moab soldiers looked down over the land, the ditches of water looked red to them. Perhaps it was the reflection of the sunrise in the water, or maybe God created a perception in their minds such that they perceived water as red as blood. The underlying factor is that it became ingrained in their thinking that the ground was covered in blood. They thought the soldiers of Judah and Israel had all killed each other during the night. So, the Moab army came running down expecting all their enemies to be dead. However, these soldiers were taken by surprise when the soldiers of Israel and Judah ran out to fight them. That day, the armies of God's people resoundingly won the battle against the army of Moab. It was akin to a walk through a park! It is interesting to note that not only did God provide the much

The Theology Behind The Manifestation of Miracle Money

needed water for His people to quench their thirst in the schorching heat of the desert but He also handed over ther enemies to them on a silver plate. This is what we call a *double doze of blessings*. This is the charecter of the God that we serve. He does not respond to our prayers based on the limitations of our needs in the natural realm but according to the riches in Christ glory available in the Heavenly realm. That is why He always provides a surplus to what we ask of Him. You ask Him for a miracle and He gives you a blessing; you ask Him for riches and He gives you wealth; you ask Him for a family and He gves you the nations, and in this seaosn, you will ask Him for provision in the desert of the World's economy and He will give you Miracle Money, glory to His Name!

From a natural perspective, a desert is the most arid place where no one would expect water to appear in abundance and in a spiritual context, it speaks of an unfavourable financial situation of dire lack or abject poverty. This implies that if you are broke, in lack or poor, then you are in a financial desert. In the context of the above scripture, the supernatural appearance of a flood of water in a desert is a clear indication that with regard to supernatural financial provision, God is not compelled to give notice of His arrival to usher an unexpected, sudden turnaround in your financial situation. In the same way a flood of water appeared supernaturally in a desert without anybody expecting it, Miracle money shall manifest widely in unexpected places even without a church song, a preaching or any *"Amen"* from the congregation. While multitudes of Christians would traditionally expect clouds to build up first in the sky and in some cases be accompanied by thunder and lightning before yielding any rain, God can manifest His sovereignty, glory and power anytime, anywhere even without you having to do anything. Therefore, the Christian traditional notion that God does not come unless you do something is an Old Testament teaching which is not applicable in this end time season.

Do you notice that the Lord Himself said that performing a miracle of this nature is an easy thing to do? Owing to ignorance and lack of revelation, while humanity in the natural realm have been erroneously taught that it is a daunting task to release certain miracles, God says, it is actually easy.

In fact there is no miracle regardless of the viscosity of its manifestation in the natural realm which can be said to be a daunting task for the Lord to perform because impossibility is not part of the vocabulary of Heaven, nor is it part of the realm in which God exist. In one of my powerful books titled, *"The Realm of Power to Raise the Dead"*, I have decoded the divinely coded mysteries on resurrection and proved both theologically and practically that it is actually easy to raise someone from the dead than it is to heal a religious Christian from a headache. As humanity steps into the realm of the undefinable, uncharted and unrecorded miracles in this last season, they shall be catapulted to a higher dimension in the spirit in which raising the dead shall become common place to God's children just like healing someone from a headache. This is because it is God's nature to perform miracles. In other words, it is naturally supernatural for God to raise the dead. Just as it is the nature of a carpenter to work on wood, just as it is the nature of a mechanic to work with machines, so it is with God. It is His nature to work miracles. Miracles are as natural to God as breathing is to us, hence raising the dead falls within the domain of the realm in which He exists, functions and operates. If God could release the resurrection power for you to raise the dead as if you are waking up people from their slumber, how would it not be possible for Him to precipitate Miracle money? This is to tell you that even releasing Miracle money is such an easy thing for the Lord to do. In the same way God declared that *"You will not see wind or rain. But this valley will be filled with water. Then you, your cattle and your other animals will have water to drink. That's an easy thing for the Lord to do. He will also hand Moab over to you."* (2 Kings 3:17-18), concerning the release of your Miracle money in this season, God is saying to you,

> *"You will not see depositor or source of finance. But this bank account will be filled with money. Then you, and your other family members will have money to spend. That's an easy thing for the Lord to do. He will also cancel off your debts."*

This is to tell you that releasing Miracle money from the spirit realm into visible manifestation in the natural realm is such an easy undertaking; it's a walk through a park as far as God is concerned.

The Theology Behind The Manifestation of Miracle Money

Do you notice that water supernaturally appeared in the desert without any notice of wind, cloud, thunder or even rain, at such a time when no one would expect it to rain? By the same token, in this end time season, Miracle money shall appear in places where no one would expect it to appear. Also note the speed and alacrity with which the flood of water appeared in the desert. It is unequivocally evident in this scenario that the realm of the spirit is the arena of speed and acceleration, hence everything happens *"suddenly"* and *"immediately."* This is what defines the distinction between *"escalation"* and *"elevation"*. In the case of escalation, there are a series of steps, phases and processes through which one migrates from one level to the next but in the case of elevation, at one point you are down and suddenly you are at the top in the next moment. This is to tell you that in this season of Miracle money, people whom the world never expected to be Millionaires or Billionaires shall arise with such an amazing financial power to take over the world's monetary system. Many of these will be emerging from obscure and isolated, backyard ministries but will rise with such an amazing financial power that will dazzle the minds of onlookers and ruffle the feathers of those comfortable with the status quo.

Do you also notice that the water did not come from a nearby tributary nor did it flow from a distant uphill but it supernaturally rained down from Heaven? This is what we describe in prophetic language as *supernatural rain*. It is divinely orchestrated in the spirit realm but is then precipitated through the avenues of the natural realm as a solid substance which could be used to meet a physical need. Taking into account the nature of its manifestation, it could be deduced that supernatural rain is a Miracle money equivalent because it doesn't give any notice of its arrival. Prophetically speaking, in the same way a flood of water appeared in a desert without any notice, symptom or sign of rain (2 Kings 3:17), in this Kairos moment, money shall supernaturally appear in people's bank accounts even without making any investments, property shall be obtained by believers even without making any deposits, believers shall win millions worth of prices in competitions they never entered, others shall be called to take up jobs they never applied for, houses shall be built without buying any land and loans shall be rendered even without applying for them and debts shall be cancelled instantaneously to give way to God's supernatural provision. When this happens, anything that can allow a man to depend on the natural for provision or obtain wealth through physical means shall be frozen in order to pave way or accentuate an avenue for the manifestation of God's supernatural provision. Moreover, long deserted accounts shall be refilled with money, houses long forsaken shall be rebuilt (Isaiah 61:4). Godly visions long forgotten or aborted shall be re-birthed. Those who shall open themselves to this final move of God and rightly position their spirits to partake of this last wave of prosperity by commanding Miracle money to appear in designated areas, shall reap alarming benefits of Millions and Billions in Miracle money.

PROPHETIC DECLARATION OF MIRACLE MONEY

In a similar fashion in which a flood of water appeared in a desert without any notice, symptom or sign of rain (2 Kings 3:17), I declare and decree that money, in the best currencies of the World, shall supernaturally appear in your bank account even without making any deposits. I declare and decree that you shall secure property even without making any investment. You shall win millions worth of prices in competitions you never entered. They will call your name where you never registered. You shall be called to take up jobs you never applied for. You shall built houses without buying any land. I declare and decree that loans shall be rendered to you even without applying for them and all your debts shall be cancelled supernaturally. Without any business endeavour, without any toiling and sweating, you shall be catapulted to the realm of Millionaires and Billionaires, in Jesus name.

THE CASE OF WATER COMING OUT OF A ROCK IN THE WILDERNESS

Have you ever wondered how water came out of the rock when God instructed Moses to hit the rock in order for the Children of Israel to quench their thirst under the scorching heat of the wilderness? (Numbers 20:11) *Where did that water come from?* In the natural realm, due to its aridity, it is impossible for a rock to produce thousands of gallons of water in a desert. This was God's supernatural provision whose manifestation was beyond human reasoning capacity and this is exactly how Miracle Money operates in the natural realm. That was a Miracle water, which came directly from Heaven to supply what the wilderness had failed to provide for His children in the natural realm! This was a demonstration of supernatural financial provision to its heightened degree, a move that not only boggles the mind but dumb-found the critics and sceptics. That is why some of the ways through which Miracle money is being demonstrated in the natural realm in this season, is something that will crack your head, dazzle your mind and leave you shocked for life. Do you have any idea how much water it would have taken to support three million Israelites in the blistering hot temperatures of the wilderness? You also have to take into account all the animals that needed to be nourished with water. Keep in mind that God's people were in a dry, arid wilderness which was a barren place, almost like a desert. The only available source of water was bitter and undrinkable, hence there was no natural source of water to nourish that huge crowd of people.

Quantitatively speaking, consider the amount of water it would have taken to adequately nourish *3,000,000 people* and all the animals in the hot and scorching temperatures of the wilderness. It would have required up to *15,000,000 gallons of water* every day just to meet their basic needs for existence as water was especially crucial in that extremely hot climate. Just one week's supply would equal approximately *100,000,000* gallons of water. Both people and animals needed much more water than they normally would and without water, they would have dried up and died in the wilderness. But because there was no natural source of water, it had to be provided for them supernaturally. It is for this reason that God told Moses to *strike the rock* (Exodus 17). When Moses obeyed, water began to supernaturally flow from the midst of that rock and it continued to flow, providing all the water needed by the people of God. What a spectacular miracle of provision!

In a spiritual sense, *"the rock"* speaks of the dryness and hardness of the economic conditions and the failing monetary system of this world. It symbolically depicts a threatening and darkening global economic outlook characterised by an incessant recession and crash in stock markets. *"Water"* coming out of the rock speaks of God's supernatural provision and flow of Miracle Money which is manifested regardless of the dryness of the economic situation. It shows that God will make a way where there is no way and that He will turnaround any situation that seem impossible in the natural realm. Impossibility is not part of the vocabulary of Heaven, nor is it part of the realm in which He exist. God can turn impossibilities into possibilities; a mess into a message; a test into a testimony; a trial into triump; a curse into a blessing; a victim into victory; a sweat into sweet and wailing into dancing, glory to Jesus! The act of *"Striking a rock"* speaks of tapping into the realm of faith to command God's supernatural provision in the form of Miracle Money to manifest or appear in places where one would not expect to find money under normal circumstances. Therefore, in this end time season, God demands that you *"strike a rock"* in order to see an abundant, torrential down pour of His miraculous or supernatural provision. In other words, God demands that you stretch your faith to command Miracle Money into manifestation and as you declare it, it shall be established for you in the realm of the spirit. It must be understood that Miracle Money manifestation is independent of the natural situations and circumstances and is not determined by the state or outlook of the economy of a country but by the size of faith, coupled with revelation which a man can fathom. Therefore, despite the harsh prevailing economic conditions, the gravity, magnitude and intensity of manifestation of Miracle Money shall be heightened in these end times such that believers in the worst economically performing nations shall rise with such amazing grace to amass humongous financial wealth in the form of Miracle Money. In a way, the Miracle Money grace shall culminate in the establishment of Godly justice and the righteousness of God as nations and people previously alienated and prejudiced shall become Kingdom Millionaires and Billionaires through the release of Miracle Money. Therefore, if you hear of the Miracle Money grace being profoundly demonstrated with intensity in lowly esteemed nations of the world, no man should be envious because God's justice and righteousness is being established prior to the second coming of Jesus as He restores all things to Himself.

PROPHETIC DECLARATION OF MIRACLE MONEY

> *In the same way God caused water to come out of a rock in the wilderness, I declare and decree that you shall flourish in the wilderness of the world's economic situation. Regardless of the darkening global economic outlook, Miracle money will locate you and unreservedly stream in your direction. I declare and decree that just like Isaac, in the dryness of the World's situation, you shall reap a hundred fold. By the mandate of Heaven, I impart the seed of greatness into your spirit. I declare and decree that you shall become great, you shall continue to be great until you are great, as the grace for Miracle money is multiplied in your life.*

THE CASE OF QUAILS (BIRDS) BEING BLOWN AWAY IN THE DIRECTION OF GOD'S PEOPLE SO THAT THEY WOULD HAVE MEAT TO EAT

There is another exhilarating record of a spectacular demonstration of God's supernatural provision which is almost similar to that of the provision of manna but this time, it involved edible birds that were alive but were supernaturally blown away by a Southerly wind in the direction of the children of God. When the children of Israel were in the wilderness as recorded in Psalms 78:26,

Unveiling The Mystery of Miracle Money

God caused a Southerly wind to blow and carry quails so that the children of Israel could eat meat.

Isn't it striking to note that God caused quails to blow in the direction of His people so that they wold gather them for meat? This is Miracle Money in its original manifestation because it involves God's supernatural provision where it would have costed millions in money to supply the same provision in the natural realm. In a Morden day world, imagine the cows and pigs being supernaturally drawn in the direction of restaurants so that the cooks and chefs could have beacon and beef! This is indeed the most fantastic miracle ever recorded in the Bible! Philosophically speaking, try to imagine what millions of quails flying right over your head would look like. The thick clouds of quails must have been dense enough to nearly block the people's view of the sun. *But the big question is: Where did all these quails come from?* They certainly didn't fly in from the wilderness. How far did these birds have to travel to reach the children of Israel? From what distance did God supernaturally call in the quail to feed the children of Israel? This phenomenon simply could not be naturally explained. It was a supernatural and miraculous provision that dazzled the mind and left those who witnessed it without any other choice except to reverence the Creator. It was just as miraculous as the 4,500 tons of manna that miraculously appeared on the ground every morning for forty years. This was Miracle money although manifesting in the form of a meat! This explains the mechanics behind the manifestation of Miracle money in the invisible realm. Do you know that in the same way God supernaturally provided these quails and nobody knew where they had come from, God provides Miracle Money to His children in this present time? As a matter of fact, the money which people receive supernaturally in their bags, wallets and other places is actually blown in their direction by the wind of Heaven to these unexpected places under the directorship of Angel tellers. It is becoming clear to me that the same forces of divinity that were at work to blow quails in the direction of the children of Israel are the same that are blowing Miracle money in the direction of God's children in these end times. It is attributable to the activities of *Angel tellers* who work in the department of Finance in Heaven.

The Theology Behind The Manifestation of Miracle Money

To cement this divine revelation with reference to quantifiable, practical evidence, how many quail do you think it would take to feed that massive group of Israelites for thirty days a month? Let me quantify it for you: It would take at least *90,000,000 quails*. Mathematically speaking, if each Israelite ate only one quail a day, in one month it would amount to *90,000,000 quails*. If they ate two quail a day, the total number needed to feed them all for thirty days would rise to *180,000,000 quails*. That's how many quails it took to feed that crowd of three million Israelites in a thirty day period. Needless to say, this was an incredible supernatural provision of God. This is a manifestation of Miracle Money because based on the above calculation, it would have taken millions of dollars to buy meat to feed all these people if God did not intervene.

A further analysis of the above narrative unveils the divine truth that God supernaturally caused a Southerly wind to blow in the direction of the children of Israel and carry quails to them. It is therefore important that in order to partake of the abundance of God's supernatural provision, you be rightly positioned to move in the direction of the Spirit because provision is located in the direction in which the Spirit is moving or blowing. The southerly wind speaks of the move of the Holy Ghost. This is the same wind that blew upon the disciples at Pentecost and left them utterly drunk in the Spirit. In this last season, we are going to experience an unprecedented avalanche or move of the Holy Ghost in ways never witnessed before. Therefore, under the directorship of the Holy Ghost, money is coming on feet in your direction. It must be understood that millions of wealth originates in the hands of the Holy Ghost in the spirit realm and these shall be blown upon the masses who are readily positioned in spirit or those whose spirits are in an upper room position to receive. Colloquially speaking, you will be walking down the street minding your own business when all of a sudden, you see wind blowing piles of paper money directly to your feet when others are just passing by. Money will just supernaturally appear from thin air and just cascade its way down to your feet as you walk through the market place and the public arena.

The fact that God caused a southerly wind to blow in the direction of the children of Israel and bring forth quails follows that in this present time God can command the same wind to blow across the Body of Christ and rain Miracle money. As a matter of fact, God uses three principal divine substances as instruments or tools to release Miracle money and these are, *the wind, the cloud and the rain* and each has a specific symbolic purpose in this Money making ministry. The cloud is what divinely orchestrates Miracle money from the spirit realm into visible manifestation in the natural realm. The wind is what moves it from one bank account to the other and the rain is what precipitates it upon the masses who are connected to God's purpose. As the Lord unveiled this revelation into my spirit, I began to see with the eyes of my spirit a cloud as small as a man's hand rising above the earth and as it moved, it grew larger and upon saturation, it emptied itself and released a rain of humongous finances upon the masses and God brought to my understanding the reality that the season for the supernatural release of Miracle money has just exploded.

> *Prophetically speaking, just like a cloud as small as a man's hand which Elijah build up in prayer, the movement of the Miracle Money grace shall begin as small as a current of water; the current will increase until it becomes a brook; the brook will grow into a great river, which will overflow and become a sea and that sea will transform into a powerful ocean. Then Miracle Money shall cover the earth as the waters cover the sea and then Jesus will come for His church.*

There is irrefutable evidence that we have just entered into a global season of *Miracle money invasion*. Prophetically speaking, in this end time season, the wind of God's provision will supernaturally blow over people's bank accounts, businesses, investments and bring forth supernatural provision in measures never seen before. Wealth in the form of money, gold, diamonds and silver shall be blown in the believers' direction and God's favours shall be manifested in every way. As attested by Isaiah 60:1-5, that *Kings shall come to the brightness of their rising*, nations of the world shall bring millions of wealth and resources to believers during this end time season for the propagation of the gospel. In the same way God caused a southerly wind to blow quails in the direction of the Children of Israel, God shall cause some countries to bring tithe to your ministry. Imagine the whole country tithing to you! God owns everything and owes nothing, hence according to the times and seasons as stipulated in the calendar of God, these end times shall be characterised by an unprecedented avalanche of wealth resources that shall be released from Heaven. Those who are rightly positioned and ready in the spirit shall be accordingly released into an unusual financial realm never to return to depend on common money again.

PROPHETIC DECLARATIONS OF MIRACLE MONEY:

In a similar vein in which God supernaturally provided quails to blow in the direction of the children of Israel, I declare and decree that God shall supernaturally provide Miracle Money for you in this present time. I release the Southerly wind of Heaven to blow Miracle money in your direction right now. I release a supernatural influence in the realm of the spirit to cause everything that you need to come to you. I declare that under the directorship of the Holy Ghost, money is coming on feet in your direction. I command the wind of God's provision to supernaturally blow over your bank account, businesses, investments and bring forth supernatural provision in measures never seen before. I command wealth in the form of money, gold, diamonds and silver to be blown in your direction, right now.

THE CASE OF A 24 HOUR TURNAROUND FINANCIAL MIRACLE IN SYRIA BY PROPHET ELISHA

The Bible further records a remarkable incident whereby God used four lepers to bring about an economic revival in Samaria following a lengthy season of drought (2 Kings 7:1). There is such a powerful revelation and provocative insight gleaned in this narrative, which can catapult you to higher realms of superabundance. Isn't it striking to note that God used four sick men to revamp the economy of a nation? God's promise through Elisha was that in 24 hours, the debilitating economic situation in Samaria would be completely reversed. Instead of scarcity, there would be such abundance that food prices would radically drop in the city. Isn't it interesting to note that in every situation facing humanity in the natural world, there is always a prophet with a solution from God? As a Prophet sent from God, Elisha declared, thus says the Lord:

"Tomorrow about this time a seah of fine flour shall be sold for a shekel, and two seahs of barley for a shekel, at the gate of Samaria".

In the midst of a darkening and saddening economic outlook hampering the city, characterised by an economic recession, as evidenced by untold inflation projections, mirrored by the skyrocketing prices of basic necessities such as flour and wheat, God dropped a prophetic word which dawned in the inner recesses of the Prophet, meant to calm down the troubling, muddy waters of the City's economic climate. A Word so accurate and precise that within 24 hours of its declaration in the realm of the spirit, it matured into a miracle that ruffled the feathers of those comfortable with the status quo and dumb-found the sceptics to their grave. As I munched over the recoded version of this Prophetic Word with the eyes of my spirit, little did I know that the same Word spoken by the prophet over thousands of generations, will reverberate in the depths of my being and turn into a double-edged sword rhema cutting through the inner recesses of my own spirit. Prophetically speaking, as I pondered over this Word and inundated my spirit with the Throne Room revelations and divine insights encapsulated therein, God said to me,

"Son, blow the trumpet, sound the horn and declare in the hearing of all the nations that the season for the global demonstration of Miracle Money has begun. In this season, Miracle money shall be demonstrated everywhere where My glory flows. Therefore, as My glory unreservedly precipitates upon the nations and covers the earth as the waters covers the seas, so shall the Miracle money grace cover the world in this season".

The Theology Behind The Manifestation of Miracle Money

It is worth exploring the divine truth that there is a sudden turnaround in the spiritual climate and atmosphere as God is unleashing His last wave of prosperity over the Body of Christ in these end times. There is a paradigm shift and turnaround in your economic and financial situation and circumstances as Miracle Money is unreservedly being loosed from the Storehouses of Heaven, to precipitate upon the masses in the extreme ends of the world. There is a mega shift that is brewing in the realm of the spirit as God is shaking the Heavens, the earth and the seas, to pave a way or accentuate an avenue for the explosion of the new move of God in these end times. In the same way Elisha declared that, *"Tomorrow about this time a seah of fine flour shall be sold for a shekel, and two seahs of barley for a shekel, at the gate of Samaria"*, I walk in the footsteps of Elisha the Prophet of God (the prophetic office) and I declare and decree a 24 hour turnaround financial miracle in your life. I proclaim and pronounce that within 24 hours from now, Miracle Money will appear supernaturally in your bank account, wallet, bag, house, car and this shall rule every provision in your life, such that you will never return to depend on common money, ever again!.

It is worth exploring the divine truth that for every move of God to prolong its manifestation in a generation, it must always be preceded by a prophetic declaration. That is why God said, *"You shall declare a thing and it shall be established,"* Why? Because a prophetic declaration is a way of divinely establishing a matter in the realm of the spirit such that its results are instantaneously manifested in the natural realm. It is for this reason that God said, *"I can do nothing unless I reveal it to My servants, the prophets"*. Why? Because it is the duty of prophets to declare God's secrets. As a prophet of God, Elisha was therefore central in spearheading this economic revival because he was used by God to declare it. Notable is the realisation that whenever God initiates a revival, He always raises two distinct breed of people for this purpose, that is, the one who will declare it and the other one who will demonstrate it. To declare a revival means to divinely orchestrate it in the realm of the spirit while to demonstrate it means to manifest its tangible results in the natural realm. In this case, *Elisha* the Prophet declared the revival in the spirit realm and the *lepers* demonstrated it in the natural realm.

In other words, Elisha orchestrated it in the spirit realm while the lepers initiated it in the physical realm, but the one who proclaims it is greater than the one who demonstrates it because revivals are pioneered first in the spirit realm before they could be manifested or demonstrated in the natural realm.

There is such a powerful principle gleaned in this narrative that when operating in the glory realm, time is not of essence when it comes to the declaration of divine phenomena. As we declare what we want and when we want to see it manifest, we move and operate outside the time dimension and eternity exerts a supernatural influence on the physical realm, culminating in a supernatural acceleration. That is why we must declare that Miracle money manifest now and we shall have whatever we say. When we declare that Miracle money manifest now, we exert a supernatural pressure in the realm of the spirit that compels all forces of divinity to act, hence Heaven is obligated to authorise the release of Miracle money in the natural realm, accompanied by a stamp of God's approval. It is for this reason that *angel tellers* swiftly, expediently and speedily move to dispatch Miracle Money in the natural realm whenever it is declared. Don't you find it interesting that in his prophetic declaration, Elisha used his prerogative as a prophet of God to specify the exact time when the financial miracle would take place? He set a maximum limit of 24 hours within which the miracle was expected to take place! What divine explanation can we ascribe to this hilarious spectacle? It's because as a new creation, we are divinely catapulted into a higher dimension in the prophetic, in which we have dominion over time in the natural realm because we were born in to the glory realm; that's where our origin and identity is, hence we are designed to function outside the time dimension just like God. It is worth unfolding the divine truth that time is not one of the characteristics of God. God is not defined by time because He lives, functions and operates in the eternal realm that is outside our time dimension. Time is not an absolute because it only exists when its parameters are defined by absolutes. The greater truth is that God set the earth in time while man was created from the eternal realm. Although man lives on earth, he doesn't operate according to earthly time because he was created in the eternal realm which falls outside the domain of time.

The Theology Behind The Manifestation of Miracle Money

Notable is the realisation that man was never designed to function according to earthly time. It was only after the fall of man in the Garden of Eden that the clock started ticking. Heaven is governed by the glory which is the realm of eternity where there is no time. That is why when we get caught up into the glory realm, we experience *"timelessness"*. The eternity realm is the womb from which time came. In other words, eternity existed before time. Time is the offspring of the eternal design. Time was created or set in creation after eternity on the fourth day. God set the sun to rule by day and the moon to rule by night, thereby establishing time and season. That is why when practically demonstrating Miracle money in the natural realm, we are able to command it to manifest instantly because we have dominion over time as we were created first in the eternal realm which is outside the time dimension of the earthly realm.

Imbued with this understanding of our dominion over time, when operating in the glory realm, the key is to learn the art of how to speak from the eternal realm into the realm of time. In the glory realm, time does not exist as we consider it on earth. The only thing that can break the cycle of time is faith. Faith is a higher law than time. It is the ascent out of time into the eternal realm. For a man who knows his rights as a citizen of Heaven, time is made to serve him. Man was not designed to serve time. Time is a part of matter, not a matter of time. Faith is God's matter, the substance or material which represents elements which are made by God to serve an eternal purpose. Time was designed and created specifically for this earth. It doesn't exist outside this planet. The reality is that when people lose track of time and step into the eternal, the eternal becomes real and the supernatural becomes your normal. In this Kairos moment, God is bridging you from time into the eternal realm whereby it is naturally supernatural to manifest Miracle money. That's when you will realise that the eternal is more real than time. The truth is that miracles are in a higher realm, without the influence of time, while our circumstances are the product of time with a beginning and an end. The greater truth is that everything in the eternal realm has already happened, miracles have already taken place and the rain of Miracle money has already been precipitated. You just have to call it from the realm in which it already exists into the realm in which it will manifest. The key is to be challenged to speak from the eternal realm into time. Therefore, when you step on any stage to demonstrate Miracle money, have the mentality that Miracle money is a done deal; it has already been made available by Angel tellers operating in the realm of the spirit. All you need to do is just turn on the switch in the natural realm and witness God in action, exploding in an arena of divine exploits that will dazzle the minds of the masses. That is why we are said to be *witnesses* because in the glory realm, we watch and see God perform His work.

Isn't it thrilling to note that in his prophetic declaration, Elisha stipulated the exact time the miracle should take place and the specific details concerning the prices at which the products will be sold? Consider what He said, *"Tomorrow about this time a seah of fine flour shall be sold for a shekel, and two seahs of barley for a shekel, at the gate of Samaria"*. Because you have dominion over time, in the glory realm, you can declare Miracle money and use your royal prerogative to stipulate the time frame when it must appear, whether in a minute, day, week or few hours. When the Bible attests that *you shall declare a thing and it shall be established for you*, it doesn't talk about flippantly declaring empty words in any direction but it talks about declaring things while in the glory realm or in an atmosphere of glory. That's when things happen. That is why those who function in higher realms of glory don't wait for things to happen, instead, they make things happen. This is because in the glory realm, it is possible for you to be instantaneously elevated to the reality of *overnight success*, whereby prayers are being answered even before you start praying. There is a new prophetic dimension in the glory whereby things are coming to pass as they are being said. In the glory realm, there is no procrastination, or delays of any nature because time is inconsequential. When God declared in an atmosphere of glory that, *let there be light*, light came forth instantly. He didn't have to wait for a manifestation to succeed His spoken word. Instead, results came forth instantaneously as words were declared. In the glory realm, there is no waiting because waiting is a process in time, of which we have dominion over time; we operate outside the time dimension because we were given birth to in the eternal realm which falls outside our time dimension. The reason why some believers experience delays in the manifestation of Miracle money is because of the absence of glory. The less you are filled with the glory, the longer it takes for you to command Miracle money into manifestation.

Note that God did not use seasoned economists, doctors, financial analysts or well educated men of renown, to spearhead an economic revival in Samaria. Instead, He choose to use the dejected, lowly esteemed and underprivileged four lepers to do that job. One would naturally expect the economically educated to be the ones at the frontline in birthing forth an economic revival because of their specialised knowledge of economic and monetary strategies but God choose to use the physically weak lepers for that purpose. Why? Those who know God very well will understand that *God calls things that are not as though they were* and His sovereignty will always prevail in divine election. In the same way God used ordinary, unschooled folks to bring forth an economic revival, God is using ordinary people with faith to demonstrate Miracle Money in this season. That is why people whom the world never thought could be used by God, are now taking over the World stage in the demonstration of Miracle money in dimensions never seen before.

The Bible records that the four leprous men at the entrance of the gate said to one another,

> *"Why are we sitting here until we die? If we say, 'We will enter the city,' the famine is in the city, and we shall die there. And if we sit here, we die also. Now therefore, come, let us surrender to the army of the Syrians. If they keep us alive, we shall live; and if they kill us, we shall only die." And they rose at twilight to go to the camp of the Syrians and when they had come to the outskirts of the Syrian camp, to their surprise no one was there.*

You see, you have a choice whether to sit and do nothing about your financial situation or plunge yourself into the pool of Miracle Money which God is using to stir the waters of His supernatural provision. Metaphorically speaking, the Miracle money grace operates on the same principle as the miracle pool of Bethsaida. Anybody who happens to be the first to step into the pool of Miracle money with a sense of urgency and expectation, receives the abundance of this grace while those who join the critical club and stand aloof as spectators, receives nothing. This truth is exemplified in the lepers' fate as they asked themselves, *"Why are we sitting here until we die?"* Their reasoning was sound because they would soon die from the famine if they had coiled themselves in their comfort zones and hibernated outside the city. If any food became available, they would certainly be the last to receive it because of their debilitating situation, hence they decided to take an action of faith and enter the city than to sit idle by and die of starvation. The city represents a place of abundance, connection and unlimited possibilities. It is for this reason that the lepers were destined for the city, because there, their circumstances would change, from death to destiny. Note that these lepers were not on the verge of death because of their leprosy per se but because of the severity of the famine. It was more of an external limitation than an internal one. Many at times, what derails people is not the limitations imposed by their physical bodies but the limitations imposed by their situations and circumstances. That is why regardless of your situations and circumstances, you can be elevated to a higher dimension in the spirit realm, in which you demonstrate Miracle money like the scattering of leaves under the influence of a storm. The narrative continues to unpack that the lepers decided that they were better off if they took an action of faith and surrendered to the Syrians than to be nonchalant about their situation. Now, you perceive that there are just two courses open to you; you can either sit idle by and do nothing about your financial situation or you could step out in faith, aggressively place a demand on the Heaven's financial provision and declare that you are a Kingdom Billionaire and everything will begin to align itself with your declaration. Accordingly, Heavens will respond by compelling all forces of divinity to partner with you such that the abundance of God manifested through a landslide of Miracle money, will stream in your direction.

The narrative further records that as these lepers took a step of faith and moved in the direction of the Syrian camp, *the Lord caused the army of the*

The Theology Behind The Manifestation of Miracle Money

Syrians to hear the noise of chariots and the noise of horses; the noise of a great army. This is what I call a divine arrangement or orchestration of circumstances in the realm of the spirit. There are several possible means through which God could have divinely orchestrated the sound of chariots. Perhaps in the invisible arena, the Lord had in some way divinely magnified the stumbling footsteps of the lepers as they made their way around the camp's opposite end, such that the Syrian army perceived them to be a sound of a large army. In a similar fashion in which God opened the spiritual eyes of Elisha's servant such that he saw battalions of angels encamping around them, God could have directly attacked the Syrian army simply by causing them to hear the noise of a real Heavenly army, marching in the realm of the spirit. In the invisible realm, God could have caused the realm of the spirit to materialise or crystallise itself into the realm of the natural such that it was transmuted as an audible noise, quaking and thundering in the ears of the Syrian army. Perhaps God did this by releasing the frequency of the noise through the Heavenly airwaves, which echoed in the natural realm in a similar vein in which a plane drives through the air but its sound is heard on the surface of the earth. The other possibility is that God could have simply created the perception of the noise in the minds of the Syrian soldiers, which boggled them into an utter state of disorientation. Whichever way God did it, it produced positive results in the natural realm. Isn't it paradoxical that the Syrian soldiers who were so spiritually blind that they could not see in the realm of the spirit, now had their spiritual eyes attuned to see in the spirit, not for them to be blessed but for their own demise! Prophetically speaking, God is releasing a sound in the spirit realm that will scatter those who have connived to devour your finances and held you captive for ages. He is magnifying your steps in the realm of the spirit such that as you move in the spirit dimension, all your enemies will be thrust into a pool of confusion.

Following the divine orchestration of this Heavenly sound which reverberated in the natural realm, it happened that the Syrian soldiers said to one another, *"Look, the King of Israel has hired against us the Kings of the Hittites and the Kings of the Egyptians to attack us!"* Therefore, they arose and fled at twilight, and left the camp intact; their tents, horses and donkeys; as they fled for their lives. This tells me that although in the natural realm Israel was powerless against this besieging army, in the spirit realm, God wasn't powerless. He was brewing and orchestrating a divine plan that would put all the cries of His children to a definite halt. The same God who struck one Syrian army so that they could not see what was there, now struck another Syrian army so that they heard things that were not there and left the camp intact. It is for this reason that the Bible concurs that *God calls things that are not as though there were.* That means He uses His royal prerogative to divinely orchestrate things in the realm of the spirit as if they were a tangible reality in the realm of the natural. Note that as the Syrian army fled, everything was left behind, leaving the unlikely lepers to spoil the camp. As a result, the siege for Samaria was over – even though no one in the city knew it or enjoyed it. In view of the above, as I officially announce the expiry date of oppression, depression and suppression in your life, I prophetically declare and decree that the days of imprisonment by the enemy are over. I proclaim and pronounce that as the enemy comes from one direction, he shall flee in seven different direction and as he flees, he shall leave behind tonnes of wealth that he has hoarded, manipulated and stolen from your hands in the days gone by.

The narrative further records that when these lepers came to the outskirts of the camp, they went into one tent and ate and drank, and carried from it silver, gold and clothing, and went and hid them; then they came back and entered another tent, and carried some from there also, and went and hid it. In the language of war, this is what we call *scooping the spoils*, which alludes to a scenario whereby you take back what is rightfully yours to the extent of even looting what belongs to the enemy. Don't you find it interesting that the weak lepers went into the tent of the ferocious Syrian army and sumptuously ate and drank as if it was a party? This is to tell you that in the realm of the spirit, battles are not won by the size of physical muscles but spiritual muscles. After the long period of famine, this was the answer to every hope and prayer they had. This was an answered prayer! They knew that their discovery of the camp could not remain a secret forever, so they hid some of the valuables so they could profit by them even when the camp was discovered by others. While the act of hiding some valuables reflects a bad conduct on the part of the lepers, the principle emphasized here is that the lepers rightly enjoyed the miracle God provided. Likewise, Miracle money is supernaturally provided for the children of God to enjoy and ease the financial burdens of life. That is why some use it to pay for their debts and buy valuables which they would never have bought in their entire life had they not been singled by God to be the recipients of Miracle money. However, recipients of Miracle money should use it wisely and be accountable for it as a valuable blessing from above.

Consider what the lepers said to one another, *"We are not doing right. This day is a day of good news, and we remain silent. If we wait until morning light, some punishment will come upon us. Now, therefore, come, let us go and tell the King's household."* In other words, it dawned in their spirit that as the ones at the frontline of economic revival, they had a responsibility to sound the horn and declare the miracle which God had orchestrated in the spirit realm. They realized that they had a responsibility to share it with others. They understood that to remain silent and to selfishly enjoy their blessings would be sin. Those who are in the habit of receiving financial breakthroughs in Miracle money, but then squander the money like the four lepers, should learn a lesson here; the money should be brought back into the house of the Lord for the furtherance of the Gospel. Note that the lepers understood that regardless of their circumstances, they had a responsibility to share the good news with others. In a similar vein, Miracle Money ought to be declared the instant it happens so that it is declared as legitimate by Heaven. In Heaven, any supernatural act that is received on earth and is not declared or testified is declared an illegal supernatural act, hence it might not last long. Moreover, testifying about the miracle in a way strengthens your faith in God and reinforces your victory over demonic forces. It is for this reason that it is recorded that *believers defeated the devil by the blood of the lamb and by the word of their testimony*. This is to tell you that God's miraculous provision is not to be kept a secret, hence the instant you receive it, you should declare or testify about it. According to the narrative, the lepers realised that it was not good to enjoy the blessings of the Lord and then remain silent and keep everything to themselves. The other important principle gleaned in this narrative is that Miracle Money is not supposed to be used for selfish gain but for Kingdom purposes. Should you receive it, you must use it wisely to expand the Kingdom so that you can provoke a further perennial flow of Miracle Money in your life. That is why the lepers were given the revelation that as much as they had been used by God as pioneers of the Economic revival, they were not supposed to use that grace for selfish gain or to enrich themselves but they were just used as vessels to propagate it to others. This is how Miracle Money grace is populated across the globe. Believers are just used as vehicles to propagate the grace to the nations, hence should handle it with wisdom. Surely, Jesus did not come to save us that we might live unto ourselves but for others.

The Bible further narrates that subsequently, the people went out in masses and plundered the tents of the Syrians: *So, a seah of fine flour was sold for a shekel, and two seahs of barley for a shekel, according to the word of the LORD.* When the good news that started with the report of the lepers was found to be true, there was no stopping the people. Because they knew their need, they were delighted to receive God's provision to meet that need. The King's officer derided the possibility of the prophet's prediction; and no doubt had plenty of adherents. But the leper's report swept away all his words to the winds. Through Elisha, God announced the exact prices in the Samarian markets, and the prophecy was proven to be precisely true. This is what I call *Forensic prophesy, Prophetic precision or Prophetic accuracy*, a realm or dimension in the spirit in which a prophet is given grace not only to foretell forthcoming, events but to meticulously ascertain with precision and accuracy, the details of when they will take place, how and for what purpose. It should come to no surprise in this season that in a ministerial context, God is using His Prophetic vessels to reveal people's cell phone numbers, home addresses, birth days, names of siblings and other accurate details that pertains to the issue at hand. Do you notice that following the invasion of the Syrian camp by four lepers and them bringing the miracle to the attention of the masses, there was a mega shift from indulgence by these lepers to multitudes? By the same token, while Miracle money has been scarcely demonstrated in select ministries across the Body of Christ, there is a mega shift that is taking place in the realm of the spirit as *Angel tellers* have now been authorised by God to unreservedly precipitating Miracle money beyond church walls to the masses in the streets, market place and the public arena. Prophetically speaking, God is in the business of raining Miracle Money and this shall get to a level whereby its manifestation shall be heightened such that it will no longer be only a few people who are demonstrating it but multitudes. In other words, Miracle Money shall move from being a scarcely demonstrated grace to a common place for God's children. In the same way there was a paradigm shift in the partaking of God's supernatural provision from the four lepers to four million people in the city of Syria, there is a paradigm shift that is taking place in the spirit realm as millions of God's people shall unreservedly demonstrate the Miracle Money grace in this end time season. It shall be such a common experience, an *"in thing"* and an order of the day in the realm of Christian prosperity. It shall get to a level of commonality whereby any believer who does not tap into God's supernatural provision by demonstrating the Miracle Money grace shall be regarded as irrelevant in the Christian fraternity.

It is disheartening to note that the glendour and glamour associated with Elisha's prophetic declaration of the 24 hour economic miracle took a sudden turn following gross criticism by one of the key government officials deployed at the gate of the city of Samaria. According to the narrative, it happened that after the prophetic declaration by Elisha concerning the forthcoming economic revival in Syria, an officer on whose hand the King leaned, answered the man of God and said, *"Look, if the LORD would make windows in Heaven, could this thing be?"* In other words, he doubted, questioned and undermined the authenticity and veracity of God's supernatural provision. Do you notice that every time God births forth a powerful revival, the devil and his crowd will always try to resist it? That is why in the midst of the global Miracle money revival, are cohorts who have been assigned in the demonic realm to try and counterfeit, oppose and undermine it. Note that we are not dealing with an ordinary officer here but the King's right hand man who had great influence in the whole city. In modern day language, he was the Mayor of the city. Because of his influential position, the devil took advantage and used him as a stronghold to resist, derail and undermine the move of God. Imagine the Breaking Nesw Headlines of the daily Newspaper in the city of Samaria saying:

> *"Tomorrow about this time, a seah of fine flour shall be sold for a shekel, and two seahs of barley for a shekel, at the gate of Samaria," Declares the Prophet of God.*

And imagine contrary Headlines surfacing in another Newspaper within the same city saying:

> *"If the LORD would make windows in Heaven, could this thing be?", Renounces City Authority.*

This is a typical scenario across the Body of Christ in this present time. While God has assigned His prophets to prophesy over cities and pursue the business of populating the grace of Miracle money in this season, there are those who have been assigned by the devil over cities to *prophe-lie* so to speak and propagate the lies of the enemy concerning Miracle money. As a result, many believers struggle to walk in the divine consciousness of God's superabundance because they tend to pay a lot of attention to negative economic reports of this fallen world's system. It all boil down to the question of which report do you believe: God's report or the devil's report? Are you not surprised that some of the words which ordinary people utter in antagonistic to the move of God, is actually the devil speaking through them? The officer's words denote the gravelly voice of the devil that hisses into the ears of unbelievers so that they are used as masquerading vessels of evil to derail the move of God. God is blessings His people in a move meant to be the last wave of prosperity but owing to ignorance, some people are questioning, to the extent of lambasting its authenticity. It is disheartening to note that in the same way the officer questioned the authenticity of God's supernatural provision, some people tend to question the divine orchestration of Miracle money, in terms of where it comes from and how it manifests. It appears that they echo or reiterate the exact words uttered by the officer saying,

> *"Look, if the LORD would make windows in Heaven, could Miracle Money be? Could God open the windows of Heaven and rain down Miracle Money?"*

It must be expressly understood that not only does God have control over money in the economy but He has power to change the whole economic and monetary system. If God could change the metabolic system of lions such that when they looked at Daniel, they lost appetite, how much more would it not be easy for Him to change the monetary system of the world? And if God could change the whole monetary and economic system, why would it be impossible for Him to release Miracle money? Those who understand Economics will concur with the fact that the economy (*Macro*) is bigger than the monetary value of any of any currency (*Micro*). Likewise, Miracle money is a smaller part of the bigger economic and monetary system of the universe which God controls. It is just a smaller picture within God's bigger picture of supernatural provision.

It is disheartening to note that like many folks around the world, the King's officer doubted the move of God, and his doubt was based on several faulty premises. Firstly, he doubted the power of God, which is the divine ability to cause changes to situations and circumstances. That is why he uttered a remark that if God willed it, He certainly could make windows in Heaven and drop down food from the sky for the hungry, besieged city of Samaria. Secondly, he doubted the creativity of God. In the mind of the King's officer, the only way food could come to the city was from above, because the city was surrounded by a hostile, besieging army. He had no idea that God could bring provision in a completely unexpected way. How often unwavering faith breaks down in this way! It knows that God is, and that

He can act but it only sees one way, and refuses to believe that such a way will be taken. However, it's striking to note that the supply came without the opening of Heaven's windows as was expected because God cannot be put in a box and would not gravitate the level of man's thinking. Thirdly, the officer doubted the messenger of God. Though the promise was admittedly hard to believe, given the dire circumstances, the King's officer could have believed it because it came from a man with an established track record of prophetic reliability. Unbelief is classed as negative spiritual gravity that deactivates or short-circuit God's power to work on behalf of humanity. It works like a hand break that tries to disable God's hand as it manoeuvres its way to intervene in the plight of humanity. It dares to question the truthfulness of God's promise itself.

Unbelief says, "This is a new thing and cannot be true." Unbelief says, "This is a sudden thing and cannot be true." Unbelief says, "There is no way to accomplish this thing." Unbelief says, "There is only one way God can work." Unbelief says, "Even if God does something, it won't be enough."

In response to the degree of contempt exhibited by the officer in question, Elisha made a counteract and said to him, *"In fact, you shall see it with your eyes, but you shall not eat of it."* This means that he would see the word fulfilled, but not benefit from its fulfilment. In the same manner in which Elisha declared to the officer who criticized the prophetic move of God, that he will surely not partake of it, those who are criticising Miracle Money are not worthy to partake of God's grace and will only be spectators instead of participators, as they will not benefit anything out of it. The principle emphasized here is that those people who are too critical, sceptical and cynical about Miracle money, will not be able to partake of this grace. In fact, as Elisha declared, *they shall only see it with their eyes, but shall not eat of it.* Through Prophet Elisha, God pronounced a harsh judgment upon the doubting officer because he attempted to stand in the way of the move of God in the same way Saphira and Ananias attempted to stand in the way of God's prosperity move and died. On the basis of the same principle, the officer had to be removed as a lesson to the masses that no one can and will ever stand in God's way. The most dangerous sin which a man can ever commit in a generation is not to steal, rob or hijack others, but to stand in the way of the move of God. In that case, God would not be left with any other option except to remove you by instant judgement. This is a valid explanation of the plight which befell the officer in question and an eye opening precaution to the masses on the dangers of resisting the new move of God.

PROPHETIC DECLARATION OF MIRACLE MONEY

Just as Elisha declared, "Tomorrow about this time a seah of fine flour shall be sold for a shekel, and two seahs of barley for a shekel, at the gate of Samaria", I walk in the footsteps of Elisha the Prophet of God (the prophetic office) and I declare and decree a 24 hour turnaround financial miracle in your life. I proclaim and pronounce that within 24 hours from now, Miracle Money will appear supernaturally in your bank account, wallet, bag, house, car and this shall rule every provision in your life. Tomorrow about this time, all your debts will be supernaturally cancelled. Tomorrow about this time, an amount of one million dollars would have been supernaturally deposited into your bank account. Strangers will call you with valid offers. By this time, you will be driving your dream car. I see the inscription of your handwriting and signature on your title deed. Tomorrow by this time, you will be owning your dream house. I hear the sound of angels calling the name of your business. Tomorrow by this time, you will receive start capital for your dream business, glory to Jesus!

THE CASE OF RAVENS FEEDING ELIJAH AND THE FOOD MULTIPLICATION THROUGH THE WIDOW OF ZAREPHATH:

The Bible records a thrilling spectacle of a demonstration of Miracle money by Prophet Elijah. The demonstration includes provision of food and water through the ravens as well as food and oil multiplication through a widow. The Bible records in 1 Kings 17:1-6 that,

God supernaturally provided ravens to bring food and drink to Elijah after he had declared the Lord's judgment against the land.

Elijah the Tishbite, of the inhabitants of Gilead, said to Ahab, *"As the Lord God of Israel lives, before whom I stand, there shall not be dew nor rain these years, except at my word."* Then the word of the Lord came to him, saying, *"Get away from here and turn eastward, and hide by the Brook Cherith, which flows into the Jordan. And it will be that you shall drink from the brook, and I have commanded the ravens to feed you there."* So, he went and did according to the word of the Lord, for he went and stayed by the Brook Cherith, which flows into the Jordan. The drought announced by Elijah in the previous verse was a great threat to the Northern Kingdom of Israel and the reign of Ahab. Therefore, his life was in danger, and God sent him to the Brook Cherith for his own safety where he was supernaturally fed by ravens.

The reality is that ever since the fall of Adam in the Garden of Eden, man has never been friendly to birds to the extent of association and even sharing food. This must be a miracle! *But the big question is: Where did the food and ravens come from?* From the Spirit realm. God has the power to command natural substances, creatures or objects to work on behalf of the Kingdom. The greater truth is that animals and other creatures were created to serve man. Note that God did not create animals first but he created man first and then animals latter so that they can serve the man he had created. God can use natural phenomena to serve you. This is the reason why they were created so that you can have dominion and command them to do whatever you want them to. This is the same reason why he commanded the donkey to speak to Balam when he was failing to cooperate with God (Numbers 22:21-39). In a similar vein, God can go to the extent of commanding natural substances such as wind, sun, rain or even creatures like birds to serve you and that is why He says *all things work together for good* (Romans 8:28). Naturally, one would have thought that God would send people or at least angels to provide food for Elijah but instead, He chose to send ravens. This is because there are millions of ways through which God can provide wealth even to the extent of using natural organisms (1 Kings 17:4-6, Matthew 17:27, Genesis 22:13-14, Psalm 50:10). Therefore, believers should be circumspect and open minded so that they are not stuck on one method which they presume God uses to provide for His children.

It is evident in this narrative that God led Elijah one step at a time. He did not tell him to go to Cherith until he first delivered the message to Ahab. He did not tell him to go to Zarephath until the brook dried up at Cherith. God led Elijah by faith, one step at a time and Elijah followed in faith. There is a powerful revelation that is gleaned in this narrative. Do you notice that it is God who told Elijah to hide by the Brook Cherith? Through this, God taught Elijah the value of the hidden life. His hiding was akin to that of David in the Cave of Pendulum; it was a training phase; a part of the Prophetic training. Elijah had just become famous as an adversary of Ahab, so mighty that his prayers could stop the rain. At the moment of his new-found fame, God wanted Elijah to hide and be alone with Him. Consider what God said to him: *And it will be that you shall drink from the brook, and I have commanded the ravens to feed you there*. Do you notice that the escape to the Brook Cherith was for more than protection? It was also to train Elijah in dependence upon the LORD. In a season of drought, he had to trust that God could keep this brook flowing. Paradoxically, as a prophet, he also had to accept food from the ravens, an unclean animal. Do you notice that God said, "*I have commanded the ravens to feed you* **there**". There is an emphasis on the word "*there*," meaning at Cherith. Of course, theoretically the ravens could feed him anywhere but God commanded that it be at Cherith. Elijah perhaps wanted to be somewhere else, or be preaching, or doing anything else, yet God wanted him there and would provide for him there. He had to go to Cherith to to find God's provision because it was **there** that God had commanded the ravens to sustain him. This is to tell you that divine specificity increases the likelihood of manifestation and prepares a breeding ground for the display of God's supernatural provision, without any reservations.

It is recorded that the ravens brought him bread and meat in the morning, and bread and meat in the evening; and he drank from the brook. Do you notice that every bit of food that came to Elijah came from the beak of an unclean animal? Elijah had to put away his traditional ideas of clean and unclean or he would die of starvation. Through this, God taught Elijah to emphasize the spirit of the law before the letter of the law. That is why it is important in this season of Miracle money that you get rid of some of the misconstrued traditional teachings which might deactivate or short-circuit the Miracle money grace from flowing into your life. The food the ravens brought to Elijah could be likened to Miracle money. God may bring Miracle money to us through unexpected sources or a spiritually unclean vessel like a raven. Have you not heard of how Tommy Williams in the USA, used to daily command birds which clustered around his house, to go and bring money and they obeyed and brought it to him? In a similar fashion, Elijah had a daily provision of bread and meat in the morning, and bread and meat in the evening: As faithfully as He provided manna for Israel in the wilderness, God provided for Elijah's needs. He came to trust more than ever in the miraculous provision of God. It is on the basis of the same principle that God provides Miracle money for His children. Contrary to what multitudes of believers across the Body of Christ presume, Miracle money is not something which ministers only demonstrate during special occasions or once a year when there is a conference because they have been fasting and praying. No! It should be a daily bread, just like how the ravens daily provided food for Elijah and God daily rained manna from Heaven for His children to eat.

To cement this revelation with reference to practical evidence, a man by the name of Tommy Williams shared several years ago how he spoke to the birds to bring him money. Based upon 1 Kings 17, Tommy started finding money around the house after he went out and hollered at the birds. They gathered around and listened to him as he exclaimed at them. *"People loose money every day. Go get it!"*. Subsequently, a 15-year-old was then inspired by this revelation such that he went out, spoke to the birds and commanded them to put the money in the backyard. The first day he discovered 65 cents, the second third day $7. Over the next two months, he found a total of $440 in the tree. Although this revelation might sound foreign to natural man's thinking the reality is that the unusual, unlimited, accelerated supply from Heaven supersedes the realm of impossibility as God has supernatural ways to fully supply every need. He makes the way when they say there is no way. We must therefore enlarge our capacity for this supernatural provision.

The narrative continues to unveil that it happened after a while that the brook dried up, because there had been no rain in the land. Elijah saw the flow of the brook slow down until it dried up. His source of water was gone. There are different kinds of drying brooks we might experience. The drying brook of money, slowly dwindling before the demands of sickness, bad debts, or other people's extravagance. Why does God let them dry? He wants to teach us not to trust in His gifts but in Himself. He wants to drain us of self, as He drained the apostles by ten days of waiting before Pentecost. He wants to loosen our roots as He removes us to some other sphere of spiritual service. He wants to put in stronger contrast the river of throne-water that never dries. Do you notice that there had been no rain in the land and paradoxically, his was the drought Elijah prayed for? He did not pray for rain to come again, even for his own survival. He kept the purpose of God first, even when it adversely affected him. This is to show you that he completely depended on God's economy and Heaven's system of provision than the natural realm, for survival.

Do you notice that God has a way of providing for His children in the event that our natural sources have dried out? This is evidenced by the narrative whereby God provided for Elijah through a widow as the economic recession was prolonged. The narrative continues to unpack that the word of the Lord came to him, saying, *"Arise, go to Zarephath, which belongs to Sidon, and dwell there. See, I have commanded a widow there to provide for you."* God led Elijah from the dry brook to a Gentile city. This was an unusual and challenging move for Elijah to make. Isn't it interesting to note that God kept transplanting Elijah from home, to Jezreel, to Cherith, and now to Zarephath? This transplanting made him stronger and anchored his prophetic mantle. You should also remember that this was the general region that the wicked queen Jezebel was from. Elijah was visiting the enemy's territory and showing the power of God in an area where Baal was worshipped. Don't you find it interesting that God spoke to the widow and commanded her to feed Elijah, yet based on her actions, she seem not to have clearly heard His voice? God said, *"See, I have commanded a widow there to provide for you"*. He didn't say, *"Go, you might come across a widow, maybe she might provide for you'*. It's amazing how God speaks to some people yet they can't even hear Him. The widow was instructed by God to take care of Elijah but there is no evidence that she heard God speak. Widows were notorious for their poverty in the ancient world but God always had a plan to meet the ends of justice. Isn't it amazing how God operates? God didn't send Elijah to the King's palace to indulge, feast sumptuously and rub shoulders with the prominent. Neither did He send him to the most resourceful and well-connected woman in the city. Instead, He told Elijah to go to a Gentile widow and receive provision, yet widows were known to be entangled in a morass of debilitating poverty. This is to tell you that God can use anything, anywhere and anyhow to get you out of your financial situation of lack, debt or poverty. That is why it should come to no surprise when you see Miracle money being greatly demonstrated in backyard ministries that are not even known in their own street.

The narrative continues to unpack that when Elijah came to the gate of the city of Zarephath, indeed a widow was there gathering sticks. And he called to her and said, *"Please bring me a little water in a cup that I may drink."* And as she was going to get it, he called to her and said, *"Please bring me a morsel of bread in your hand."* The act of the widow gathering sticks shows that she was a poor woman, gathering meagre scraps for firewood. Elijah perhaps thought that God would lead him to a palace where the rich dwells, but God led him to a poor Gentile widow. You learn this from the fact that she didn't even have firewood. Now, there was no reason why she should not have had wood even in time of famine of bread, for there was no famine of wood, unless she had been extremely poor. It is strikingly interesting to note that God told Elijah that He commanded the widow to feed the prophet, yet this woman seemed unaware of the command. This shows how God's unseen hand often works. She does not appear to have been at all aware that she was to feed a prophet. She went out that morning to gather sticks, not to meet a guest. She was thinking about feeding her son and herself upon the last cake. Certainly, she had no idea of sustaining a man of God out of that all but empty barrel of meal. Yet the Lord, who never lies, spoke a solemn truth when he said, *'I have commanded a widow there.'* God had so operated upon her mind to prepare her to obey the command of His servant, the prophet.

Don't you find it strange that Elijah made an unusual request for the widow to bring him a morsel of bread in her hand? Elijah boldly put this request in faith. Common sense and circumstances told him that the widow would not give so generously to a Jewish stranger, but faith made him ask. This was certainly putting the widow's faith to an extraordinary trial, to take and give to a stranger, of whom she knew nothing, the small pittance requisite to keep her child from perishing, was too much to be expected. God indeed chose this woman, but He chose her for more than a miracle. He chose her for service. The choice of this woman, while it brought such blessings to her, involved service. She was not elected merely to be saved in the famine, but to feed the prophet. She must be a woman of faith; she must make the little cake first, and afterwards she shall have the multiplication of the meal and of the oil. So, the grace of God does not choose men to sleep and wake up in Heaven, nor choose them to live in sin and find themselves absolved at the last; nor choose them to be idle and go about their own worldly business, and yet to win a reward at the last for which they never toiled. No! The sovereign electing grace of God chooses us to repentance, to faith, and afterwards to holiness of living, to Christian service, to zeal and to devotion.

Notice the response of the widow of Zarephath. She said, *"As the Lord your God lives, I do not have bread, only a handful of flour in a bin, and a little oil in a jar; and see, I am gathering a couple of sticks that I may go in and prepare it for myself and my son, that we may eat it, and die."* This polite address showed that she respected God, yet recognized that the God of Israel was Elijah's God and not her own. Elijah quickly found out that she was not only poor, but desperately poor. Elijah found her right before she was going to prepare her last morsel of food for herself and her son and then resign themselves to death. And Elijah said to her, *"Do not fear; go and do as you have said, but make me a small cake from it first, and bring it to me; and afterward make some for yourself and your son. For thus says the Lord God of Israel: 'The bin of flour shall not be used up, nor shall the jar of oil run dry, until the day the Lord sends rain on the earth."* God's first word to the widow through Elijah was *"Do not fear"*. Her present crisis rightly made her afraid, and God wanted her to put away fear and put trust in Him. Consider what Elijah said to the widow: *"Go and do as you have said, but make me a small cake from it first"*. This was an audaciously bold request from the prophet. He asked this destitute widow to first give him something from her last bit of food. This seemed like the worst kind of predatory fund-raising, so to speak, yet the end was worthwhile. Now, consider the prophetic word which God spoke through the mouth of His Prophet:

"The bin of flour shall not be used up, nor shall the jar of oil run dry, until the day the Lord sends rain on the earth".

This shows why Elijah could make such an audacious request. It was because God told him that He would provide a never-ending supply of food for the widow, her son, and Elijah himself. By faith, he asked the widow to put her trust in this great promise of God. Look at how the widow's obedience provoked an endless stream flow of God's great blessing into her life: She went away and did according to the word of Elijah; hence, she and her household ate for many days. She was willingly gave at great risk, based on her trust in the promise of God and the results were quite overwhelming: The bin of flour was not used up, nor did the jar of oil run dry, according to the word of the Lord which He spoke by Elijah. Do you notice that it says she and her household ate for many days? This is to tell you that once the grace for Miracle money is poured upon your life, it functions like a running tap of water; it keeps pouring upon you until you become a Kingdom Millionaire, glory to God! God fulfilled the promise to the widow, her son, and Elijah. God used her as a channel of supply and her needs were met as a result. Why didn't God give her a granary full of meal at once, and a vat full of oil instantly? It was not merely because of God's intent to try her, but there was wisdom here. Suppose he had given her a granary full of meal, how much of it would have been left by the next day? I question whether any would have remained, for in days of famine, men are sharp of scent, and it would soon have been noised about the city that "the old widow who lives in such-and-such a street, has a great store of food". Consequently, the people of the city would have caused a riot, and robbed the house, and perhaps, have killed the woman and her son. She would have been despoiled of her treasure, and in four and twenty hours the barrel of meal would have been as empty as it was at first, and the cruse of oil would have been spilled upon the ground." The opposite of what the Prophet had declared would have happened, hence God, in His wisdom divinely orchestrated the miracle exactly as it transpired.

In view of the above, the demonstration of this miracle by the hand of Prophet Elijah, culminated in a scenario in which the flour and oil did not run out of the jars. In other words, there was a perennial stream flow of Heaven's provision in the natural realm. This is exactly what God is doing for believers in this end time season. Operating at this dimension, believers shall buy things which are supernaturally paid for, eat in restaurant but before you get to the till, someone has already paid, put fuel in the car and someone walks to the attendant and pays the bill. There is a realm in God's supernatural provision that it doesn't matter what you spend, your money, fuel or airtime just doesn't get finished. In the natural realm people take insurance to cover themselves but at that level, it's as if there is a perennial supply and flow of money into your bank account and all other avenues through which money can flow. I have seen people who have driven their cars for some time without fuel, in other words they had their empty fuel gauges resurfacing as they drive. Some went to the extent of making cell phone calls without anytime. At that realm, whatever it is that you need or require, Heaven will supernaturally provide. For example, if you need a lawyer, even without paying for the services rendered, a man will just come from nowhere and volunteer to take the job. If you need finances, people will just come from nowhere and volunteer to pay for all your debts. All your bills get paid continuously. This is the realm of *financial recharge*. Every time you withdraw, the same amount you have withdrawn will still appear in the bank. When you pour petrol, whatever you use will be resurface as you drive.

PROPHETIC DECLARATION OF MIRACLE MONEY

As Prophet Elijah declared: "The bin of flour shall not be used up, nor shall the jar of oil run dry, until the day the Lord sends rain on the earth", I walk in the footsteps of Elijah, the Prophet of God and I declare and decree that the money in your bank account or wallet shall not be used up. As you use it to purchase property, the same amount of money will appear in your bank accounts or wallet again. It will never be finished. I declare and decree that your debts are cancelled supernaturally and money in Millions and Billions of dollars is being supernaturally transferred into your account, right now. I declare and decree that the fuel in your car shall not be used up. The fuel gauge shall resurface the more you drive. I declare and decree that the grocery in your cardboard shall not be finished. You shall cook plenty food everyday yet it shall resurface again. I declare and decree that the airtime in your cell phone will never be used up. You shall make thousands of phone calls yet it shall never be finished. I declare and decree that your clothes will not wear out. You shall wear them a thousand times, yet they shall forever stay new. Glory to Jesus!

THE CASE OF A RAM BEING CAUGHT BY ITS HORNS SO THAT ABRAHAM COULD USE IT FOR A SACRIFICE

There is yet another incident recorded in the Bible which unequivocally denotes God's sovereign control over all things. It opens our eyes to see how God manoeuvres His hand in the invisible arena in order to supernaturally provide for His children. The Bible records in Genesis 22:6-14 that,

God supernaturally provided a ram for sacrifice instead of Isaac, hence Abraham called the name of that place, "Jehovah Jireh, meaning, "The Lord will provide."

The Theology Behind The Manifestation of Miracle Money

While this is one of the most inspirational accounts of God's supernatural provision, one might be tempted to ask: *But where did that ram come from?* It must be noted that God has millions of ways through which He provides for His children. God can either move financial wealth from the natural realm into the hands of believers in the case of one receiving an investment or He can precipitate money directly from the spirit realm into the physical realm. In this case, the ram came from the spirit realm and was manifested in the physical realm. However, the natural mind does not understand the things of the spirit for they are spiritually discerned, hence the mind and logic breaks on account of spiritual matters. Therefore, if anybody questions the credibility of Miracle money in terms of where it comes from, I would also like to ask him to tell me where the ram which Abraham used for slaughter instead of Isaac, came from. If you can precisely tell me where that ram came from, I can also precisely tell you where Miracle Money comes from. Think about it!

Prophetically speaking, in this season money will appear supernaturally in people's bank accounts, bag and cars in the same way a ram appeared in the bushes and Abraham used it for sacrifice. The ram was a prophetic picture of God's redemptive plan of how God would save lost humanity through sacrificing His own so Jesus Christ. However, instead of Abraham sacrificing his own son, God provided a ram so that Abraham will use it for sacrifice. By the same token, instead of struggling to find your own finances to finance the gospel, business or family, God shall supernaturally provide Miracle money from Heaven so that you can use it for the furtherance of the gospel. This unusual money shall rule every provision, vision, ministry, need, desire, purpose, plan in matters relating to the fulfilment of Kingdom plans and purposes. When this happens, no longer shall you return to depend on common money again.

THE CASE OF FOOD MULTIPLICATION BY PROPHET ELISHA

Another notable miracle that demonstrates God's grace of supernatural provision is the multiplication of loaves by Elisha (2 kings 4:42-44). According to this narrative, a man came from Baal Shalisha, and brought the man of God bread of the first fruits, twenty loaves of barley bread, and newly ripened grain in his knapsack. Elisha then said, *"Give it to the people that they may eat."* But his servant said, *"What? Shall I set this before one hundred men?"* He prophet of God insisted, *"Give it to the people, that they may eat; for thus says the LORD: 'They shall eat and have some left over.'* Elisha's assurance of a financial miracle did not depend on a careful survey of the food available but on the power of God to provide for His people. Instead of using the offering as food for himself as he would be privileged to do (Numbers 18:13), Elisha told his servant to give the food to the people. These people are probably the *"sons of the prophets"* mentioned in verses 1 and 38. So, he set it before them; and they ate and had some left over, according to the word of the LORD. This is akin to how Jesus multiplied two loaves and five fish and fed five thousand people. Do you note that in a crowd that anticipated Jesus' miracle of feeding the 5,000, Elisha commanded that a small amount of bread be served to 100 men? In the context of this scripture, *"A hundred men"* doesn't represent a head count, but it's a way of referring to a large crowd. The supply of bread and grain appeared to be inadequate to feed such a large group. The real problem, however, was not the lack of food but the lack of faith. Indeed, there are many things in this narrative that ties with Jesus's financial miracle of feeding five thousand people, hence Elisha might be more aptly considered a type of Jesus. God promised not only to provide, but to provide beyond the immediate need. Elisha trusted the promise of God, acted upon it, and saw the promise miraculously fulfilled.

Conclusively, the above flood of revelations based on scriptural reference is ample evidence that Miracle money is real and that God can supernaturally cause money to rain down directly from Heaven. It is therefore imperative

The Theology Behind The Manifestation of Miracle Money

that believers should be circumspect and get rid of some misconstrued traditional teachings that have been holding Christians away from God's financial blessings for a long time. You need to stand your ground so that you can overthrow Satan's conspiracy to limit your money and keep you from receiving the *Miracle money* God has set aside for you. Miracle money is usually manifested to a heightened degree when natural avenues of provision have all stopped up in the natural realm. For example, Isaac received a hundred fold supernatural increase at such a time when all his natural sources of provision had been exhausted. The Bible states in Genesis 26:15 that shortly before he supernaturally received his hundred fold release of wealth, *all the wells which his father's servants had dug in the days of Abraham his father, the Philistines had stopped them, and filled them with earth.* In other words, as long as you are still clinging on to the natural realm as your major source of provision, you might not see the hand of God moving mightily on your behalf in the arena of Miracle money. This hundred fold release is not a one-time event that happened only to Isaac in the distant land, but a continuous phenomenon in the realm of God's prosperity. Jesus corroborated this divine truth when He declared in Mark 10:29,30 that *there is no man who has left his house or lands, for my sake, and the gospel's who shall not receive a hundred fold now in this time.* This was a prophetic instruction from the Lord himself concerning the hundred fold supernatural release which God is unreservedly pouring out upon His children in these end times. However, obedience to the voice of God with regard to financial matters is also highly imperative in this *season of financial overflow.*

CHAPTER THREE

THE SEVEN SUPERNATURAL DIMENSIONS OF FINANCIAL PROSPERITY

Divergent Forms of Manifestation of Miracle Money

In What Form Does Miracle Money Manifest In The Natural Realm?

There are various ways of manifesting Miracle money in the natural realm and believers must not be confined or limited to one method. God has more than a million ways to manifest His grace, hence He cannot be put in a box. Believers are therefore advised to explore these myriad of ways of manifesting this special grace in the natural realm. When God pronounced that *No eye has seen nor ear heard, nor has it entered into the heart of man what God has prepared for those who love Him* (1 Corinthians 2:9), He alluded to these manifestations of the Spirit which shall characterise this end time season. Miracle money is one of those special miracles which God prepared before the foundations of this world for believers to manifest in this end time season. Bear in mind that God also made a public declaration saying, *"I will give you treasures of darkness, and hidden riches of secret places"* (Isaiah 45:3).

Miracle Money is one of those treasures which God is unveiling to His people in this final chapter of human history. To the critics and sceptics, Miracle money will always remain a mystery and unfathomable phenomenon but to those who are open to the last wave and move of God, it is no longer a secret. The Bible speaks of the length, width and breath of the love of Christ (Ephesian 3:18). Miracle Money is one of those dimensions which reveal God's love for His people especially in this season just before He closes the curtain at the end of age.

Prophetically speaking, a time will come shortly whereby the manifestation of Miracle money shall become a common occurrence in the church just like praying for a headache. This shall culminate into what I call a *supernatural invasion* as the spirit realm invades the natural realm. In essence, Miracle money is a product of the supernatural invasion of God's glory in the earthly realm. As the glory of God is revealed more and more, things are going to be more exciting as miracles of such a heightened magnitude never seen before shall be unfolded from the Throne Room of Heaven. Depending on the gravity of manifestation, some shall breed awe, wonder and amazement while some shall trigger or provoke just cries of joy and celebration. Believers have indeed been plunged into a season of new things where there shall witness the unspeakable as the spirit realm manifest itself in the natural in intensity. Although these are many ways through which this grace shall be unreservedly poured upon the masses, there are key ways through which it shall manifest in its intensity and viscosity.

In the natural realm, there are divergent ways of releasing money from a central economic harbour. For example, there is *a bank transfer* whereby money is transferred from one bank account to the other; there is *a financial deposit* where money us directly deposited into an account; there is a *financial withdrawal*, whereby one just withdraws money from an ATM or bank account; there is a *Direct stop and debit order* whereby the account holder instructs a bank to send money to other account; there is a *financial exchange*, whereby money is converted into another currency and lastly there is *a financial access*, whereby a client receives money directly from An ATM even without the use of a debit card. As it is in the natural, so it is in the spirit.

The banking system in the natural world is an exact representation of the banking system in the spirit because the things which are seen were created from the things which are not seen. There is an *angelic deposit* whereby angel tellers deposit money directly into the account of a believer; there is *a wealth transfer* whereby money is supernaturally transferred from one account of an unbeliever into that of a believer; there is a *supernatural debt cancellation* whereby a believer's debts are supernaturally cancelled; and then there is a *supernatural financial withdrawal* whereby a believer steps out in faith to command an ATM to supernaturally release whatever amount he needs. The truth is that angels utilise the same technology and processes that we use in the natural financial or banking system although the transaction takes place in the spirit realm. If they were not using the same processes, then money would not eventually find its way to appear in our bank accounts. Just like when the Lord Jesus Christ came into the world, He didn't come through mysterious means but he had to come through the natural processes of birth as the Holy Ghost overshadowed Marry, hence she gave birth to a child. If Jesus had just dropped down from Heaven as a King, many would have found it difficult to accept Him. So, the truth is that God uses the natural phenomena and processes which people are used to in order to bring forth the supernatural into manifestations. The following are therefore divergent ways through which money is supernaturally transferred into the natural realm by the hand of angels: These are *supernatural wealth transfer, supernatural angelic deposits and financial receipts, supernatural debt cancellation, supernatural financial rain, supernatural financial multiplication and financial withdrawal and the golden rain.* These are what we call the **Seven supernatural dimensions of financial prosperity.** This is because they are the current means through which God is sending prosperity to His children. Therefore, if you are to receive money from Heaven today, expect it to come through any one of these 7 dimensions or a combination of some.

THE FIRST DIMENSION

SUPERNATURAL ANGELIC DEPOSITS:

An angelic deposit represents a direct supernatural deposit of money by angels of finances into people's bank accounts, wallets, pockets or bags, usually during worship sessions or spiritual gatherings, without a trace of how it got there in the natural realm.

This is a direct supernatural deposit of money into people's bank accounts especially during worship or demonstration sessions by *angel tellers* operating in the spirit realm. In the realm of God's prosperity, angels regulates the economy of the Kingdom of God and are actively involved in the invisible realm by supernaturally depositing money in the bank accounts of believers. Hence, there is in the realm of prosperity such a thing as *angelic deposits*. In the light of this revelation, believers must therefore be awakened to the reality that money is spiritual and as much as it is widely used in the natural realm as a medium of exchange, the original blue print of it is in Heaven, hence angels have control and access to distribute and deposit money supernaturally. Angelic deposits are therefore one of the ways through which God distributes millions of wealth in this end time dispensation to its intended purpose. During such sacred moments in God's presence, as a minister demonstrates Miracle money, either through commanding it into manifestation, blowing it forth through a microphone or waving hands towards the people, the congregation instantly receives messages in their phones alerting them of money that has been deposited. This is a supernatural work of angels in the invisible realm whose effects or results are visibly and tangibly seen in the physical realm. It transcends the realm of senses, hence it cannot be comprehended, mastered or fathomed by the human mind. Even the world's most intelligent Banker cannot trace Miracle Money because it is a divine orchestration that supersedes human wisdom. God's wisdom is greater that the most intelligent banker in this world. It happens that as people are worshiping and the grace for supernatural manifestation of Miracle money is demonstrated, money falls physically into people's bags, pockets and wallets and as they are instructed by the minister to search, they find it slipped in unexpected places. In some instances, a minister can even be catapulted to a dimension of *forensic prophecy* or prophetic accuracy whereby he declares the exact amount of money which should appear, where it should appear, and the exact currency in which it should manifest. This is the supernatural work of God which defies human reasoning and dazzle the minds of spectators. Behind the scenes, as people are gathered in worship, angels are activated or released in the invisible realm such that they start depositing money into these unexpected places. To authenticate the validity of Miracle money, in some case, *angel feathers* representing the presence of angels are found lying of the floor, hanging on people's clothes or floating in the air in territories where Miracle money would have been manifested. This is similar to the sudden appearance of water in a desert without a sign of rain, as recorded in the scriptures (2 Kings 3:17). This implies that there was a supernatural transfer of rain or water from the spirit realm into the natural for people to partake of. Remember that *Manna* the food of angels was released directly from Heaven into the natural realm to be used as food for the people to eat. It was not something that was manufactured in the earthly realm and then given to people. Instead, it came directly from Heaven, just like the falling of rain.

The Bible declares in Hagai 2:8; Joshua 6:19 that *Silver and gold belongs to God and that He has given it to the Son.* This implies that in the capacity of sons of God and co-heirs with Christ, we are entitled to a full possession of money or wealth in all its currencies under Heaven. Therefore, God can supernaturally deposit that wealth anytime, anywhere and in whatever form through the work of angels as we take up our positions of son-ship to place a demand on it by faith.

The greater truth is that Angel Tellers play a key role in making Angelic deposits in the same way Bank Tellers process deposits and other financial transactions in the natural realm.

The greatest challenge facing the masses is that lack of revelation and ignorance is what robs people of their right to fully partake or participate in the supernatural manifestation of the blessings of God because you cannot walk into what has not been revealed to you. The major challenge in the Body of Christ today besides issues of denominational tension is lack of understanding of God's system of governance and financial provision. According to God's system of governance, He has placed the money in the spirit realm under the close supervision of angels. The problem is that many believers are crying out to God for financial breakthrough but they don't know where the real money is. It's tantamount to a civilian who cries to the President of a country to help him withdraw his money from a bank, but then runs the risk of not receiving any help. This is because although the President owns the country, the money might not be directly in his hands but committed to the Reserve Bank under the close supervision of the Governor. This is a quintessence of the system in God's economy because as it is the natural, so it is in the spirit realm.

The greater truth is that the money that you need to impact the world is in the realm of the spirit, governed and committed into the hands of angels of finances, hence you need to rigorously engage angels of God for its release. Knowing where the money is and in whose hands the wealth of the Kingdom has been committed is such an important element to the release of your financial breakthrough. In most cases, the person who deposits the money might not necessarily be the owner of the money but a messenger sent to deposit it, in the same way angels are sent to distribute Miracle money. Knowing how to get the money from God's hand is therefore an imperative action. It must be understood therefore that God will not change His laws to accommodate your ignorance. Instead, He has established spiritual laws and set in place a system by which He governs the whole universe, hence it's up to you to know His system of governance so that you can operate accordingly. Developing a high level of sensitivity to angelic presence and knowing how to recognise and commission angels to go and gather your blessings is such a vital key to the ultimate manifestation of your millions of wealth in the form of Miracle money.

There is another dimension of Angelic deposits called *Supernatural Financial Cash receipts*. This involves the act of receiving Miracle money directly from the hands of angels in a direct natural encounter in the physical realm. This entails a visible appearance of angels handing over money into the hands of believers in a confrontational physical encounter in the natural realm. In this end time season, the spirit realm is no longer a mystery to believers any more. Instead, angels shall be seen in broad day light and they shall no longer be a mystery as Heaven is manifesting itself directly on the earthly realm. As this grace intensifies and Heavens manifest itself unreservedly on earth, culminating in what seems to be a *Heaven-on-earth sphere of existence,* some people shall physically receive money from the hands of angels. Angelic encounters shall be come a common experience and Miracle money, the order of the day. In the same way an angel baked nice cakes for Elijah, angels shall manifest in the physical realm to visibly hand over money and food parcels to believers in need. In some cases, believers shall meet people whom they have never seen before who shall hand over millions in money into their hands and then disappear even without saying a word.

Paul cautioned us as believers *never to forget to entertain angels for some entertained strangers unaware* (Hebrews 13:2). But how can someone mistake an angel for a stranger? It's because at times not only do angels appear in an aparition form but in bodily form just like humans. This denotes a transition from a *Hazah* to a *Mara* experience in the angelic realm. In this end time seasons, angelic manifestation will be heightened to a level whereby angels manifest in a physical form to give money to God's people. However, it is important that one be opened and sensitive to their visitation so that he may not miss out on some crucial financial blessings. When an angel cooked cakes for Elijah, this was a preview of the greater manifestation of angelic activity in the end times. The greater truth is that every miracle that happened in Old Testament is always pointing to something powerful yet to take place in the end times. The Bible records an incident whereby angels opened the prison gate and took Paul out of prison. In a like manner, angels shall manifest visibly in the natural realm such that they will take believers out of the prison of their financial lack into the realm of abundance. In this end time season characterised by a heightened degree of angelic manifestation in which God is expediting His work, many believers shall meet, talk, work and walk with angels in a natural setting. No longer shall angels be a mystery but a common phenomenon as believers walk in the supernatural. In a similar fashion in which Elijah encountered an angel who baked cakes and presented him with water, many shall encounter angels who shall present them with money, food, gifts and other financial resources in a natural setting. In that realm, you will not have to pray or see a vision in order to experience an angelic encounter because angels will be physically littering the streets, market places and the public arena. This angelic manifestation and visibility shall become a wide spread global phenomenon to the extent that some will be visiting churches, people's homes and other unexpected territories. You will encounter angels and communicate with them as if you are communicating with people in the natural realm.

THE SECOND DIMENSION

SUPERNATURAL WEALTH TRANSFER

This involves a supernatural transfer of money or financial resources from the hands of the wicked (unbelievers, sinners, devil's cohorts) into the hands of the righteous (believers, elect, called) in such a way that is inexplicable in the natural realm. This Biblical phenomenon denotes a supernatural transfer of Heaven's wealth and resources in the form of money, gold, silver, oil, investments, property and a myriad of other riches in glory from the worldly systems in possession of unbelievers into the hands of believers whom God has ordained or set apart to finance His end time agenda, plans and purposes (Job 27:13; 16-17; Proverbs 13:22; Proverbs 15: 6; Haggai 2:7-9).

It is worth noting that we are living in the most critical and momentous days in the history of the earth. This is a special end time season whereby God is lifting up His people especially in the arena of financial provision so that they can quickly expedite His divine plans and purpose on earth. It must be understood that while it is possible for God to rain Miracle money directly from Heaven, some of the financial resources which God is going to unleash upon His people will not come directly from Heaven as in the case of Money rain. Instead, they are already located in the earthly realm yet in possession of unbelievers. What God simply does is to supernaturally transfer, shift or move these finances from corrupt, bogus, wicked people of this world into the hands of His children who are ready to use them to propagate the gospel of the Lord Jesus to the extreme ends of the world. This supernatural transfer of wealth will take place in a way that ordinary people of this world will not understand. Even Bank experts with all their specialised Accounting knowledge, will not be able to comprehend the dynamics of this divine phenomenon. This shall be a time when God distinctively separates the righteous from the wicked. The Bible records a spectacular incident in Exodus 10:21-11:10 whereby on a given day, while there was thick darkness which covered the whole of Egypt, there lights in Goshen, which was the land inhabited by the Children of Israel. In other words, there was a transfer of light from the wicked to the righteous. This is the same principle by which God uses to transfer wealth from hands of the wicked to the righteous. While there is financial darkness engulfing the wicked in the World economy, characterised by a crash in stock markets and loss of humongous wealth, there shall be abundance, increase and profits for the righteous. Therefore, the accounting principle for Miracle money is to *credit* Satanic warehouses and *debit* Godly warehouses, since the wealth of the wicked is laid up for the righteous.

To quantify and enhance a significant level of understanding of this concept, let's take a glance at the following humongous wealth that is in the hands of Worldly people:

THE PROFILE OF THE TOP 10 RICHEST PEOPLE IN THIS WORLD IN 2016

1. CARLOS SLIM HELU- $53.5 billion in telecommunications - Mexico

2. BILL GATES- $53 billion in Microsoft - USA

3. WARREN BUFFET- $47 billion in investment - USA

4. MUKESH AMBANI- $29 billion in petrochemicals, oil and gas - India

5. LAKSHMI MITTAL- $28.7 billion in steel - India

6. LAWRENCE ELLISON- $28 billion in Oracle - USA

7. BERNARD ARNAULT- $27.5 billion in luxury goods - France

8. EIKE BATISTA- $27 billion in Mining oil - Brazil

9. AMANCIO ORTEGA- $25 billion in Fashion retail - France

10. Karl ALbrecht- $23.5 billion in Supermarkets - Germany

    Do you notice that a huge chunk of $342.2 Billion is in the hands of just 10 people in this world? And how many of these World top ten business tycoons are believers? In view of the above statistics, it is evident that the bulk of this world's wealth is in the hands of unbelievers. This is a quintessence of the wealth that God is supernaturally transfering from the hands of wicked man into the hands of the righteous in this season, for the furtherance of the Gospel of His Son, Jesus Christ. This is what Prophet Isaiah in the past generations saw by prophetic perception in the realm of the spirit and then decoded it in prophetic language as a *new thing* (Isaiah 43:19). It is a new thing in the sense that it's a prosperity wave that is currently sweeping across the Body of Christ as multitudes are thrust into the new reality of God's supernatural provision. However, as far as God is concerned, wealth transfer is not a new Biblical concept in the realm of prosperity but a divine phenomenon that has transpired across past generations. However, the gravity and intensity of its manifestation shall be heightened in this end times in what I call the *final wave of prosperity*. There is a divine prophetic revelation in the realm of prosperity that in the end time dispensation, the church shall gather humongous wealth and resources from Heaven, so that it can use them for the proliferation, propagation and furtherance of the gospel. This supernatural transfer of wealth is based on the following catalogue of God's prophetic words declared through the voice of Prophet Isaiah, saying,

'The wealth on the seas will be brought to you, to you the riches of the nations will come. (Isaiah 60:11) 'Your gates will always stand open, they will never be shut, day or night, so that men may bring the wealth of the nations (Isaiah 61:6). 'You will feed on the wealth of nations, and in their riches you will boast'. (Isaiah 66:12) 'I will extend peace to her like a river, and the wealth of nations like a flooding stream'.

In a Biblical context, this phenomenon of wealth transfer has already transpired six times. The *First Wealth Transfer* took place in Genesis 12:10 in Egypt whereby famine struck the land, compelling Abram to go down to Egypt. While there, the Egyptians saw Sarai's beauty and spoke highly of her to Pharaoh, who decided to take her for a wife. Believing that Sarai was Abram's sister, Pharaoh entreated Abram and gave him sheep, oxen, servants, cattle, and much wealth. After the Lord had plagued Pharaoh and he discovered that Sarai was actually Abram's wife, he eventually gave her back. But Pharaoh never asked for the wealth back. Pharaoh then gave Abraham a lot of wealth such that he left Egypt a very rich man in cattle, in silver, and in gold (Genesis 13:1-2), which were the highest measure of wealth in the world at that time. This was the first recorded wealth transfer from the wicked to the righteous.

The Second Wealth Transfer took place in Genesis 26:1 when Isaac was about to go to Egypt and God interrupted him and through a divine arrangement of circumstances in the realm of the spirit, He caused him to meet Abimelech of the Philistines and God transferred the Great wealth of Abimelech to Isaac. Consider what the following scripture has to say about Isaac: *"Then Isaac sowed in that land, and received in the same year a hundredfold and the* LORD *blessed him. And the man waxed great, and went forward, and grew until he became very great. For he had possession of flocks, and possession of herds, and great store of servants and the Philistines envied him*" (Genesis 26: 12-14). Here again we see a wealth transfer taking place. Not only did Isaac inherit the wealth from his father Abraham, but he also received a great wealth transfer from Abimelech— so much that the Philistines told Isaac, "*Go from us, for you are much mightier than us*" (verse 16).Note that both Abraham's and Isaac's wealth transfers took place in times of famine. This is to tell you that your prosperity is not dependent upon the world's economic conditions. Instead, it is dependent upon the Word of God, which is an infallible manual by which we access all financial resources from Heaven!

The *Third Wealth Transfer* took place in Genesis 30:25-31 when God blessed Jacob after working for Laban for seven years and God gave Jacob the wealth of Laban. This is evident in Jacob's confession to his wife Rachel: "*You know that with all my power I have served your father. And your father has deceived me, and changed my wages ten times, but God suffered him not to hurt me. If he said thus, the speckled shall be your wages; then all the cattle bare speckled: and if he said thus, the ring straked shall be your hire; then bare all the cattle ring straked. Thus God has taken away the cattle of your father, and given them to me*" (Genesis 31:6-9). When Laban cheated Jacob by making him work for another 7 years, although in thenatural realm that seemed to be an unfair act, God used it as an avenue, leeway and reason to transfer wealth from Laban to Jacob. Subsequently, the *Fourth Wealth Transfer* transpired in Genesis 41 when God gave Joseph favour to interpret dreams and became the wealthiest man in Egypt within a flip of a moment. Joseph received the wealth of the *superpower Egypt. Consider how Pharoah handed over the wealth of Egypt to Joseph, on a silver plate:* "*Forasmuch as God has shown you all this, there is none so discreet and wise as you are. You shall be over my house, and according to your word shall all my people be ruled. Only in the throne will I be greater than you. And Pharaoh said to Joseph, See, I have set you over all the land of Egypt. And Pharaoh took off his ring from his hand, and put it upon Joseph's hand, and arrayed him in vestures of fine linen, and put a gold chain about his neck; and he made him to ride in the second chariot which he had, and they bowed before him and he made him ruler over all the land of Egypt. And Pharaoh said to Joseph, I am Pharaoh, and without you shall no man lift up his hand or foot in all the land of Egypt*" (Genesis 41:39-44). Imagine God gave His servant Joseph the wealth of the entire nation of Egypt was the richest in the world at that time! Pharaoh even gave Joseph control of all of Egypt's business and economy. This was indeed an enthralling wealth transfer in action.

The *Fifth Wealth Transfer* is recorded in Exodus 12: 35-36 when the children of Israel stripped the Egyptians of humongous wealth that belonged to them and left Egypt with alarming wealth after being in bondage for four hundred years in Egypt. David also speaks of this supernatural wealth transfer when he testifies in Psalms 105:37-38 that the children of Israel brought silver and gold out of the land of Egypt. This was a fulfilment of scripture because God had promised Moses that when the Israelites come out of Egypt, they would leave with the wealth of the Egyptians. This is what God had ascertained: "*I am sure that the king of Egypt will not let you go, no, not by a mighty hand. And I will stretch out my hand, and smite Egypt with all my wonders which I will do in the midst thereof, and after that he will let you go. And I will give this people favor in the sight of the Egyptians, and it shall come to pass, that, when you go, you shall not go empty: But every woman shall borrow of her neighbor, and of her that sojourned in her house, jewels of silver, and jewels of gold, and raiment: and you shall put them upon your sons, and upon your daughters; and ye shall spoil the Egyptians*" (Exodus 3:19-22). Can you imagine what happened that night after God had slain all the firstborn males throughout Egypt? Think of what it was like when the Israelites went to the Egyptians, who had just lost sons and been ruined by all the plagues, yet these same Egyptians gave them their wealth. That was truly a miracle of transfer! The *Sixth Biblical Wealth Transfer* took place in 1 Chronicles 1:11-12 when God gave Solomon the wealth of the nations and made him the richest man in the world. In the *six wealth transfer*, God Almighty not only gave Solomon the wealth of one nation, but the wealth of the nations of the world. King Solomon exceeded all the Kings of the earth in riches and wisdom (1 Kings 10:23). Think about it! He was the richest man on the planet because of God's great wealth and favor!

The *Seventh Wealth Transfer* is the portion of the end time dispensation. It is the one which God is abundantly pouring out upon the church in this present hour. It is the blessing of the last dispensation and marks the beginning of the final wave of prosperity. Next in line for this great wealth transfer is you! Remember that the wealth of the sinner is laid up for the just (Proverbs 13:22). The Lord wants to give you the wealth of the sinner to establish His covenant: *"Thou shall remember the* LORD *thy God: for it is he that giveth thee power to get wealth, that He may establish his covenant which He swore unto thy fathers, as it is this day"* (Deuteronomy 8:18). His covenant is the Gospel of Jesus Christ, His Son, for the nations! God will give you the wealth of the sinner so that you can support the preaching of the Gospel to the extreme ends of the world! This wealth transfer is just around the corner! Concerning the wicked possessing the World's wealth, the Lord said, *"Though he heap up silver as the dust, and prepare raiment as the clay, He may prepare it, but the just shall put it on, and the innocent shall divide the silver"* (Job 27:16-17). Therefore, get ready for this alarming wealth that is going to rain upon your life and catapult you to the realm of billionaires in this end time season.

It is of paramount significance to highlight in this regard the greater truth that God's desire has always been to transfer wealth and riches from unbelievers into the hands of believers so that they can carry out His divine plans and purposes on earth on behalf of the Kingdom. To substantiate this divine truth, the Bible declares in Proverbs 13:22 that *the wealth of the sinner is laid up for the Just.* I like the Amplified version because it puts this concept of wealth transfer in its correct divine perspective. It states that *the wealth of the sinner [finds its way eventually] into the hands of the righteous, for whom it was laid up.* This speaks of an automatic wealth transfer agenda divinely orchestrated directed from Heaven, to move alarming levels of wealth, property and money from unbelievers into the hands of believers for them to be elevated to the realm of End Time Kingdom Millionaires and Billionaires. Moreover, in a related scripture in Job 27:16-17 (NIV) God declared that *"Though the unbeliever heaps up silver like dust and clothes like piles of clay, what he lays up the righteous will wear and the innocent will divide his silver"*. The international version expresses this in a very powerful way. It says,

"Evil people may have piles of money and may store away mounds of clothing. But the righteous will wear that clothing, and the innocent will divide that money."

The narrative continues in Verse 19 (NLT) to emphasize that, *"The wicked go to bed rich but wake up to find that all their wealth is gone."* This is the divine concept of supernatural wealth transfer which God is unveiling in this present hour. Through this programme, agents of darkness such as Satanists, devil worshipers, magicians, worldly men and demons who have been specialising in twisting, manipulating and stealing the finances of believers shall loose humongous wealth into the hands of believers. Moreover, the Bible declares in Ecclesiastes 2:26 (NIV) that, *"To the person who pleases Him, God gives wisdom, knowledge and happiness, but to the sinner, He gives the task of gathering and storing up wealth to hand it over to the one who pleases God"*. The New International Version expresses it in a more informative way by stating that*"If a sinner becomes wealthy, God takes the wealth away and gives it to those who please Him."* Proverbs 28:8 (NLT) expresses this divine concept of wealth transfer in a different but enlightening way. It states that, *"Income from charging high interest rates will end up in the pocket of someone who is kind to the poor."* This implies that as a believer, the wealth of the wicked is looking for you, hence you need to rightly position yourself in the spirit so that it can locate you. Therefore, in this season, divine favour, supernatural ideas, wisdom, supernatural connections, divine opportunities and divine arrangement of circumstances and supernatural doors shall align themselves to you.

This implies that there shall be a mega shift, sudden transition and revolutionary leap from Worldly Billionaires into God's Billionaires as wealth and property supernaturally slips from the hands of unbelievers into believers for the furtherance of the gospel. *The question you are probably asking yourself is: How will this transfer take place*? Firstly, investment or business doors will be shut against the wicked unbelievers while opportunities are supernaturally opened and available to believers in the natural realm. This process shall be well managed by angels such that there shall be no flaws. Unbelievers will just wake up and in a flip of a moment all their millions and billions worth of investments will be gone. When this happens, no theory or monetary policy shall be able to provide a viable explanation, solution or answer to this phenomenon. Believers shall therefore rise with such alarming financial power to direct the world economy through establishing banks, malls, trade centres, and be in possession of the best properties and assets in the word. Secondly there shall be an unexpected crash in the global stock markets such that at the end of the process, humongous investments would have supernaturally slipped into the accounts of believers. Thirdly, this shall be made possible through a supernatural appearance of Miracle money directly into the accounts of believers through *angelic deposits*. This is indeed the best time for one to become a Kingdom Millionaire. Therefore the above stated scriptural reference is ample evidence of the reality of wealth transfer which God has planned for His church in these end times.

Prophetically speaking, there is coming the greatest financial invasion ever witnessed in the history of humanity. The manifestation of this blessing is at an all-time high and imminent as we are approaching a *"Blessing manifestation of glory"* which is a supernatural explosion of wealth in ways and intensity that the human race has never seen before. In the current end time dispensation, there are a multitude of wealth reservoirs that shall be taped and drained into the gospel of Jesus Christ as the Lord is restoring the earth to its rightful position of possession of wealth and resources. There shall therefore be an explosion of wealth into the Body of Christ such as never seen before. There shall be a large scale supernatural transfer of wealth into the bank accounts, investments, houses, bags, wallets and even clothes of Christians for the purpose of propagating the gospel of Christ. Everything the world has and is using it for evil shall be claimed by believers and used for the propagation of the gospel across the world, just before the Master returns for the Grand Finale of the earth.

A SEVEN-FOLD PROPHETIC REVELATION OF THE AFTER MARTHS OR REPERCUSSIONS OF THE END TIME WEALTH TRANSFER

- Unbelievers in possession of a large proportion of the world's wealth and resources shall supernaturally loose humongous wealth, property and investments in ways that will defy natural laws of finance and confound the wisdom of the most intelligent World Bankers, Economists and Financial Experts (Proverbs 13:22). In other words, money shall be supernaturally credited on the account of the unbelievers and debited on the accounts of believers in such a way that the books in the banks and economy will remain balancing from an accounting point of view. This shall instantaneously give birth to Kingdom Millionaires and Billionaires who shall be elevated to the centre of the world stage to dominate the best of the world's investment and most lucrative properties.

- Multitudes of believers shall supernaturally obtain wealth in their bank accounts, wallets, houses and other unexpected areas (Ecclesiastes 2:26). In other words, millions in Miracle money shall supernaturally appear in places where people never thought it could. This shall be used for the furtherance of the gospel. No scientist, accountant, or even the most intellectual professor will be able to provide a comprehensive explanation of where this Miracle money came from, how it manifested in the natural realm and why it was transferred.

- The economies of the world shall be shaken to their very foundations to pave a way or accentuate an avenue for a smooth wealth transfer process. A global crash of stock markets and unexpected loss of wealth through investments by unbelievers shall characterise this wealth transfer season (Proverb 13:22) and the process shall be well managed and regulated by angel tellers such that there shall be nothing questionable from a natural perspective. The *"Invisible hand"* which economists emphasises as being responsible for regulating the economy and prices of stock markets shall be turned into *"God's Visible hand"* as He moves and manoeuvres the monetary and economic system in favour of believers.

- There shall be a sudden, unexpected and hilarious rise of Kingdom Millionaires and Billionaires from every sphere of life in the Christian realm and it shall be evident that wealth is now in the hands of believers. People whom the world had undermined, subjugated and held in contempt for a long time shall be instantaneously catapulted to the realm of control and possession of the world's humongous wealth and riches. This shall transpire in the same way God used the four lepers to bring forth an economic revival in Syria by looting the camp of the Syrian soldiers (2 Kings 7:1). As Prophet Elisha descibed in prophetic language, unbelievers shall only see it but not partake of it.

- Godly justice and equitable distribution of wealth shall be fostered as believers are elevated to a position of control, possession and ownership of wealth. As a way of prophetic fulfilment of the scripture that the earth waits in earnest expectation for the manifestation of the sons of God (Romans 8:19), believers shall use their financial power to take over where the governments of the world has dismally failed to render services to the poor, needy and orphans. Therefore, there shall be widespread works of charity, donations just like the wealth revival during the early church where believers brought forth their wealth to distribute to the poor, such that no one lacked anything. God ordained ministries shall receive tithes from certain countries and global financial institutions shall give alarming wealth to the church in the form of donations. Companies' social responsibility projects shall be directed towards the church in this critical end time season.

- Demonic powers and forces confined to the second Heaven, shall be severely shaken. In other words, a season of great spiritual shaking or awakening shall invade the world's monetary and economic system as God declared through the voice of Prophet Hagai saying, *"Once more and in a little while I will shake the Heaven, I will shake the earth and I will shake the sea and the earth shall be filled with My glory"* (Hagai 2:6-7). Wealth transfer shall be a product of this end time shaking. In other words, agents of the devil such as Satanists, devil worshipers and magicians who possesses a large portion of the World's wealth, businesses and companies and are using them for manufacturing satanic products, shall be dethroned and taken out of business (Proverbs 28:8). A season of widespread unusual miracles, signs and wonders that shall culminate in the raising of the dead, shall proceed the dismantling of these satanic forces, paving a way for millions of wealth to stream in the direction of the righteous, to the extent that it shall be common to see believers owning millions of wealth and property.

- A season of distinction shall be birthed in which believers are separated from unbelievers and genuine Christians are separated from pretenders or fake ones and those who are using the name of God to pursue their own deceitful interests shall be exposed. Believers shall be clearly known by their degree of prosperity and the magnitude of wealth they have amassed. They will begin to prosper and continue to prosper until they have reached the brink of prosperity (Genesis 26:13-23). This shall accentuate an avenue for the coming of the Lord Jesus Christ as the church shall be brought to a level of perfection and sanctification.

THE THIRD DIMENSION

SUPERNATURAL DEBT CANCELLATION

This invokes a complete supernatural removal, termination or payment of a debt a person owes others, without a trace of how it transpired in the natural realm

Contrary to what multitudes of people presume, debt cancellation is not a new Biblical concept. Its origin dates way back as far as the Old Testament days. In essence, God's original master plan for humanity has always been to set His people free from the entanglement of debt (Deuteronomy 15:1-2; Philemon 18-19; 1 Samuel 17:25, 22:2 2 Kings 4:7; Matthew 18:27, 6:12; Leviticus 25:10; Nehemiah 5:3-4, 11-12). The most severe disadvantage of debt is that it keeps God's children bound, sabotaged, caged, imprisoned and oppressed. To make matters worse, it drives their attention away from worshiping God in the fullness of the spirit. Echoing the voice of the prophet Isaiah, Jesus proclaimed in Luke 4:18—19 saying, *"The spirit of the Lord is upon me because He has anointed me to preach the gospel to the poor; He has sent me to heal the broken hearted, to preach deliverance to the captives, and recovering of sight to the blind, to set at liberty them that are bruised, to preach the acceptable year of the Lord."* The Amplified Version states it explicitly as: *"The day when salvation and the free favors of God profusely abound."* In the context of this scripture, the acceptable year of the Lord is the year of Jubilee, the year when all debts were cancelled. This is because debt is part of the world's system of finance and it's a system devised by the devil to keep the children of God in bondage to the fallen world (Deuteronomy 28:15, 43-44; Proverbs 22:7). Jesus, however, has redeemed us from the curse of the law, and we are now free to walk in fullness of the blessing of Abraham (Galatians 3:13-14). Moreover, the scripture above unveils the reality that the spirit of the Lord has anointed me *to preach the good news to the poor*. This implies that the permanent solution to poverty is the Word of God because it provides ultimate answers and solutions on how to escape the debilitating morass of lack caused by debt. Therefore, as far as God is concerned, the poor don't have to be poor anymore and they don't have to lack anything or be hamstrung by debt anymore.

It is worth mentioning that multitudes of believers are supposed to be millionaires by now but some have been hamstrung by debt. Hence, they have not been able to move forward to amass humongous wealth from Heaven. It is a typical scenario across a broad spectrum of Christian cycles to find children of God who live from hand to mouth on borrowed income to the extent that they get entangled in a web of debt. The wicked thing about debt is that it exacerbates poverty and breeds a negative spiritual gravity that nails one to continuous pain, suffering and debilitating poverty. Therefore, in the same way God provides Miracle money, the other divine orchestration which Heavens renders free of charge is divine intervention through supernatural debt cancelation.

In order to enhance a significant level of understanding of the divine concept of debt cancellation, it is of paramount importance that we derive ample references on incidences touching debt cancelation scenarios in the word of God. The Bible records in 2 Kings 4:1-7; 6:5-6 that *God supernaturally provided supernatural debt cancellation for a widow* when He worked miracles of supernatural financial provision by the hands of Elijah. After the death of her husband, the widow owed many people a lump sum of money and was on the verge of losing both her sons to the creditor but Elijah gave her a prophetic instruction to keep pouring oil from a small pot into as many empty vessels as they could find and then sell the oil to pay the debt. To present the background of this narrative, a certain woman of the wives of the sons of the prophets cried out to Elisha, saying,

> *"Your servant my husband is dead, and you know that your servant feared the LORD. And the creditor is coming to take my two sons to be his slaves." So, Elisha said to her, "What shall I do for you? Tell me, what do you have in the house?" And she said, "Your maidservant has nothing in the house but a jar of oil." Then he said, "Go, borrow vessels from everywhere, from all your neighbors; empty vessels; do not gather just a few. And when you have come in, you shall shut the door behind you and your sons; then pour it into all those vessels, and set aside the full ones."*

According to the narrative, she went from him and shut the door behind her and her sons, who brought the vessels to her; and she poured it out. Now, it came to pass when the vessels were full that she said to her son, *"Bring me another vessel."* And he said to her, *"There is not another vessel."* So, the oil ceased. Then she came and told the man of God and he said, *"Go, sell the oil and pay your debt; and you and your sons live on the rest."* This was a supernatural bail out from debt through *prophetic instruction*. Isn't it interesting to note the integral role which prophets played in the olden days in terms of solving the problems of the masses? Although derailed by religious dogma, prophets should continue to play an integral role in the society today. In this season dominated by a darkening global economic outlook, many children of God somehow find themselves entangled in a web of debt and subsequently hamstrung in ministry due to lack of finances. Under the circumstances, God uses supernatural debt cancellation to bail them out of their situation.

In retrospect to this narrative, it is worth noting that this widowed wife of one of the sons of the prophets had debts and no means to pay them. The legal system in Israel at that time would not allow her to declare bankruptcy. She had to involuntarily handover her sons as indentured servants to her creditor as payment for the debts. However, inhumane this might seem, the creditor was within his rights, for Mosaic Law allowed him to enslave the debtor and his children as far as the Year of Jubilee in order to work off the debt. By commanding her to go and borrow vessels from neighbours, Elisha made this woman commit herself in faith to God's supernatural provision. To borrow vessels in this manner invited awkward questions, but she did as the word of God through His prophet commanded her. She did what she was commanded to do and she did it in faith, hence the result answered the end. Notable is the realisation that God takes care to deliver His servants in ways that involve the exercise of their faith. He would not have them be little in faith, for *faith is the currency of Heaven and the wealth of the Heavenly life* since *you have God in the measure in which you desire Him*. Only remember that the desire that brings God must be more than a feeble, fleeting wish. Wishing is one thing but willing is quite another. Lazily wishing and strenuously desiring are two entirely different postures of mind. The former gets nothing while the latter gets everything, including God and all that God can bring.

As aforementioned, notice that the woman was instructed to pour oil into all those vessels, and set aside the full ones. Elisha told the woman to take all that she had and pour it out in faith into the borrowed vessels. As she did this, the oil miraculously kept pouring from the original vessel until all the borrowed vessels were filled. At the end of it, she had a surplus oil. That is a remarkable miracle! Note that Elisha did not gather the vessels and pour the oil himself, but he prophetically instructed the woman to do it herself, thereby strengthening her faith in God. This was a prophetic action of faith in response to prophetic instruction. The original vessel of oil, the one the woman had in her house was a smaller vessel that held only oil for anointing. This means that the distribution of the oil into the other vessels required constant pouring and allowing the oil to supernaturally fill the small vessel again. The vessels also had to be empty before they could be filled with oil. It did no good to bring the widow full vessels. Philosophically speaking, a full Christ is for empty sinners and as long as there is a really empty soul in a congregation so long will a blessing go forth with the word, and no longer. It is not our emptiness, but our fullness which can hinder the outpourings of free grace.

The narrative continues to unpack that once all the jars were filled, the oil ceased. This tells me that the miracle was given according to the measure of the woman's previous faith in borrowing vessels. She did borrow enough so the excess oil was sold and provided money to pay the debt to the creditor and to provide for the future. It is interesting to note that had she borrowed more, more would have been provided. On the other hand, had she gathered less, less would have been provided. If she borrowed few vessels, she would have but little oil but if she borrowed many vessels, they would all be filled such that she should have much oil. She herself was to measure out what she should have. It is unequivocally evident that in matters of spiritual blessings from God, you have more to do with the measurement of your mercies than you think. The extent to which you can be filled with the blessings of God depends on your capacity to contain those blessings. The principle of this miracle is that the level of man's commitment to the materialisation of the miracle determines the amount of blessing and provision actually received. In most cases, we make our blessings little, because our prayers are little. Note that the oil did not pour out on the ground or simply flow about. It was intended for a prepared vessel. Each vessel had to be prepared by being gathered, assembled, emptied and put in the right position. Strikingly, when there was no more prepared vessel, the oil stopped. This is to tell you that when you no longer avail yourself as a prepared vessel of honour to be used by God, the anointing stops from flowing into your life. How empty you are as a vessel determines how much anointing will flow into your life.

It is evident in the narrative that this woman was in a very desperate situation. Back then, when someone had a debt they could not pay, they had to offer themselves or their children as slaves to work until the debt was paid off. The only thing she owned that had any value was some oil, but it was almost gone, then she would be left with nothing. However, the Lord took the little which the woman had and multiplied it. He not only gave her enough money to pay her debt and keep her children from becoming slaves but he also gave her plenty extra so that she could buy food, clothing, and everything else they would need in the future. How do we know that the woman believed that God would intervene in her desperate situation? She collected jars from her neighbours. If she had not believed God, she would not have bothered the neighbours and risked being embarrassed if nothing happened. God invited this woman to be a part of His plan and her actions of faith gave proof of her trust in God. Isn't this story a beautiful picture of how much God cares for His children? This is to tell you that no problem is too great or too small for our loving God! If this woman could believe God to that extent, you too can believe God for Miracle money in this season.

As corroborated by scriptural evidence, there are three principal ways through which God supernaturally terminates, nullifies or invalidates debt. Firstly, God spontaneously and supernaturally provides the required finances just like in the above-mentioned case of the widow who was instructed to sell the olive oil and pay for her debts and she and her sons lived on what was left over (2 Kings 4:1-7). The other scenario is the one involving the taxes which were paid by extracting money from a fish's mouth (Matthew 17:24-27). In other words, God can release money supernaturally into one's account to cover for the outstanding debt. You might be shocked when some day you decide to check your account and then find a lump sum of money whose depositor or origin is untraceable. This is how debt cancellation works. Even the most intelligent banker will not be able to trace the origin of an angelic deposit, yet all the books will be balancing as per accounting procedures. Secondly, God cancels, nullifies or removes the debt in the same way He used Nehemiah to cancel all the debts of the poor Jews (Nehemiah 5:1-13). Another quintessential example is the one that pertains to a King who forgave his servant and cancelled his debt worth 10,000 talents (Matthew 18:23-27). In a similar fashion, God can cause those whom you owe to irresistibly make a decision to voluntarily cancel the debt for no apparent reason. For instance, a Bank or insurance company that you owe an amount of five hundred thousand dollars can call you out of the blue and tell you that your debt has been cancelled, hence you don't owe them anything. Thirdly, God moves upon others to pay your debt just like in the case of Paul who promised to pay the debts of the saints in full and have it charged to his account if they owed anything (Philemon 18-19). The other scenario involves the Samaritan who took out two pence and gave them to the owner of the Inn and said to him, *"Take care of him. Whatever else you have to spend, I will pay it back in full when I return"* (Luke 10:30-37). In other words, God can move others even the people you have never met in life to voluntarily pay for the outstanding debt. However, believers must not try and put God in a box by limiting themselves to only one method for God has a million ways of supernatural provision. Whichever way God uses, the bottom line is that God is in the business of debt cancellation, hence if you could only open yourself to His supernatural ways of provision, you shall have all your debts cancelled within a flip of a moment so that you can begin to pave your way to becoming the world's next top Billionaire.

HOW TO BECOME DEBT FREE

Becoming debt free is something every Christian should thrive to acheive. The Bible admonishes us in Romans 13:8 to *"keep out of debt and owe no man anything, except to love one another"* (*The Amplified Bible*). In fact, as believers, we should be the lender, not the borrower (Deuteronomy 28:12).The following are therefore practical guidelines unveiled by revelation on how believers can get out of the yoke and bondage of debt. It must be expressly understood in this regard that my solemn intent is not to create any doctrine on the subject of debt cancelation but to provide practical guidelines which believers could apply to supernaturally escape the horrendous plight of debt.

Make up your mind to get out of debt and live debt free.

A vital point of departure to the supernatural escape from debt involves giving the Word of God first place in your life, and by making it your final authority. Confession, meditation and visualization works hand in glove, hence it is imperative that you confess and meditate on the Word and then see yourself getting out of debt because if you can't see it, then you can't have it (Psalms 1:1-3; Joshua 1:8). With that being said, you must therefore pay undivided attention to Romans 13:8 and believe God to be your source for all your needs and desires. Regardless of the gravity of your circumstances, be determined to be single-minded (James 1:8, 22-25), and remain grounded on the truth of God's word. Then start talking your way out of debt and the results of your confession shall speedily manifest in your life.

Prioritize God's interests in your financial affairs.

It is imperative that you take God first in your finances because the dimension of God's supernatural provision will not work where God is not involved. Therefore, decide that no matter what comes your way, you will obey God's Word and tithe, as well as be a generous giver (Malachi 3:8-12; II Corinthians 9:6-15). Tithing lays a solid foundation for your financial breakthrough, success and opens supernatural doors of impossibility because it is the only area in the Bible whereby God removes boundary lines and grants humanity the prerogative to test Him. Therefore, the people who must tithe or give the most are those who are in debt because giving provides an immediate supernatural escape from debt.

Consistently believe God for your daily bread (Matthew 6:11).

People who easily experience an immediate supernatural escape from debt are those who are determined to heavily rely on God for the supply of their daily provision. This is the money you need for your household to function every day. Your tithes and giving should be included in this, but don't cheat yourself. It is important to decide that you are living to give (Ephesians 4:28). Live on the increase from your giving, that is, reach for the place in your financial life where the income from your job or business becomes your seed for giving. And as you sow, believe for a hundredfold harvest.

You will be a blessing to others and be out of debt. You will become a live demonstration of scripture that God will bless you and make all grace abound toward you; that you, always having all sufficiency in all things, may abound to every good work.

Lay hold of it by faith.

It is worth exploring that as far as God is concerned, Christ has already redeemed us from debt but should you accidentally find yourself still entangled in a web of debt, you need to start claiming or appropriating the work which Christ has already done for you on the cross. Therefore, practically apply the principles set out in Mark 11:23-24. Believe in your heart and confess with your mouth that your needs are met and that you are out of debt. Prophetically decree that the windows of Heaven are opened to you, that the hundredfold return is yours in this lifetime and that you operate financially according to the wisdom of God. (Proverbs 2:1-10, 3:13-18.) As you speak it forth, it shall be established according to your word and the results shall manifest speedily and before you know it, someone will be knocking on your door to hand over a fat cheque reflecting that all your debts have been fully paid for.

Bind the devil in the Name of Jesus

It is important that you understand that while it is in the confines of God's will for you to get a supernatural escape from debt, it is also Satan's desire to keep you caged and see you humstrung by debt (Matthew 18:18; Mark 16:17; James 4:7; Ephesians 6:10-18). In some cases, the reason why some children of God found themselves entrapped in the cage of debt is because Satan has stolen, twisted and manipulated their financial blessings in the high places where some blessings are exchanged for evil and given to people for which they were not originally intended by God. Moreover, Satan works through his agents' such as witches and manipulates the monetary system of this world to lock people into a morass of unescapable debt. Therefore, you need to lift up the shield of faith and take a very aggressive stance towards the enemy and in Jesus' Name, order Satan and all his forces out of your financial affairs. Bind every demon that is responsible for you being in debt and cast out the monitoring spirits assigned to ensure that you stay locked in debt. By the power of the Holy Ghost and through the blood of Jesus, release yourself from the yoke of debt into which the devil has locked you and declare your liberty in the name of Jesus. It is possible that some people might never become millionaires because of demons who are holding them but the minute they go for deliverance and have the demons cast out, their millions of wealth starts to manifest speedily.

Loose the forces of Heaven into your financial affairs

The Bible declares in Matthew 18:18 that *whatever we bind on earth shall be bound in Heaven and whatever we release on earth shall be released in Heaven*. It is therefore important that as much as we bind the demonic forces who want to devour our finances, it is equally important that we release the forces of divinity to work on our behalf. However, a multitude of believers usually make a grave mistake in this area because their prayers are dominated by biding demonic forces yet they hardly get to release their millions of wealth into their bank accounts. Their finances are free because they have bound the demons, good enough, but they have not released anything into their accounts, hence their financial status quo remains the same. In Heaven, unless you release something, it remains tied up. One of the Heavenly forces that must be released is the work of angels of war. It must be understood that angels play a pivotal role in our deliverance from debt by breaking the rod of wickedness centered on debt, thereby liberating the children of God from this bondage. (Hebrews 1:14; Psalms 103:20). The angels of God are your ministering spirits and they too will assist you. Therefore, ask God to send the angels of war to deliver you from your situation and it shall be done according to your request.

Praise God for the manifestation of His power in your financial affairs

Some people wait to get out of debt so that when things are now fine, they can start praising God. As long as they are stuck in debt, they would not see the reason why they should praise God. This is a grave mistake because praise is one such powerful force that can break down the walls of debt within a flip of a moment (Psalms 9:1-4, 67:5-6, 68:19). Praise releases an atmosphere that is responsible to penetrate every limitation or wall of resistance to bring you out of the cage of debt. Praise keeps the door to abundance wide open. When the channel between you and God is clear, you can receive His promises. Even when it seems in the natural that your circumstances have not changed, refuse to operate in the realm of senses but keep praising God and you will be thrilled in the midst of your praise to be interrupted by an anonymous call that your debt worth thousands has been paid in full.

THE FOURTH DIMENSION

SUPERNATURAL FINANCIAL MULTIPLICATION

This is a direct multiplication or recreation of the substance of money by either speaking it into existence or supernaturally transmuting and converting a natural substance into another form in which it appears quantified in the natural realm. It entails the supernatural multiplication of money, food, property and other natural substances under the influence of the Holy Spirit and the invisible work of angels.

It is worth exploring the truth that in this end time season which marks the last wave of prosperity revival, believers shall be catapulted into God's creative power to speak money into existence or convert any tangible or visible substances into multiple dimensions. For example, you can use your royal prerogative as a son of God by taking a twenty dollar note and multiplying it into twenty thousand dollar notes. What a spectacle! But how possible is that in the natural realm? You see, the instant you speak to money and command it to multiply, in the invisible realm, angels will start populating the money into multiple dimensions. I'm conscious of the fact that I'm about to step on some religious toes especially of those who are more devil-conscious of the power of magic and less Christ-conscious of the power of God. The truth is that some of the miracles which God is unfolding from the Throne Room of Heaven at this time will ruffle the minds of those comfortable with the status quo. Although it boggles the mind, this is the same dimension of creative power in which God operated when He spoke to the darkness of the earth in Genesis 1:3 and said, *"Let there be light"* and light came forth.

Therefore, as believers, we have the same creative power of God in our spirit such that we are able to speak anything we want to see into manifestation in the physical realm and it shall be established in the realm of the spirit. During the creation, God did not use one method to create the world. In some cases, He spoke the word and material substances appeared. In some cases, He took material substances and converted them into another form. For example, He took dust and converted into a human being called *Adam*. In a similar fashion, believers have the power to create money from any natural substances which they might wish to. For example, converting books into piles of paper money. I know that I'm already stepping on some religious toes especially those of religious charlatans and those who are sailing their boats through shallow streams of spiritual understanding. As believers step into the realm of the undefinable, uncharted and unrecorded signs and wonders in this last season, some of these miracles demonstrated will be so deep such that the spiritually uneducated will just look at them and think it is the devil behind their manifestation yet it's God. This is in view of the fact that in some cases, people's level of faith is not so much developed that they are not aware that we can operate like God on earth and follow the exact pattern which He followed to create substances of the Universe.

There is another dimension of financial prosperity whereby the little wealth, money or property in your possession just supernaturally multiplies, doubles, triples or quadruples into quantities, measures and volumes you never imagined before. This is the supernatural multiplication of wealth. It is a realm of creating something humongous from a very little substance (John 6:11; 2 Kings 4:7; Luke 5:5-7). Have you not heard of how God supernaturally provided a perennial supply of food for the widow of Zerephath in the midst of a famine? The Bible records in 1 Kings 17:8-16, that the barrel of meal and the bottle of oil would not be depleted until the rain returned and she and her house did eat for the whole year. In other words, no matter how much they used, there was always enough left over in the containers. In a similar manner in which Elijah caused the flour and oil of the widow of Zerephath to multiply, the season has come whereby believers across the Body of Christ will speak to the little money, food, grocery, clothes, products or any other resources they have and command it to multiply to any level of abundance they desire and it shall happen exactly as they declare it. In the context of this revelation, believers whom by profession functions in the realm of business, sales and marketing shall touch and speak to their products and have them multiplied beyond measure. Owners of supermarkets shall sell their grocery products for the whole year without running out of stock and accordingly believers acting in the capacity of customers shall buy grocery products and use them on a daily basis without them being depleted.

Prophetically speaking, there shall be such an instantaneous manifestation of a hundred, thousand and million fold increase in everything that believers sows, declares or invest. In the morning, one will deposit a hundred pound in a bank and then withdraw a thousand pounds by the evening, the other will invest a thousand pound by day but then receive a return on investment of million pounds by night. In other words, divine arrangement of circumstances as catalysed by angels shall cause all forces of divinity to work on behalf of believers and everything shall align itself to the sovereign will of God. Moreover, after using your debit card to purchase items from shops, you shall command the money to get back into your account and it shall be as you say it. Furthermore, you shall continue using your bank card to purchase anything while the balance in your account does not change at all. This is not fraud but God' grace coupled with His favour manifesting in an unusual way. When God declared in Deuteronomy 3:23, 7:11 that you shall occupy houses which you never build, He meant that believers will be elevated into this realm whereby they receive God supernatural provision of finances in every sphere of life even without doing anything. In this season God is relocating you from a nation called lack into the realm of super abundance. Your grocery will not run out, the few eggs left in your cardboard will not run out, you will eat and eat but they will not run out of supply. To substnatiate this revelation, a lady from South Africa, Melissa Simon by name testifies about how money multiplied right in front of her own eyes. After failing to pay my monthly rent, collectively church members dug into their pockets and blessed her with R1 700. She was then asked to count the money before she leaves, hence she double checked and confirmed that she had the exact amount needed. When she got home, she recounted the money, only to realise that there was an extra R200 note. Baffled by this, she counted the money again and was still left with an extra R200. She thought that it was fake money, so, she rubbed the brown R200 note together and, miraculously, the R200 note split into two R200 notes, hence she had an additional R400. Overwhelmed by what she had just witnessed, she checked the money once again and verified it by recounting it carefully. This time around, there was an additional R300 notes. It was as if the money multiplied just like Jesus multiplied two fish and five loaves to feed the thousands!. In total, she had now been blessed by the Lord with an additional R700. This was indeed an enthralling money multiplication miracle!

The Bible further presents a thrilling scenario in John 6:5-14, in which Jesus supernaturally multiplied fish and loaves into dozens of bread and multiple fish which fed five thousand men. In other words, Jesus used the little they had as a point of contact to bring forth a thousand fold.

Prophetically speaking, in this end time season, the little resources that people have as their last resort such as food, money, offerings, gifts, sacrifices will multiply supernaturally in ways that the human mind will fail to comprehend. In this season, you are going to be at the frontline of a Miracle money revival to feed the masses following people's demise due to the incidence of natural disasters, outbreak of water and other calamities which might befall humanity. In some cases, you are not even going to need a lot of money to buy food but you are just going to take one little meal and divide it in the same manner in which Jesus touched the loaves and fish and they supernaturally multiplied. In communities where the governments of nations have dismally failed to render basic services, believers shall take responsibility to feed the masses though supernatural multiplication of wealth. This shall be a fulfilment of the scripture in Romans 8:19 that *the earth waiteth in earnest expectation for the manifestation of the sons of God.* As sons of God are manifested, not only will they heal the sick but they will also rise with such amazing power and mountain moving faith to command the supernatural multiplication of natural substances in a view to accomplish tasks which the government of nations have failed to, hence the masses in every facet of human existence shall acknowledge the sovereignty of God.

Have you not heard of miracles of harvest multiplication which God performed on behalf of Isaac? The Bible records a spectacular incident in Genesis 26:12-14 (NLT) that *When Isaac planted his crops that year (in the midst of a famine), he harvested a hundred times more grain than he planted, for the Lord blessed him.* In other words, God supernaturally multiplied his harvest. What the Bible describes as a hundred-fold increase was actually a multiplication of the seed which Isaac sowed. As a consequence, he became the richest man alive at that time. He acquired so many flocks of sheep and goats, herds of cattle, and servants that the Philistines became jealous of him. This is what a supernatural multiplication of wealth does. There are two dimensions of sowing unveiled in this scripture, firstly, the one which involves the spiritual act of giving to the work of ministry and secondly, the one which involves the natural act of sowing seeds by farmers. In a spiritual context, as believers sow their financial seeds in this season, finances shall begin to supernaturally multiply in offering baskets, banks and wallets and handbags and it shall be used for the furtherance of the gospel. In a natural context, believers who shall sow seeds in their farms shall supernaturally reap a thousands and million fold increase just like Isaac and this shall be used to feed the masses across the globe who are entangles in a morass of debilitating poverty as a result of satanic slavery. Just as surely as God gave Isaac the miracle of a hundredfold release when he needed it the most, God wants to do the same for you. Paul concurs in 2 Corinthians 9:10 (NLT) that God is the one who provides seed for the farmer and bread to eat. In the same way, He shall provide and increase your resources and produce a great harvest of generosity in you. In other words, Paul alerts us that God is the source of all supernatural multiplications of wealth, hence no one should view this end time supernatural financial revival with suspicion. Moreover, God declared in Leviticus 26:4-5, 9-10 (AMP) that,

"I will give you rain in due season, and the land shall yield her increase and the trees of the field yield their fruit. And your threshing [time] shall reach to the vintage and the vintage [time] shall reach to the sowing time, and you shall eat your bread to the full and dwell in your land securely. For I will be leaning toward you with favor and regard for you, rendering you fruitful, multiplying you, and establishing and ratifying My covenant with you. And you shall eat the [abundant] old store of produce long kept, and clear out the old [to make room] for the new."

For clarity of purpose, allow me to refer to different versions of the Bible so that you can feel the impact of what God is saying here. (NLT): *"You will have such a surplus of crops that you will need to get rid of the leftovers from the previous year to make room for each new harvest."* (NIV): *"You will still be eating last year's harvest when you will have to move it out to make room for the new".* This is the essence of the supernatural multiplication of wealth. The Bible further declares in Deuteronomy 28:8, 11-12 (AMP): *"The Lord shall command the blessing upon you in your storehouse and in all that you undertake. And He will bless you in the land which the Lord your God gives you. And the Lord shall make you have surplus of prosperity, through the fruit of your body, of your livestock, and of your ground, in the land which the Lord swore to your fathers to give you. The Lord shall open to you His good treasury, the heavens to give the rain of your land in its season and to bless all the work of your hands; and you shall lend to many nations, but you shall not borrow"*. The above mentioned scriptural reference is therefore ample evidence of the dimension of supernatural multiplication of wealth which God is lavishing upon believers in this end time season.

There is another dimension in the realm of Miracle money which involves creating a new substance through the exercise of the God kind of faith (Genesis 1:1; Hebrews 11:1-3; Romans 4:17; John 2:7-10; Luke 3:8). It is worth exploring the divine truth that in the realm of the spirit, things are created by the spoken words. As far as God is concerned, words were not primarily given for communication purposes only but for the release of the supernatural creative power of God. For instance, when God created the world, He spoke and said *light be* and the Holy Ghost proceeded from the father, went forth and brought those things which He spoke into manifestation. As a child of God, born of the spirit of God, you have received an impartation of an inherent creative power and ability into your spirit to speak things into existence, not only in the spirit but into physical manifestation. It is important to note that in this end time season, not only shall believers speak substances into existence but they shall also recreate substances or convert them from one form of matter into the other. Prophetically speaking, as we have been launched into the final season which marks the final move of God and the final wave of prosperity, believers are going to experience extraordinary manifestations of God's power in the area of translation of natural substances.

Have you not heard of how in John 2:1-11, Jesus supernaturally turned water into wine and filled dozens of gallons of wine? This is the dimension of recreation of a natural substance which Jesus taped into to meet a human need in the natural realm. It is possible for the realm of the spirit to transmute itself into the natural. For example, some believers across a broad spectrum of Christian faith have been able to tap into the realm of the supernatural to transfer the healing power of God into water so that those who happen to drink or come into contact with it are instantaneously healed. However, many have not been able to catch a divine revelation that even the substance of water itself can be turned into a another substance that can be used for

Kingdom purposes in the same way Jesus turned water into wine. If water could be turned into wine, then an overdraft can be turned into a draft of millions. In this era, while it might not be necessary for you to turn water into wine, water can be turned into any other substance that can meet a human need. For example, it can be turned into fuel and used for transportation purposes or converted into oil for lubrication purposes or even turned into juice for consumption purposes. In these most harsh economic times in which the prices of oil and petrol are skyrocketing on a daily basis, God can allow you to turn water into petrol so that it can be used to transport believers all over the world to propagate the gospel of the Lord Jesus Christ. Moreover, in the same way Jesus changed water into wine because there was a need, God can change any substance into physical money when needed. For example, it is possible for one to turn a book into piles of valid and authentic money. I am not talking about magic but the supernatural power of God on display. As a matter of fact, many of those things which magicians have done which breeds awe and amazement to the spectators are actually an imitation because Satan has nothing original by himself but photocopies what He sees Going doing. If you could only decide to live by heavenly understanding, you will realise that in the spirit realm, anything can be changed into everything. If you need clothes, you can command just one piece to turn into a line of clothes; if you need food, you can command any reasonable substance to turn into food and it shall be established for you in the realm of the spirit. That is why the Bible says you shall declare a thing and it shall be established for you. In the context of this scripture the word *"thing"* represents anything. Imbued with this understanding, you realise that it is possible to convert any natural substance into anything.

THE FIFTH DIMENSION

SUPERNATURAL MONEY RAIN:

This comprises of a direct visible raining down of money from Heaven upon those who place a demand by faith for such a manifestation by making a pulling on the supernatural.

Contrary to what some folks presume, it is absolutely possible for money to fall or rain directly from Heaven in a visible and tangible form in broad day light upon those who believe God for the impossible. This is what I call *Money Rain*. I'm not talking about money falling from trees but on people whose level of faith has been cultivated and rightly positioned to make a pulling on the supernatural by transmuting the spiritual substance of money from the spirit realm into a visible and tangible manifestation in the natural realm. This alludes to the divine truth that Miracle money is manifested through a divine phenomenon called *supernatural rain*. This involves the precipitation of showers of rain from the spirit realm into the natural realm. By supernatural rains, I'm not referring to the normal rain which comes during the rainy season. Instead, I'm talking about the rain that comes from the spirit and is manifested in the natural realm as if it is natural. The difference between the rain of the spirit and natural rain is that natural rain comes from the *clouds* while the rain of the spirit comes from *Heaven*. And it is this supernatural rain of the spirit that breeds Miracle money into visible and tangible manifestation in the natural realm. While many manifestations of Miracle money have taken place supernaturally without people seeing it, this grace shall intensify in this season to such an extent that many believers shall physically and visibly see money raining down from Heaven. Others shall be catapulted to the realm of open vision and behold Heaven opening up and angels pouring out the rain of Miracle money down to earth upon the masses who are connected to His purpose. This is the extent to which the viscosity of this grace shall be heightened in these days. The Bible records a remarkable incident which took place at Cornelius's house in Acts 10:1. It states that *as Peter began to speak, the Holy Ghost fell upon all those who heard the word.* The act of the Holy Ghost "*falling*" describes the rain of the Spirit as it precipitated from the Throne Room of Heaven. In a similar manner in which the rain of the Spirit fell upon the masses who were connected to God's word, in this season, as believers gather in worship and the word is preached, at the sound of the minister's voice, the rain of Miracle money shall fall upon the masses who are connected to God's word.

The Seven Supernatural Dimensions of Financial Prosperity

In a similar fashion in which Elijah the Prophet declared, *"I Hear the sound of the abundance of heavy rain"* (1 Kings 18:41) and *"It came to pass in the meanwhile, that the Heavens were black with clouds and wind, and there was a great rain"*, I walk in the footsteps of Elijah the prophet and I declare and decree that, **"I hear the sound of the abundance of Money rain"**. As I echo and reiterate the voice of the prophet in this prophetic season, I proclaim and pronounce that there are Heavenly waves of glory approaching the earth that have never been seen before and their current is changing as these waves are breaking forth on the surface of the earth, causing explosive tides of Money rain precipitating to the extreme ends of the world. There is a supernatural invasion of Heaven on earth as the current is changing, waves are shifting, and the clouds are raging, heralding the unfolding of a new season of Miracle money. In the same way that immediately there was a torrential downpour of heavy rain that overtook King Ahab and his chariot, suddenly the torrential downpour of the heavy rain of Miracle money will precipitate upon the masses to the extent of overtaking the leaders of government of nations such that they will be streaming in the direction of the church clamouring to know more about this new move of God so that they can find means to support it financially. Note that before Prophet Elijah was catapulted to the realm of *prophetic perception* to declare the abundance of rain, he first saw a *cloud* as small as a man's hand and it was upon saturation of that small cloud that heavy rains invaded the natural realm. By the same token, the *Miracle money cloud* (which is a Glory cloud) as small as the man's hand has already unravelled in the atmosphere as we have already felt the first sprinkles of a Miracle money revival sweeping right across the Body of Christ. It is unequivocally evident in this season that the atmosphere is ripe for believers to step into the realm of the undefinable, uncharted and unrecorded signs and wonders. The Miracle money cloud has been saturated such that it is ready to heavily precipitate upon the masses in the extreme ends of the earth. Heaven is pregnant with the possibilities of God. God is about to explode in the demonstration of Miracle money that will unravel the debilitating morass of poverty in which the masses have been entangled. This is unequivocally a ripe season for Miracle Money. I can sense it in the very atmosphere. Something unfamiliar to your status quo is about to unfold from the Throne Room. What a spectacular season to be alive and witness the enthralling move of the Spirit!

To substantiate this revelation with further reference to scriptural evidence, when God declared in Zechariah 10:1 that *Ask me during the time of rain and I will give you showers of rain,* He was talking about the abundant move of God and the unprecedented avalanche of the last wave of signs and wonders on earth. He was alluding in metaphoric language to the new manifestations of the Spirit which are unfolding from the Throne Room of Heaven and precipitating directly upon the masses on earth like heavy rain. Miracle money is one of the new manifestations of this end time grace which shall fall directly from the Heaven like rain (Zechariah 10:1). The other translation reads *"Ask the Lord for rain in the springtime, it is the Lord who sends the thunderstorms. He gives showers of rain to all people, and plants of the field to everyone."* Therefore, God says in this season of Miracle money, believers must be open enough to believe God to do the impossible and step up in faith to ask God for the rain of Miracle money from Heaven. As a demand for Miracle money is placed on Heaven by faith, God shall release torrents of Money rain to curtail the dryness of the earth's economic climate. To cement this revelation with reference to further scriptural evidence, God further declared that,

> *'I will make them and the places around my hill a blessing, and I will cause the shower to come down in this season, there shall be showers of blessing. And the tree of the field shall yield her fruit, and the earth shall yield her increase, and they shall be safe in their land, and shall know that I am the Lord."*

In the context of this scripture, the word *"shower"* does not refer to the misconstrued *"light shower"* that religious people have taught or stigmatised. Instead, it means to shower financial rain or pour down Heaven's financial blessings violently, hence there is such a thing as a *rain or torrents of financial blessings.* It describes the falling of financial blessings from the air in thick succession, a copious supply, abundant, plentiful, full, and rich, a falling of financial blessings from Heaven in great and large quantities. It speaks of a divine outpouring of Heaven's humongous financial wealth upon the masses who believe God for the impossible. Therefore, as believers, we should be rightly positioned in the spirit to receive this downpour and torrent of abundant, liberal, excessive prosperity and provision coming down violently in thick succession from the floodgates of Heaven. Oral Roberts, a man who functioned in the realm of God's prosperity for decades to the extent of building a World renowned university, concurs with this revelation and thus reiterates that God's financial blessings are *"Not just a trickle, not a stream, not a river but a flood."*

While in the natural realm folks would traditionally expect clouds to build up first in the sky and in some cases be accompanied by thunder and lightning before yielding any rain, in the realm of the spirit, God can manifest His sovereignty, glory and power anytime, anywhere even without you having to do anything. In a similar fashion in which a flood of water appeared supernaturally in a desert without anybody expecting it, Miracle money shall manifest widely in unexpected places even without a church song, a preaching or any *"Amen"* from the congregation. Do you notice that water supernaturally appeared in the desert without any notice of wind, cloud, thunder or even rain, at such a time when no one would expect it to rain? By the same token, in this end time season, Miracle money shall appear in places and areas where no one would expect it to appear. In the same way a flood of water appeared in a desert without any notice, symptom or sign of rain (2 Kings 3:17), in this Kairos moment, money shall supernaturally appear in people's bank accounts even without making any investments and property shall be obtained by believers even without making any deposits, glory to God!.

THE SIXTH DIMENSION

SUPERNATURAL FINANCIAL PROPHETIC INSTRUCTION

This involves stepping out in faith and dominion to command natural subjects such as birds, animals, wind, clouds, rain

or any other living or non-living creatures to supernaturally bring forth Miracle money to you.

It implies taking dominion to use natural phenomena as channels to bring Miracle money. It precisely entails giving divine authorisation or prophetic instruction to natural subjects in your sphere of contact such as birds of the air, the fish of the sea, and some creeping animals of the land, to go and get the much needed Miracle money and bring it to you. This is in view of the fact that according to Genesis 1:6, God gave us dominion over all these, meaning we have the prerogative to send them to go and perform certain tasks just like how Adam used to engage them. It works almost on the basis of the same principle as a debit order in which you instruct the bank to debit money into your account for a specific season. Because there is financial instruction, authority and command exhibited, it is also called a *Supernatural money order*. We are using financial terms here because we are dealing with money. In this end time season, believers shall step up to their authority to command natural subjects to bring money and it shall be established in the realm of the spirit. In some cases, birds can be even commanded to go and bring Miracle money and they will populate your yard with piles of Miracle money. On another dimension, believers can speak and command wind, clouds, rain or any other natural substance to bring forth Miracle money and it shall be established in the realm of the spirit. Does it amaze you that we can speak to wind and command it to blow in a specific direction? Have you not heard about how Jesus spoke to the boisterous winds of the sea and commanded them to be quiet and they obeyed? If the winds could be commanded to be quiet, it follows that they can also be commanded to move in a specific direction. Just like how wind was instructed by God to blow quails in the direction of the children of Israel for them to eat, wind can be commanded to blow money in a specific direction in order to meet a specific need. The Bible concurs that *we shall declare a thing and it shall be established*. This is because God has given us dominion over the birds of the air and the fish of the sea and every creature of the land such that we can command them to bring Miracle money. This is the dimension in which Jesus operated when He instructed Peter to go and obtain money from a fish. A fish represents the means or channel of manifestation. However, believers must be enlightened that supernatural manifestation is not only limited to the use of a fish but any other animals or birds can be used as a channel to bring Miracle money.

A man by the name of Tommy Williams shared several years ago how he spoke to the birds to bring him money. Basing his unwavering faith on 1 Kings 17, Tommy started finding money around his house after he went out and hollered at the birds. They gathered around and listened to him as he exclaimed at them. *"People lose money every day. Go get it!"*. Subsequently, a 15-year-old was then inspired by this revelation such that he went out, spoke to the birds and commanded them to put the money in the backyard. The first day he discovered 65 cents, the second third day $7. Over the next two months, he found a total of $440 in the tree. Although this revelation might sound foreign to natural man's thinking, the reality is that the unusual, unlimited and accelerated supply from Heaven supersedes the realm of impossibility as God has supernatural ways to supply every human need in the natural realm. He makes the way when they say there is no way. We must therefore enlarge our capacity for this financial supernatural provision.

The Bible records an incident whereby Joshua commanded the sun to go backwards. In a similar fashion, we have the same authority to command money into manifestation and it shall be established. Jesus demonstrated this ability when He spoke to the winds and ordered them to be still and it was so. Elijah prayed and commanded the Heavens to release rain and it happened exactly as he had declared. In a like manner, believers shall command a rain of Miracle money to fall upon the masses and this shall be used for Kingdom expansion purposes. Accordingly winds or storms of lack, poverty and suffering shall be commanded to depart from the masses so that the new wave of Miracle money could be ushered. This is what I call *taking authority over money*.

Do you know that the Body of Christ has the same authority over money that they have over sickness and disease? In the same way Jesus commanded a woman with an infirmity whose back was bent down for over thirty eight years to be strengthened and it was so, we can also command money to strengthen itself and move in our direction as occasion demands. Beyond any shadow of doubt, we have authority over money and can make demands on money and that money would obey us. The greater truth is that divine prosperity works exactly the same way as divine healing. This means that you can believe God for Miracle money just as you believe Him for divine health. Both blessings already belong to you and are legally yours. You just have to step up in faith to appropriate them. Therefore, you should refuse lack just as quickly as you refuse sickness. Only if you could decide to live by Heavenly understanding and make up your mind that you are not going to be broke or live in lack another day, but that you are goingto live in divine prosperity and abundance of Miracle money. Satan cannot stop the torrential or stream flow of God's financial blessings upon your life. Therefore, you need to catch a revelation of how to take authority over money and make money obey you. Did you know that you can talk to money, and money will have to turn and come your way? Money is one of the most submissive substances in the universe, which when called or placed a demand upon, it quickly and swiftly comes on feet in your direction. Money has no authority in itself; it must do what you tell it to do only if you know how to take authority over money and "loose" it so you can get in your life in million measures.

The greater truth is that as much as you have dominion over the natural environment, the birds of the air, the fish and vegetation, you also have the dominion and audacity to exercise authority over money and release humongous wealth.

It must be expressly understood that the same way you cut and tree and use it for wood or furniture, is the same way you call money to come and use it for the Kingdom purposes. The Bible records in Genesis 1:26 that when God created man, He said, *"Let us make man in our image, after our likeness: and let them have dominion over the fish of the sea, and over the fowl of the air, and over the cattle, and over all the earth, and over every creeping thing that creepeth upon the earth"*. God set Adam up to have dominion. Notice the word *"over"* in the above-mentioned verse. God gave Adam dominion *over* fish, fowl, cattle, and over all the earth. Money, silver and gold, is included in that statement! We know that Adam lost or gave up his dominion when he disobeyed God and sold out to Satan. But the Second Adam, Jesus Christ (1 Cor. 15:22, 45), came that we might take back our dominion over certain things—over Satan and circumstances. As believers today, we are supposed to have dominion over money. Yet money has been dominating us by our not having enough. Jesus has given us all this authority, but it is largely going to waste. Remember we read that the silver and the gold are the Lord's (Haggai 2:8). Well, where is the gold and silver that are the Lord's? It's in the earth. If we'll learn to cooperate with Him, He'll put us right back in the Garden of Eden, so to speak, where we can have more than enough of everything we need!

That is what I call *taking authority over money!* Jesus talked to the waves and the wind, and they obeyed Him. He talked to bread, and it multiplied. Jesus talked to someone who was in the grave four days, and the man got up and came out of that grave! And Jesus talked to a fish, and that fish brought Peter some money! This is to tell you that money can be loosed unto you; you can make money obey you. Money doesn't have to be resistant to you. Getting money loosed unto you can be the easiest thing. Money will have to turn toward you when you make your declaration in faith, "Money, thou art loosed in my life!" Now what am I saying when I say, *"Money, thou art loosed in my life"?* I'm saying, *"Satan, you have to turn my money loose. I know my authority. I am not an ignorant Christian. And you have to turn mine loose!"* This is how Miracle money is released in the spirit realm.

THE SEVENTH DIMENSION

THE GOLDEN RAIN

This is the supernatural manifestation of the wealth of Heaven on earth as evidenced by the falling or raining down of precious stones such as gold dust, silver and diamond stones and supernatural oil from Heaven.

Unveiling The Mystery of Miracle Money

A supernatural phenomenon in the realm of God's prosperity that has been happening for quite some time in the Body of Christ is gold dust supernaturally appearing on people as a sign of the manifestation of the wealth of Heaven on earth and the unveiling of higher realms of God's glory from the deepest territories of the Glory Realm. The reality is that while paper notes are widely accepted as a measure of wealth, Miracle money doesn't always have to manifest in the form of paper notes and coins. In some instances, it can manifest in the form of gold dust, diamonds, silver stones and other precious stones, which represent the wealth of Heaven. These have the same monetary value just like any other currency in the world. This is what we call the *Golden Rain*. This wealth of Heaven has been manifested supernaturally in divergent ways evidenced by the appearance of gold dust, silver and diamond stones and supernatural oil soaked on people's bodies, on the ground or on buildings where saints gather for worship. Naturally, there have been strong speculations about the origin of this divine phenomenon and it seems that the main questions arising pertaining to these miracles are firstly, what is the source and secondly what is the purpose? However, it must be fully understood that these are end time manifestations of God's glory. The supernatural manifestation of Gold dust, silver and diamond stones is this most recent wave of glory and prosperity that is sweeping the world. We have been ushered right into the very special divine moments in the calendar of God where we are feeling the first sprinkles of the greatest revival of miracles, signs and wonders ever recorded since the Book of Acts. This is the result of the highest level of concentration of the glory of God being manifested upon the Earth. This wave of revival shall be greater than any other because we are entering the culmination of time, when we will experience the former rains and the latter rains of revival glory combined. Some of the things we are experiencing are familiar, but many things are brand new. This, too, was foretold in God's Word concerning the last days. A season of exploration and discovery has just exploded as great mysteries are being rediscovered that will unleash the greatest outpouring of God's glory and harvest since the days of the early church.

The Seven Supernatural Dimensions of Financial Prosperity

It is of paramount importance to highlight right from the onset the divine truth that contrary to what multitudes of believers presume, the manifestation of *gold dust* and other precious stones is not a new phenomenon in the realm of God's prosperity. Taking centre stage recently in packed churches is a new phenomenon that really is not that new. It is the appearance of *"gold dust"* and the transformation of fillings or crowns into *"gold."* These transformations have been hailed as a new move of God that is sweeping the charismatic churches worldwide. Throughout ages, the wealth of Heaven and God's supernatural provision has been manifested in divergent ways, whether it be, gold dust, gold fakes or gold teeth. However, the gravity and intensity of its manifestation is heightened in these last days in what I call *"a new wave of gold manifestations"*. The truth of the matter is that the unparalleled degree of manifestation of gold dust in this end time season is not intended to be just a *Church phenomenon*, but a *Church revelation*. It is worth exploring the divine truth that in every new move of God, there are different people who play different roles. There are those who *reveal it*, those who *teach about* it and those who *write about it*. Revelation of divine phenomenon is essential in terms of reinforcing a significant level of understanding so that multitudes of people across the globe can abundantly partake of the grace which God is currently unleashing upon the church.

Consider the following prophecy spoken through the voice of Prophet Isaiah:

> *" For behold, darkness will cover the earth and deep darkness the peoples; But the LORD will rise upon you and His glory will appear upon you."* (Isaiah 60:2).

Today, this scripture is being fulfilled as the tangibility and visibility of God's glory is grossly manifested upon people. It must be understood therefore that God can use whatever He pleases to show himself real to His people. That is why He is raining down gold dust upon His people in the natural realm. Did you know that gold dust represents the wealth of Heaven? To substantiate this divine truth, the Bible concurs in Ephesians 1:3 that *we are blessed with all spiritual blessings in the heavenly places* and gold dust is a visible and tangible evidence of manifestation of these blessings. Therefore, the miraculous appearance of gold dust and other precious stones most frequently during times of worship and prayer, when hearts are focused on God's splendour and majesty, is a reflection of the spiritual truth that God is majestic and rich in spiritual blessings. Do you remember that God declared in Deuteronomy 31:6-8 saying, *"I will never leave you nor forsake you"*? These supernatural manifestations of gold dust are an incontestable or undeniable evidence that God is with us. In fact, when the gold dust manifests, this truth is confirmed and our hearts soar in praise of our Royal King as He gives us a glimpse of His power and greatness.

Pertaining to the Greater Gory in the end time dispensation, God declared in Hagai 2:8. 7, that,

> *'I will shake all the nations; and they will come with the wealth of all nations, and I will fill this house with glory,' Says the LORD of hosts. The silver is mine and the gold is mine,* 'declares the LORD of hosts. *The latter glory of this house will be greater than the former,' says the LORD of hosts.*

Note that in the context of the above-mentioned scripture, God talks about Gold dust and silver after emphasizing the shaking. In actual fact, there are three things which God unveils in this scripture. Firstly, the *spiritual shaking,* then the *silver and gold manifestation* and lastly *the appearance of the glory*. This implies that the manifestation of gold dust is a sign of a great shaking, spiritual awakening and the supernatural move of God. It is a visible and tangible manifestation of God's glory in these end times. When Heaven is shaken off, it releases an uninterrupted flow of wealth in the form of gold dust, diamonds, silver and other precious stones. Do you notice that in our opening scripture, God mentions that glory will be greater. That means, there is a connection between gold dust and the glory. This implies that gold dust is a manifestation of the latter glory. In actual fact, it is the Glory of God that rains gold dust and diamonds in church. Therefore, when God said, *"The glory of the latter house shall exceed the former",* He actually spoke of these new waves of signs and wonders which shall invade the natural realm in this last dispensation.

The Seven Supernatural Dimensions of Financial Prosperity

It is worth mentioning that as an unchanging God, the Lord will continue to orchestrate, manifest and release these new waves of miracles at ever increasing glory. As these precious stones shall continue to fall and oil oozes out supernaturally from the atmosphere, it is as if God is revealing a glimpse of His glory to His church. He is revealing Himself as a supernatural God on behalf of His children while worldly people shall see but not partake of this grace. Prophetically speaking, as ministers across the globe delve into the deeeper revelation of Isaiah 60:2 encapsulated in this publication, gold dust, oil and precious stones shall begin to fall and appear in the hands of their congregants in greater intensity. It is worth exploring the divine truth that Gold dust is a sign of God's majesty, wealth and glory present in our lives. It is a spontaneous manifestation of the wealth of Heaven on earth. However, some people erreneously presume that it is strange that God would reveal His majesty in this way, but we should try to let God out of the box since He has every right to display His glory and reveal Himself in whatever way He sees fit! The Bible tells us that gold is used to pave the streets of Heaven. We think this is amazing, but if God wants to use gold to pave the streets who are we to tell him that He shouldn't? Have you not heard of how Moses and the elders of Israel went up Mount Sinai and when they came into the glorious presence of God, the pavement under their feet was made of sapphire? This is to tell you that you shouldn't insist that God does things your way. Philosophically speaking, God doesn't have to use cement or asphalt on His Heavenly roads. He can use sapphire, gold, silver or whatever precious stones He chooses. He doesn't have to use human means of communication to prophetically convey a message to His people. Althaugh humanity living so much in the lower plane of life are acclamatised to the use of words and pictures, if God wants to use gold, diamonds and gems to communicate with His children, then who are we to tell Him that He is doing it wrong? In the realm of the spirit, creativity is not only expressed through words and pictures but through prophetic actions. That is why in the realm of the spirit, it is possible to communicate without the use of words. In prophetic language, this is what we call *dramatic prophecy*. Imbued with this understanding, you suddenly realise that we should not be surprised that God is making gold dust and gems appear out of thin air because nothing is too difficult for God to do. All He has to do is speak and it is done. Therefore, our onus is to praise Him for choosing extravagant and creative ways to reveal Himself to us.

Pertaining to the proliferation of gold dust in the natural realm, God proclaimed in Job 22:21-25 saying,

> *Now, acquaint yourself with him, and be at peace, so that good things shall come to you. Receive the law from his mouth, and lay up his words in your heart. If you return to the Almighty, you shall be built up, you shall put away iniquity far from your tabernacles. Then shall you lay up gold as dust, and the gold of Ophir as the stones of the brooks. Yea, the Almighty shall be your defence, and you shall have plenty of silver.*

This brings one to sudden realisation that there are also many beautiful and useful elements underground such as gold, silver, gems, coal, and oil which God has created. I don't see it as contrary to His nature throughout the centuries for Him to bestow the actual physical elements of gold, silver, gems, oil or other gifts supernaturally whenever He might choose. The Bible makes it explicitly clear that God created all things and owns everything. In Psalm 104:24, David declares: *"The earth is full of Your possessions."* In 1 Chronicles 29:11, it reads, *"Yours, O LORD, is the greatness, the power and the glory, the victory and the majesty; for all that is in heaven and in earth is Yours."* Everything in the ground, above the ground, in the air, and all that passes through it, ultimately belongs to God. He owns the cattle on a thousand hills and the wealth in every mine, althaugh He has committed it into our hands. This is to tell you that wealth is a stewardship from God. Whether it's money, land or possessions, we will never be rightly related to what we have until we recognize that it belongs to God.

Prophetically speaking, in this end time dispensation, there shall be a wide spread global manifestations of gold, silver dust and gemstones appearing upon people mainly during church meetings. Supernatural oil shall be seen visibly dripping from hands and figures of people, some of which shall receive gold coins, jewels, gems, diamond or silver. It must be expressly understood that these precious stones are not limited to Gold dust and silver stones only but to other supernatural experiences of other precious stones such as sapphires, topaz, emerald and rubies. In this season, God has sent the *angel of precious stones* for His people to experience manifestations of diamonds, topaz, emerald, rubies as well as gemstones falling from the atmosphere, inside churches by the hands of angels. The scriptural reference to this supernatural phenomenon is found in Exodus 13:30 where it is recorded that *the High Priest wore breastplates adorned with twelve precious stones*. Therefore, gold dust, silver and diamond stones are just exactly like the twelve stones of the Ephod, the twelve stones of the twelve tribes of Israel. In an endeavour to ascertain the credibility and authenticity of this supernatural phenomenon, some diamonds were taken to experts who analysed and examined them and accordingly declared that the cutting of these stones was so perfect, that they couldn't give them value for the percentage of the diamond stones for there were none like that on earth.

Coupled with this wave of gold dust manifestations is a heightened degree of angelic activity, visitation and manifestation. Multitudes of believers shall encounter these beautiful transparent figures or spirit beings not in an expanded or aparition form as is the norm in Christian fratenity, but in a visible form in the natural realm just like human beings. In other words, angels shall physically appear, not raining gold dust per se but precipitating real gold and diamond stones upon God's people so that they can sell them and advance the preachig of the gospel. However, the degree, intensity and magnitude of manifestation of these spiritual experiences shall all depend on the degree of adoration, level of sensitivity and openness to this spiritual phenomena as well as the depth of worship by believers. However, this phenomenon shall spill over to people's houses, homes and yards, businesses, schools, in the streets and market places where God manifest the visibility and tangibility of His glory to all creation. In the face of a darkening global economic outlook, God has a contingent plan to render His people a supernatural bail out from poverty, lack and debt. It is for this reason that believers shall sell the gem stones and diamond stones they are receiving supernaturally, so that they can obtain money to pay off debts. This is akin to a divine scenario in the Old Testament, whereby the Children of Israel needed food miraculously. They couldn't use money at that time as there was no food to buy. So, God provided the manna for that time and that need was met. By the same token, God shall provide gems or gold coins (*as some have received*) to be sold to buy food or meet our material needs and give us enough to help others whenever He chooses to. Strange as it may sound, we may personally need these items someday soon, hence it is best not to limit God in any way. Some of these precious stones shall be sold for a value worth of millions of rands and this shall create a platform for many believers across the world to be elevated into the realm of Kingdom Millionaires.

Althaugh these supernatural manifestations breed awe and amazement to spectators, and ruffles the feathers of those whose minds are intricately interwoven in the monetary system of this fallen world, the Bible foretold that signs and wonders of such a great magnitude would be seen in the last days, and the manifestation of gold dust, diamonds, silver as well as other precious stones is one of them. Over the last few years, there has been a lot of reports of gold and silver dust appearing upon people, mainly in charismatic Christian meetings. Some have also received gold coins, gems, as well as oil dripping from hands of individuals in their homes. Others are receiving angelic manifestations seen above them as flowing beautiful transparent figures and circles of faint light referred to as *angel orbs*. Moreover, angels' feathers, gemstones, coloured sparkle and gold dust are accelerating. Many are attaching prophetic significance to this current wave of gold manifestations, heralding a new phase in the church, being prophetic of the establishment of God's Kingdom on earth, or being symbolic of the transference of wealth from the wicked into the Church. The Angels of precious stones who works in conjunction with Angels of prosperity shall be seen on the rise, visibly manifesting and engulfing the scene where God is worshiped in truth and in spirit, infesting it with the glory of His presence.

To cement the revelation of this divine phenomenon with reference to practical evidence, manifestations of *gold dust"* on hands and other parts of the body has been reported occasionally in some of our meetings. These are what appears to be tiny specks of gold appearing in the hands, where wiping the hands has the effect of depositing the gold specks on clothing. This manifestation appears to be transferrable, either by prayer or by simple contact, others do exhibit this manifestation. The *law of contagious experience* seem to have taken its course in this new move of God. For example, during one of our meetings, gold dust started appearing in the hands of one lady. Upon wiping her hands on her clothing, the gold dust appeared to have been deposited upon her clothing and yet the amount of the dust on her hands seem to remain constant as if the gold dust spontaneously reappeared after wiping on clothing. This woman then started laying her hands on anyone around her lining up to receive the blessing and many others reported the appearance of gold dust on their own hands. Moreover, Gold dust was reportedly appearing not only in hands, but also on the face and in the hair of the congregants. There were even reports of *gold flakes* appearing in the pages of people's bibles, cars, bags and houses. Not only gold, but manifestations of silver and even diamonds and other precious stones such as onyx, pearl, jasper and emerald has also been reported. Others found the gold dust in the prayer rooms and on worship instruments and it was constantly appearing further and further back along the walls until it finally met at the back doors of the sanctuary. Moreover, people reported gold appearing spontaneously in their teeth. In some cases, the dark amalgam fillings in the teeth appears to have transmuted itself into gold fillings. In other cases, gold in the shape of crosses appeared in teeth, and also gold crowns covering the teeth. Along with the *"gold teeth"* manifestations, occurrences of gold dust, gold fakes are increasing worldwide. Shiny sparkles of diamond dust and silver dust were received during services as people received the gold inlays and silver fillings, some in the form of a cross and the actuality of gemstones falling from the atmosphere, inside churches. Accompanying this divine manifestation, it has been further reported that a *"Glory Cloud"* appeared during worship services. In short, a cloud of gold-like dust was hovering up by the roof. It caused some hysteria during worship as multitudes of people were crowding together in exhilaration underneath the glory cloud, with some falling hysterically under the power.

To substantiate this supernatural manifestation with reference to scriptural evidence, God declared in His word that *behold I'm doing a new thing. Can't you perceive it as it springs forth?* Gold dust is one of the new manifestations which are encapsulated in this revelation. The reason why God calls this manifestation a *"new things"* is because it is fresh from the Throne Room of God and do not have a name as yet in the natural realm. Moreover, God declared in Jeremiah 33:3 that *"Call unto me, and I will answer thee, and show thee great and mighty things, which thou knowest not."* This implies that there are newer, deeper and higher things in God which the world has not discovered yet but God unfolds them to His children through the power of the Holy Spirit. Therefore, in this end time season, we have been catapulted into a *realm of new things*. The greater truth is that in every generation, God unleashes or reveals His hidden wisdom through the revelation of new things. These are divine substances which are released from Heaven to earth, which unveils the reality of God's presence. It seems that the Lord is now doing very unusual things which simply don't have any physical explanation. Since God is still a Creator, He is still in the business of creating new things and each new move of His Spirit has its own mark upon it.

The Bible declares in Isaiah 40:5 that *the glory of God shall be revealed and all flesh shall see it*. This implies that this is the season of visitation of the glory of God. Every eye is beginning to see the glory of God manifested through wide spread demonstrations of Miracle money and gold dust across the globe. The glory is no longer hidden but publicly manifested in the streets, market places and public arena. This divine trruth is corroborated by Habakkuk 2:14 that *the earth shall be filled with the knowledge of the glory of God*. In this last wave of signs and wonders, God is therefore raining down gold dust as a new spiritual substance in the same way He rained manna down in the wilderness for the children of Israel to eat. When God rained down manna, it was a completely brand new spiritual substance to the children of Israel just like the gold dust appearing these last days. Through these new things or supernatural appearance, God is proving Himself as a visible and tangible God who is not far away from His people but is practically involved in the affairs of humanity of on a daily basis. In this end time season, God is therefore doing a new thing, and sharing with His people the glory of His face, and a little of His splendour is rubbing off in the form of dust, so that the individual may be edified, as with tongues, the Church strengthened, and the lost brought into the Kingdom of God.

The greater truth is that God will do whatever it takes to get our attention and gold dust manifestations are a wakeup call that is only going to intensify in this end time season. He is shocking His Body, and at the same time testing the waters as to who will be open to His workings of supernatural provision. *"Why did Jesus Christ walk on water when he could use the available boats? "Why turn fish and bread into thousands while the disciple could go and buy food?"* These are not miracles, they are signs and wonders. God does them to prove a point. Therefore, gold dust is a sign that God is present. God said we should expect signs that would point to Himself. He declared *"I will show wonders in the Heaven above and signs on the earth below, blood and fire and billows of smoke"* (Acts 2:19). The manifestation of gold is a sign and wonder that points to His internal and external qualities, part of a visible representation of an invisible God.

In its original form, gold dust represents the wealth of Heaven which God is unreservedly manifesting on the earth in the last days. God declared that, *"Silver is Mine, and the gold is Mine. The glory of this latter temple shall be greater than the former,"* (Haggai 2:8-9). Moreover, the Bible says that wealth belongs to God and He has given it to the son. The Bible further says in Job 22:24 that,

Then shalll you lay up gold as dust, and the gold of Ophir as the stones of the brooks. If you lay gold in the dust, and gold of Ophir among the stones of the torrent-bed, then the Almighty will be your gold and your precious silver.

This is where the divine revelation of gold dust stems from. This implies that God owns everything and does not owe anything, hence He has freely given or lavished such humongous wealth upon His children. This wealth is manifested in the form of gold dust and other precious stones. This means that a global revival which by far exceed any other revivals ever manifested in the history of humanity, accompanied by manifestations of gold dust and other precious stones, has just exploded. However, it is of paramount importance to note that the gold dust is not an end in itself but a means to an end. It is only a sign of what is to come. The end is that an avalanche of billions of souls will be saved across the globe. When the gold appears, it is an indication that the spiritual climate is ripe and the atmosphere in a meeting is charged for miracles, hence anything can happen that can lead to a stream flow of multitudes of souls into the Kingdom. This is the same anointing in which Jesus operated when He raised the dead and moved in signs and wonders which practically demonstrated miraculous provision. By sending this unusual manifestation into our midst in this present time, God is saying to us that we can expect to see greater things than these in this season.

The question is: Why does God rain gold dust and other precious stones on earth in this time?

Spiritually speaking, Gold is the *colour of harvest,* hence the heightened degree of manifestation of gold dust represents the fact that the harvest of billions of souls across the globe in this end time season is ripe. As God pours out His Spirit in this unusual and unprecedented way, the golden glory is attracting, magnetising and drawing multitudes into the Kingdom in record numbers. As a matter of fact, the manifestation of gold dust has proven to be a most powerful tool for evangelism and reach out campaigns in these last days. This is because the nature of this generation is such that people are generally curious, and would want to see something tangible and visible for their faith to be strengthened in God and this manifestation is the exact kind of recipe that draws the curious into the Kingdom. Gold is therefore a visible sign heralding that the glory of God has returned to His people, and that the glory is no longer a mysterious, invisible or distant phenomenon but a reality of this age. The ordinary men, who previously *"sinned and came short of the glory of God"* are now being drawn to the glory of God, so to speak, when they see it manifesting in the natural realm. When they see it manifested, they are drawn to repentance and are saved. The prophet foretold: *Arise, shine; for your light has come! And the glory of the LORD is risen upon you* (Isaiah 60:1). When the glory of God is seen upon us, people are attracted to it like metal to a magnet, thereby positioning us for a harvest.

The manifestation of gold dust signifies the revelation of the visible and tangible latter glory of God.

It is an irrefutable fact that gold dust is a product of God's glory. Whenever the glory of God manifests in a tangible and visible way, gold dust usually appears as an evidence of its manifestation. Whenever the glory of God used to appear or manifest in the Old Testament, thunder, clouds, smoke and lightning would accompany its manifestations. These were not the glory but the symptoms or signs which show that the glory is present. While God has million ways of manifesting His glory, in this end time season, He chooses to rain down gold dust and other precious stones as evidence or signs of the presence of His glory. I recall vividly the day when I preached on Isaiah 60:2, and suddenly gold dust, supernatural oil and other precious stones began to fall and flow through the hands of many who were present and since then, it has continued to manifest in all our meetings.

Gold dust is meant to draw multitudes of people to God.

This is what the Bible mean when it concurs *that the Gentiles shall come to your light, and Kings to the brightness of your rising.* This means that as the *light* which represents the glory of God is displayed through gold dust manifestations, millions of souls shall stream to the Kingdom, to worship God. In the context of the above-mentioned scripture, the *brightness of your rising* speaks of the glorious gold dust anointing which is elevating you to a higher realm of dominion and sonship in Christ. When it says *"Lift up your eyes all around, and see; they all gather together, they come to you; your sons shall come from afar, and your daughters shall be nursed at your side* (Isaiah 60:3-4)." It is actually talking about an unprecedented avalanche of billions of souls from every sphere of human existence, streaming into the Kingdom as the glory of God is manifested through gold dust and draws every creation to the father. Therefore, the manifestation of the glory of God through gold dust leads to a harvest of souls as the *rain of the Spirit* produces a bumper harvest.

Prophetically speaking, in this season, the viscisity of the glory of God shall be manifested to the extent of spilling over and gushing beyond the church doors and bars into the streets, market place and public arena. This divine spectacle shall culminate in a scenario in which even hard core unbelivers and drug addicts shall be drawn to the glory and be saved. In some cases, as beleivers gather to honour the Lord through worship, the golden rain shall come down so thick like snow and gold fakes shall appear everywhere, all over the carpets, bibles, on the chairs, on the floor, and on the hands and faces of people or even at home to the extent that such manifestations shall inevitably culminate in government officials of nations constitutionally endorsing Jesus Christ as their Saviour.

Through the gold dust manifestations, our number one agenda in this season is to make God more real and being born again a fashionable experience right across the whole world. The message we are sending across is that no one should be left behind clinging on the shore line, standing at the bus stop or packed at the parking lot when God is visibly and tangibly moving on behalf of all humanity.

However, it is worth mentioning that the gold dust phenomenon has suffered severe criticism by sceptics who lack revelation and are sailing their boats through shallow streams of spiritual understanding. I too was a bit uncertain about it when it first unraveled from the horizon until the Lord led me to Haggai 2:8-9, where He says, *"The silver is Mine and the gold is Mine. The glory of the latter house will be greater than the former."* The Lord then told me that the latter house is the present church and that His glory is associated with God's presence intensely manifested in every believer which shall invade every sphere of life in this end times. It is for this reason that I strongly believe the manifestation of gold dust and other precious stones is a sign of the imminence of Christ's second coming. The viscosity of Shekinah glory dust is manifesting like showers of golden rain which are ushering us into the Grand Finale of the earth. Therefore, concerning our urgency to respond to this glory that is being unreservedly being poured out from the Heavens, God is echoing the same Word which He spoke through the voice of Prophet Isaiah and He is saying:

"Arise, shine, for your light has come, and the glory of the Lord rises upon you. See, darkness covers the earth and thick darkness the people, but the Lord rises upon you"

In other words, although darkness covers the sceptics, critics and those who reject the glory of God, gold dust shall fall upon you like rain. Put differently, althaugh the financial darkness hovers over ordinary folks, who have been enslaved by the failing economic system of this world, upon you, the glory of Miracle money and gold dust manifestations is rising. For clarity of purpose, let us refer to another scripture in Zechariah 10:1, where it says,

> *"Ask rain from the Lord in the season of the spring rain, from the Lord who makes the storm clouds, and he will give them showers of rain"*

This implies that anybody who shall open up to this new wave of signs and wonders shall qualify to be a recipient of this glorious phenomenon. However, those who shall resist, criticise and condemn it, will in a way shut a door against themselves, hence shall only see but not partake of it. However, in a view to reinforce the veracity and authenticity of evidence of this supernatural manifestation, the following are *"tests"* to determine if a manifestation of gold dust is a genuine work of the Holy Spirit: No. 1. *Does it honour the person of Jesus Christ?* No. 2. *Does it produce a greater hatred of sin and a greater love for righteousness?* No. 3. *Does it produce a greater regard for Scripture?* No. 4. *Does it lead people into truth?* No. 5. *Does it produce a greater love for God and man?* If the answer to all the above questions is yes, then the gold dust manifestation is directly from God.

In view of ample scriptural evidence unraveled above, it is unequivocally clear that this supernatural golden substance is a sign of the glory of God coming upon His people. In essence, gold represents the glory of God. In the Old Testament, the children of Israel brought their riches of gold, silver, and jewels into the wilderness tabernacle. The tabernacle was filled with these symbols of the glory of God. When the Lord gave instruction for Solomon's temple, He told them to overlay everything with gold, including the walls and ceiling. Even the veil that separated the manifest glory of God from the rest of the temple had golden thread woven into it. It is strikingly interesting to note that God has always chosen to represent His glory with a golden substance. Isn't it amazing to realize that as New Testament believers, we are now the carriers of God's glory? We carry His presence here on Earth; we are His temples. If the glory of the Old Testament was just a fading glory (2 Corinthians 3:7-11), then how much more does the Lord want to cover us in the presence of His glory today! I believe that these things we are experiencing are simply prophetic signs of the glory of God being released upon the earth. It is therefore undeniably true that God wants us to display His glory in the earth in these days of His outpouring!

OTHER PECULIAR MANIFESTATIONS OF THE SPIRIT WHICH ACCOMPANY MIRACLE MONEY

ANGEL FEATHERS

A heightened degree of visible angelic manifestation and visitation evidenced by Angel feathers falling on people during worship sessions.

Owing to a heightened degree of God's glory which they carry, angels have been entrusted with the propagation of Miracle money in the physical realm on behalf of Heaven. Mind you, angels have the ability and capacity to contain glory, move in the glory, propagate it and impart it upon mankind according to God's will. It is for this reason that angles play a key and integral role in the manifestation of Miracle money because Miracle money is a product of God's glory. Without the direct, active involvement and work of angles, Miracle money would not manifest. Angles are the ones whom God has entrusted with the responsibility to despatch or propagate Miracle money to earth so as to fulfil His end time purpose and divinely orchestrated Kingdom plans. Believers are therefore advised to be circumspect, vigilant and sensitive to the work of angels if ever they want to be recipients of millions in Miracle money. It is for this reason that Paul cautioned the believers in Ephesus not to forget to entertain strangers for some entertained angels unaware. Sensitivity to angelic operations means acknowledging the work of angels, cooperating with their presence as well as provoking their manifestation in the same manner in which Abraham engaged two angels who were purporting to be passing by. Therefore, if ever you want to abundantly partake of this special grace, it is of paramount importance that you actively engage angels.

It is striking to note that whenever Miracle money is demonstrated, *Angel feathers* are found either floating in the air or resting on the floor in the territory in which Miracle money would have supernaturally appeared. This is meant to reinforce the credibility and authenticity of manifestation of this divine phenomenon. If you can't see angels manifesting in the natural realm, at least angel feathers gives evidence of their presence so that your faith can be strengthened in God. This leaves us with no other question except to ask: *Do angels have wings?* Emphatically yes! There are different species and breed of angels within the same angelic kind. By God's Grand design, others have wings while others do not have them, depending on the functions which they were designed to perfom in the realm of the spirit. So, when they leave angel feathers behind, it's a part of their being that serves as an undeniable evidence of their presence in our meetings.

SUPERNATURAL OIL

The perrenial flow of supernatural oil usually on people's hands during worship sessions.

The glory of God can also be manifested through supernatural oil and this is increasingly becoming a common occurrence in the Body of Christ in these end times. The manifestation of God's glory though supernatural oil is an evidence of the presence of the Holy Spirit since He is the one who administers the anointing. The oil of Scripture is directly related to the

Holy Spirit's work in our lives (2 Corinthians 1:21-22). The anointing is a supernatural impartation of God's ability on a vessel and with the anointing, comes an enablement to accomplish tasks with speed. The Holy Spirit, by His anointing and presence, confirms what He is—the Spirit of Truth, of Holiness, of Wisdom. David concurs with this divine truth when he testifies in Psalm 23:5 that *"You have anointed my head with [fresh] oil."* This is to tell you that God is anointing us with a fresh new impartation from His Spirit! The Lord also wants to anoint those who have been overcome by the spirit of mourning with the oil of rejoicing. That anointing brings the lifting of our heads with the refreshing of seeing beyond today—not with superficial optimism, but with a deep abiding of hope that has been begotten in us by God.

In our ministry, we experienced an unusual supernatural occurrence of appearance of oil from Heaven which rained down and covered the ceiling of the church and then gracefully dripped or oozed down its walls and eventually soaked the carpet until it became wet with oil. This supernatural oil initially began to saturate and pour out of the atmosphere with the smell of rose. After that it started flowing with the smell of nard. Then it continued flowing out but this time with a new fragrance of myrrh. As if that was not enough, all sudden diamond stones started falling heavily on people's heads during worship sessions like hail stones. Sometimes during my sacred moments in God's presence, as I stand in the glory, my hands and feet will begin to drip with supernatural oil, representing the anointing of God. Many times, I would use this supernatural oil to pray for the sick and have seen tremendous miracles of healing taking place. The supernatural oil that flows from my hands often carries a Heavenly aroma – the fragrance of Jesus, as penned in Song of Songs 2:1. Other times, during the sacred moments in the glory of God, I have seen tiny sparkles appear in the air or on people. Sometimes the glory would come as a shower of golden rain; sometimes this golden substance will come out from the pores of my skin and starts dripping down profusely.

CREATIVE MIRACLES

A heightened degree of signs and wonders manifested through creative miracles.

It has been noted that in tandem with Miracle money manifestations, is the rain of creative miracles in which the original blue print of body parts supernaturally appears in bodily territories where they previously did not exist. The truth is that all creative miracles are given birth to in the glory of God and these shall become a common experience that manifests in parallel with Miracle money in these end times. Germination of hair on bald heads, growing of teeth, supernatural increase in height, supernatural development of body parts, miracle repairs of malfunctioning electric gadgets and supernatural airtime recharge, are just but a few examples of creative miracles of the end times as the viscosity of the glory of God is intensely manifested in this very hour. The greater truth is that anything that comes into contact with the glory of God whether living or non-living, comes to life, whether it be a dead body, coughing car, a dysfunctional cell phone or a malfunctioning refrigerator. This is what we call *Miracle repairs.* Other manifestations which are surfacing in the Body of Christ involves people being divinely transported or translated from one place to other, disappearance and reappearance of human vessels in the spirit realm (Inside-the-body and outside-the-body experiences), being caught up in the spirit dimension (Throne Room visitations) as well as people falling under the power in the streets without a preacher, as the glory of God invades the streets, market places and the public arena.

By definition, a creative miracle *is an impartation of a completely brand new organ or body part upon either an individual, machine or plant in territories where they previous did not exist.* It is a creative miracle in the very sense of the word; to create means to bring forth into manifestation or existence something that was previously not there. It is therefore a creative miracle in the sense that an organ did not exist at all in the body but now a brand new one has been imparted from Heaven. For example, the creation of flesh and bones where there was previously nothing, the growth and infilling of new gold teeth, appearance of hair on bold heads, supernatural appearance of miracle money in people's accounts, wallets or bags, instantaneous supernatural loss of weight as well as the appearance of eyes, hands, legs and other body parts in areas where there was completely nothing. Provocative miracles demonstrated in the Body of Christ in this season which have been hailed as controversial but powerful involves a Miracle height (a situation in which short people instantaneously get taller), Miracle pregnancy (the instantantaneous development of a pregnancy) evidenced by a growth of a big tummy, Miracle babies (giving birth to a baby within three days of pregnancy). Other thrilling miracles emerging on the horizon include Miracle repairs, Miracle airtime recharge, Miracle fuel, Miracle clothes and food parcels, Miracle cheques and Miracle angelic music in which angels joins believers during worship session with a divine aura of Heavenly music, reverberating through the atmosphere, and nailing every impossibility in the natural realm to a definite halt.

As this wave of creative miracles continues to blow in the Body of Christ across the globe, some believers will encounter strangers who will emerge from nowhere and hand over car keys and say this car is yours! or surrender a genuine bag full of diamonds and paper money worth millions of dollars and after that disappear into thin air. It is becoming evident in this season of the proliferation of the glory of God that not only do human beings receive creative miracles but machinery and plants as well. It is also striking to note that miracles can either be human, electrical, chemical, mechanical and biological. *Human* in the sense of people receiving new body parts; *Mechanical* in the sense of machines, equipment and gardets receiving new body parts, an equivalent to what we call *Miracle repairs*; *Electrical* in the sense of gardets functioning normally without them being connected to any source of electricity; *Chemical* in the sense of a substance being supernaturally converted into another brand new form, just like water being converted into wine and *Biological* in the sense of plants or crops receiving newness of life, which is the opposite of what Jesus did to the figtree.

The rationale behind creative miracles is that there is an original blue print of every body part in Heaven's Power House such that in the event that someone loses one of his body parts due to either accident, misfortune or complications at conception, birth or any other calamity of life, their parts can be instantly reinstated, imparted or restored to their original position of normal perfection. It should therefore be understood that in Heaven, there is a Power House that consists of an original blue print of all body parts, making it possible for one to tap into the realm of the miraculous and command that specific body part to be imparted upon an individual who has a missing organ in his body. I'm not talking about a situation whereby God restores a body organ to its proper function but a case where God creates something that was completely not there. In a practical sense, one could command a person's left hand to shorten and be pushed back in Jesus' Name to conform to the person's original blueprint found in Heaven. For example, if God has created you to be 5 feet 10 inches, and you are slightly deformed and are only 5 feet 7 inches, then under the anointing of the Holy Spirit, one can command your backbone to be straightened up and reach your ideal height according to the blueprint God made you to be. However, although possible, it is not necessary for one to pray that you grow to be 8 feet because that is not your original blueprint in Heaven.

Prophetically speaking, taking into account the nature of this end time dispensation, God wants us to migrate or graduate from the realm of ordinary miracles to the realm of creative miracles. However, it is worth admonishing that during ministerial sessions, ministers of the Gospel should strike a balance between the aspects of *possibility* and *necessity* because there are certain miracles which are possible but not necessay. *Possible* in the sense that there is God's power available for their demonstration and *unecessary* in the sense that their manifestaion does not either glorify God or make an impact or positive change to the lives of those who experience it. It is for this reason that Paul says everything is permissible but not everthing is beneficial. A miracle is said to be unbeneficial when it's manifestation breeds confusion and uneccessary skepticism and in some cases, the miracle itself might glorify the one who demonstrates it instead of God. That is why it's not every man who demonstrates miracles who is used of God because there is in the realm of God's power, what we call *channelling of the anointing*. This is a divine scenario in which the minister is given a divine prerogative as a son of God, to channel God's power in a specific direction that will impact or change the lives of the recepients of the miracle. It is for this reason that God holds every minister accountable for the supernatural power which Heaven releases on behalf of the masses who are desperately starving for God's power.

THRONE ROOM ENCOUNTERS

Increased visitations to the Throne Room in Heaven.

In these last days, divine transportation and translation in the realm of the spirit shall become a common experience as believers are caught up to the Third Heaven, as Apostle Paul penned. It should come to no surprise that some believers shall be caught up in the spirit dimension to minister in other countries and after that be divinely transported back in this critical season. There shall be heightened manifestations of God's glory whereby believers will function under an extreme degree of an open Heaven such that they will go to public places and supernaturally know specific conditions of certain people, cities or nations. This is a realm that we can tap into when we have walked, fellowshipped and communed with God so much such that by His grace, He grants us permission to temporarily visit His Throne in Heaven, in order to get a foretaste or glimpse of how things are there. Prophetically speaking, this is a characteristic feature of the end time dispensation and in *this season of visitation*, many believers will be catapulted right into the Throne Room of Heaven, on a study tour, to explore the glory of God and perambulate in the deepest territores of the Glory Realm. This is the realm that Paul tapped into in 2 Corinthians 12:2, when *he was caught up to the Third Heavens*. We also have a catalogue of testimonies of some believers around the world who are still entering that realm as God wills. For example, the seven Columbian youths whom Jesus took to both Heaven and hell to see what is happening there, have provided an irrefutable evidence of the realities of the spirit world.

This is akin to the spiritual manifestations taking place in our ministry in which after being laid hands on and lying breathlessly on the floor, believers are catapulted into the spirit world, where they go to either Heaven or hell. Upon coming back, many are able to testify to the masses about the current happenings in Heaven or hell. Others have brought informative, inspiring and prophetic messages from Heaven concerning people's destinies on earth, while others have seen people they know in hell, including former freinds, relatives and some other people who used to be Christians during their life time on earth. In some cases, these people clarify how they missed Heaven and provides enlightenment on why they eventually got to be in hell. This reinforces the faith of those whose trust in God is still wavering, such that everybody's faith in God is strengthened.

THE RISE OF KINGDOM MILLIONAIRES AND BILLIONAIRES:

The emergence of a distinct breed of believers who shall unreservedly tap into God's unlimited grace by manifesting Millions and Billions in Miracle money in the natural realm

One key characteristic feature of this last wave of prosperity revival is that it has culminated in the birth of newly emerging Millionaires and Billionaires as this wave of generosity swells with Kingdom wealth. When I was growing up in the things of God, I used to think that being a millionaire was a daunting task and a mission impossible but when I began to launch deeper in fellowship with the Holy Ghost and voraciously munched over God's prophetic Word to secure deeper revelations on supernatural financial provision, I realised that becoming a Millionaire is the easiest accomplishment which a man can ever attain in a generation. I was awakened to a fresh and new reality that contrary to how multitudes of believers think, *it is actually more difficult to be a poor man that it is to be rich*. This is because the difference between a rich man and a poor man is not determined by the level of education or affluence of the economy of the country in which you live. Instead, it is determined by the level of *revelation* which you have about God's word concerning financial prosperity. Revelation knowledge is the Master key to unlocking Heaven's Store Houses and a secret to amassing humungous wealth from God's Throne Room. That is why after the masses have inundated their spirit with revelations of God's Word encapsulated in one of my anointed books on Kingdom Finance titled, *"How To Become A Kingdom Millionaire"*, I have received inspiring testimonies and provocative reports on how some believers in the Body of Christ across the globe have been elevated to the realm of Kingdom Millionaires and ammassed humungous wealth on behalf of the Kingdom. The most striking testimony was that of a Business man in the USA who testified that following a conscienteous application of the revelational principles encapsulted in this book, divine oportunities had opened on his way to becoming a Billionaire, Glory to God!

Many at times we are erreneously taught that faith is solitarily the bottom line and a key that opens every door in the realm of the spirit and as a result, we stretch our faith to the limit yet there is no revelation to make it produce the results of what the Word talks about. It's like toiling from task till dawn ploughing on dry ground yet there are no rains to water it and cause it to produce a bumper harvest. When you have done everything that you know best in the name of faith and you seem not to get a breakthrough, it means that there is another ingredient that is lacking, which is *revelation*. Faith is what plants the seed on the ground but revelation is what provides nourishment for the seed to grow. Did you know that Solomon was the richest man in the world in gold, silver, money, property and wealth? Do you know how he obtained that wealth? It was simply through *revelation*. He received a revelation from God on how to deal decisively with cases facing the people he governed, and humungous wealth was committed into his hands, such that he became a Billionaire overnight. By the same token, it is through revelation that as this last prosperity wave blows Miracle money, gold dust and Heavenly precious stones across the Body of Christ, people who would never have become Millionaires due to limitations of the monetary system of this fallen world, will rise with such amazing financial power such that they will literally take over the world economy. I'm talking about a situation whereby believers own and control banks, multinational companies, global finacial institutions and eventually the whole world, glory to Jesus!

CHAPTER FOUR

SPIRITUAL LAWS AND PRINCIPLES THAT PROVOKE MIRACLE MONEY INTO MANIFESTATION IN THE NATURAL REALM

What Key Principles Do I Need To Unlock The River of Miracle Money?

How Do I Receive The Anointing For Miracle Money?

Most Christians believe that God does release Miracle money, but simply believing that God is able to do it is not enough. You must know the parameters and principles of how to receive it, manifest or demonstrate it in the natural realm. There are key spiritual laws that you can tap into in order to release Miracle money. There are certain principles that one can tap into in order to walk into the deeper realities of God's power in the arena of supernatural financial provision. Just like there are laws of gravity which governs how to operate in the natural realm, there are also spiritual laws that govern the spirit realm or how to operate in the realm of the miraculous. These laws of the supernatural complement each other and are progressions to enter into the greater depths of God. Each of these laws has a specific manifestation that produces something special. These should be applied correctly in order to produce the results of what the Word of God talks about. If you correctly apply these principles, you will provoke an unprecedented flow of Miracle money in your life and ministry than ever before. However, it is unfortunate that many believers are failing to operate in the realm of the miraculous because they do not understand spiritual laws and principles which they could take advantage of to generate positive results. Spiritual laws and principles are therefore vital keys that unlock the doors into the supernatural and accentuate an avenue through which the power of God can flow.

The Law of Divine Impartation

It is an undeniable fact that spiritual things are received through impartation. Paul concurs with this divine truth when he says *Brethren, I long to see you so that I can impart a spiritual gift so that at the end you may be established* (Romans 1:11). This is the same principle by which the grace for Miracle money spreads. While it is true that revelation always begins with one person, however, there is a tendency for it to spread and impartation is one of the key divine processes which God uses to transfer His grace. It is possible for one to receive the grace to demonstrate miracle money through the laying of hands. Impartation necessitates the transfer of God's grace, hence Miracle money should not only be demonstrated within the four walls of the church. In fact, there are two ways of impartation. That is *impartation by divine transportation* and *impartation by point of contact.* and both are evident in Paul's ministry. When Paul attested that *Brethren, I long to see you so that I can impart a spiritual gift so that at the end you may be established* (Romans 1:11), he spoke of impartation by point of contact and when he testified saying, *"For though I am absent in the flesh, yet I am with you in spirit, rejoicing to see your good order and the steadfastness of your faith in Christ"* (Colossians 2: 5), he spoke of impartation by divine transportation whereby his spirit was divinely transported into the Colossian churches and he could see, understand experience and know what was happening in the church by a *supernatural visitation*. Impartation by point of contact is *direct impartation* popularly administered through the laying of hands while impartation by divine transportation is an *indirect impartation* whereby Miracle money anointing is divinely transported and carried by the tidal waves of the air, cutting right across through space and time into visible and tangible manifestation in the natural realm. As believers are watching DVDs or CDs in the comfort of their homes, they can receive miracle money in an instant, even though they were not present at a meeting where Miracle money was demonstrated. What explanation can one give for this phenomenon? You see, the glory of God *(carrying Miracle money)* can be divinely transported by invisible sound waves travelling through time and space. That is why it is possible for you to watch a miracle crusade on television that was filmed 3 months back and you receive Miracle money while watching it. It's because the glory has travelled through time and space to you. Even though you were not there when the actual crusade took place, whenever you watch it, the same glory is reactivated and you receive the same impartation or blessing as if you had been there 3 months ago. The glory of the meeting that took place at a particular time is frozen and reactivated the moment you watch it. So, the voice waves of the one speaking, the worship and the very atmosphere which released Miracle money in that meeting can be contained in sound and light in the form of images and can be reactivated. That is why it is important to watch DVDs of anointed man of God because there is an impartation from these meetings frozen in time, waiting for you to receive it and release it by just pushing the play button of the DVD player.

This is the same principle by which the Bones of Elisha held a reservoir of glory and sound waves of power such that a man who was thrown into the same grave where Elisha had been buried more than four hundred years back was instantly resurrected (1 Kings 13:21). This is simply because the glory travels through space and time and in this case, it had travelled ahead more than four hundred into the future such that the same degree of resurrection glory which soaked into Elisha's body during his life time on earth was still present to raise the dead. As Elisha was now in a higher realm of glory in Heaven, his body was now the only point of contact to transmit the glory between Heaven and earth. This is what we call *Elisha glory,* when a torch of the last generation is passed to the next generation with even greater power. This is to tell you that the glory travels through time and space, which is why in in the glory realm, one can be divinely transported in the spirit dimension to other places just like the experience of Philip in Azotus. That is why multitudes of believers shall experience *divine transportation* in the spirit in the end times days.

It is by the same principle of the divine transportation of sound waves that the Miracle money grace will be widely demonstrated in this season. In some cases, even as friends and colleagues are talking about miracle money in their offices, it shall manifest right there. It shall grow a lever whereby if you were to drive your neighbours' car, you can receive miracle money, while playing a tap listening to a man of God, miracle money shall appear, even as a teacher is teaching in a class, miracle money shall appear in the classroom, while a farmer is still planting crops, miracle money shall appear. In other words, miracle money shall manifest unreservedly in every sphere of human endeavour as God reveals the fullness of His saving grace to humanity. It must be understood that the spirit realm operates differently from the physical realm. What people perceive to be expensive and wealthy such as money or gold, in heaven it is a surplus. That is why in Heaven, there are streets of gold. Money is just a surplus commodity in Heaven, hence God can populate it in billions in the natural realm. Therefore, you must migrate from the traditional thinking of receiving just few hundreds or thousands to millions and billions of rands, as this grace intensifies and as believers across the globe embrace it.

The Law of Contagious Association

The law of contagious association states that spiritual things are transferred or imparted through association. That is why Paul said *imitate me as I imitate Jesus* (1 Corinthians 11:1). Through this divine principle, power was able to flow from Paul to the churches. As they emulated him, they were thrust into the same degree of power at which he was operating. This does not speak of mere imitation in the case of copying one's style of doing things but it speaks of a rubbing or receptivity of spiritual substances and blessings by virtue of associating yourself with the source of blessings. If you want to receive and manifest the grace for Miracle money, it is imperative that you partner or associate with a man of God whom God has given the grace to manifest Miracle money. This is in view of the divine truth that God manifests Himself according to how you perceive Him as *Deep calleth unto deep*. Therefore, if you associate yourself with a man who demonstrates the grace for Miracle money, you will receive Miracle money, if you associate yourself with the one who raises the dead, you will also raise the dead. Spiritual things work by association. The Bible says *when disciples spoke, people realised that they had been with Jesus*. In the context of this scripture, the phrase, "*had been with Jesus*" speaks of the *law of association*. In other words, it is because of their association with Jesus that people took heed of their message Just by associating with Jesus, disciples were able to learn to the extent of doing exactly as Jesus did. Therefore, continuously staying in the presence of God will also ensure that you draw from the source of power. However, the power does not only flow when you are connected to God but when you are connected to those upon whom the Lord has made an investment of His power. Our blessings and destiny are closely related with those to whom God has connected you. God will connect you to specific people, hence we must be a wise discerner of relationships. It is through relationships that we capture the mantles and blessings upon those whom God has connected us. On the other hand, if you disconnect yourself from a spiritual covering, you lose the anointing because one would have been cut off from the atmosphere, association and influence, in the same way a branch is cut off from a tree. It was because of his association with Moses that the people hearkened to the voice of Joshua. Every time they looked at Joshua, they saw Moses in him. This is just how powerful the law of contagious association is. Moreover, Elisha received the mantle by virtue of association with Elijah. If it wasn't for association, I don't believe he would have received even the *double portion* from him. He followed Elijah closely as he ate from his hand until the reward time came and Elisha scooped the spoils.

The law of contagious experience states that whenever the power of God is flowing and everyone is connected in the spirit, if one person catches the power or manifestations, the rest will catch it too. By virtue of association, even the blessings of God can spill over to touch those close to you in your sphere of contact in the same way Lot got blessed by virtue of his association with Abraham and Laban got blessed because of Jacob (Genesis 30:25-43). Do you know that if one person demonstrates Miracle money in your church, other members and churches in the neighbourhood will catch it too such that within a twinkling of an eye, the whole city will be in a Holy Ghost Miracle money flame. The manifestations of the spirit are contagious in the sense that they are easily transmitted to other people. Some manifestations are common or popular amongst certain ministries as a result of the application of the law of contagious experience. There is a spiritual law in principle that we don't really know anything until we have experienced it. You can know something through somebody else's sharing or through reading the Word of God but we do not really know the matter until we have experienced it. God is a person and He wants us to experience Him as a person. For example, your relationship with your wife is a legal relationship but at the same time, it is a personal relationship. A house is a house but the relationships within the house make it a home. Christianity is a true-life relationship with God. When you experience God, you experience Him in the spiritual world, which has a side effect on our soul and on our body. Likewise, we can never really understand working with angels until we have had a spiritual contact and experience with them. However, we cannot base theology on experience. Theology must be based on the Word of God. But the experience helps us to look at the Word in a different way. Without the experience, I believe none of us will look at the Word in a different way.

The Law of expectation

The expectancy level is such a powerful key that can provoke the power of God into manifestation. The Bible says in Acts 3:5, that when Peter and

John came across a crippled man at the Beautiful gate of the temple, he gave them attention expecting to receive something and that is the reason why he received his healing on that day. In fact, every day, they had passed by that man on their way to the temple and this was not the first time. But on that day, the man was in a better position to receive. Sometimes, when you remain in an atmosphere of faith, your faith grows until you are expectant enough to receive. Likewise, on that day he passed by the Beautiful gate, Peter sensed that the man was expectant and rightly positioned in the spirit to receive, hence he healed him. The truth is that regardless of the level of anointing upon a vessel, no one can give you what you are not ready to receive. As a believer, you must expect to receive Miracle money whenever you get to a place where the presence of God is moving. Unfortunately, there are certain preachers who struggle to help even their own congregation to receive Miracle money because they themselves lack genuine expectancy. A high level of expectancy places a demand on the anointing and produces tremendous results of power. Miracles tend to intensify when the expectancy level is high. The law of expectation is such a powerful divine principle in that miracles do not happen where they are needed but they occur where they are expected. The higher the level of expectation, the greater the dimension of miracles, signs and wonders.

There is however an intricate connection between *expectancy level* and the *law of response*. For example, to respond to the power of God, we need to expect something supernatural to happen. If we do not expect anything, then we will be unable to respond when there is a manifestation of God's power. God is extending His hand to give us the supernatural in the form of Miracle money but we also have to extend our hands in return to receive it. The reason why God demands in Exodus 23:15 that *no man should come into His presence empty handed* is because He knows that if you come empty handed, you will not expect to receive anything from Him, hence He challenges you to bring something so as to stir up your faith level. In a ministerial context, as you minister, you must watch the response of the people because how the congregation responds is vital for the smooth flow of God's power. Stirring up their readiness can be done in different ways, for example by declaring

Spiritual Laws And Principles That Provoke Miracle Money

"Are you ready for Miracle money?" How they respond will tell you whether they are really ready and rightly positioned in the sprit to receive or not. Keep declaring that if there is anyone on wheel chair, there must stand up; if there is any blind person, their eyes will open up and if there are any people who are on the verge of death on sick beds, declare that they will come back to life and that the congregation will receive Miracle money. As you declare these words, the expectancy level will provoke faith in their spirits such that some will even begin to rise up without you touching them. This is the power behind the *law of expectation*.

Prophetically speaking, the glory of God is hovering over the church and it's starting to unravel in this end time season. In the same way a famer is expecting the seed he planted in the soil to bring forth fruits, everything within me is leaping in excitement as I sense a shifting in the atmosphere. The Holy Ghost is about to explode in the demonstration of signs and wonders that will ruffle the feathers of those comfortable with the status quo. There has never been a time like now when Heaven is so aligned with the earth as it is now. You can smell it in the very atmosphere. There is expectancy in the air that corresponds to the Heavens for what God wants to do on earth. The spiritual atmosphere is full of expectation right now. Like a pregnant woman expecting the imminent delivery of her baby, the womb of the spirit is pregnant and ready for the birth of something new. Expectancy is the breeding ground for miracles, signs and wonders. When you are expectant, Heavens releases a corresponding divine energy or supernatural influence to bring the abundance of Miracle money into manifestation in the natural realm.

The Law of receptivity

The law of receptivity is such an important divine principle in matters of demonstration of Miracle money because it is what determines how much money a man can receive from God. In Mark 8:27-30, Jesus once asked His disciples a simple question,*" Who do people say that I am?"* This is the essence of the *law of reception*. The reason why Jesus asked His disciples this rhetoric question is not because He wanted to know how popular He was. Instead, it's because He wanted to establish how people received Him because how people receive you as a minister determines the effectiveness of the message you preach to them. Moreover, your ability or capacity to receive from God will automatically determine how much of His blessings can be imparted into your spirit. It is unfortunate that many believers tend to overemphasise the idea of giving but they never focus on the art of how to receive. This is because receiving is as equally important as giving. If you only know how to give but you don't know how to receive you will find yourself losing more but never gaining anything. It is a typical scenario in the body of Christ that many people are eager to stand and participate in the presence of God but the greatest challenge is that they do not know how to receive from the presence of God. In some cases, while the spirit of God is moving and imparting the anointing and other spiritual substances, people are also busy praying and preoccupied with their own agendas and programs and in the process, they are not able to receive what the Spirit of God is appropriating in the meeting. Some people do not receive because their conductivity level is low, meaning that they are poor conductors of the power of God while others are good conductors of the same power.

Some people do not receive because their spirits are closed. The power of God is flowing but their spirits are closed. On the other hand, others are able to receive because they are rightly positioned in the spirit to receive. Some people do not receive because they are in the realm of flesh and not in the spirit and they tend to conceptualise how to receive from a carnal perspective. The Bible declares in John 3:27 *that a man cannot receive anything unless it is given from above*. The extent to which one's spirit is activated or developed will determine how much he will receive from God. That is why spiritual exercises such as prayer and fasting opens and aligns our spirits and makes it easy to receive from God.

The law of atmosphere

A conducive atmosphere, ambiance and spiritual climate must be fostered in an endeavour to trigger the flow of Miracle money in the natural realm. God has always been known to speak from the cloud of His glory, hence it is important to know how to build a spiritual atmosphere. The spiritual atmosphere is the cloud of God's presence that surrounds us and Miracle money has its own cloud. We must therefore create a celestial atmosphere for miracles, signs and wonders through the word we speak. When you get to a level where your faith cannot operate, change the atmosphere. Unfortunately, many people are in places where the supernatural power is non-existent because a divine atmosphere was never generated. The atmosphere is generated through a myriad of spiritual exercises such as praise and worship, prayer and intercession which build the tabernacle where God's glory can manifest. After man was disconnected from the glory of God as a result of sin, the only way to bring it back was through praise and worship. However, the duration of praise and worship depends on the extent to which the environment or atmosphere is cultivated. If the atmosphere is hard to pierce, it will take longer to build the throne but where an atmosphere already exists, one can go directly into worship. Moreover, it is also important to discern the atmosphere whether it is for miracles, healing, deliverance or something else after that speak into that atmosphere in order to make what you declare come to pass. In Genesis 1:1-10, when God spoke and said *let there be light*, the Holy Spirit who had already created a conducive atmosphere by brooding over the face of the deep, acted on the word which God spoke and brought those things which God spoke into manifestation. This is the same principle by which we operate in the realm of the miraculous whenever we want to provoke a greater flow of God's power.

The Law of Release

The law of release is such a powerful divine prophetic principle which when tapped into, can result in an avalanche of Miracle money from the realm of the spirit into the natural realm. Do you remember when God declared in Zechariah 10:1 that, *"Ask for rain in the time of the latter rain and I shall give you showers of abundant rain"*? This is the essence of the *law of release*. Rain speaks of the anointing and in the context of supernatural power, this implies that if you need an unprecedented flow or avalanche of Miracle money in the natural realm, you must release it during the right time when the power of God is moving or flowing. This spiritual law awakens us to the consciousness that it is advisable to release God's supernatural power when people are ready to receive or when the spiritual atmosphere is conducive enough to unleash or release the power of God. Hence, there are two critical prerequisites for the release of God's power and that is; the extent to which the atmosphere and spiritual climate is pregnant with the possibilities of God and the extent to which people are ready to receive from God. The Bible further declares in Ecclesiastics 11:3 that *when clouds are full of rain, they empty themselves on earth.* Knowing when to release the power is one such a vital key to the flow of God's power. That is why Paul advises in 1 Timothy 5:22 that *no one must not be quick to lay hands* because at times the anointing might be building up like a cloud or accumulating until a particular point. Making haste to release the power under such circumstances might not produce expected results. The expectancy level of people somehow is a determining factor to the law of release. You only release the power when your faith level and expectancy levels of people are high.

This implies that we cannot declare the word if we don't have foreknowledge of what will happen. For example, if you are going to speak to a blind person yet you don't expect his sight to return, then rather don't say anything and if you are going to tell the lame to stand up yet you don't expect anything to happen, you rather not say anything at all. Apostolic revelation breaks new ground by declaring what the father is saying and doing at this moment in time. This causes the Heavens to loose what God has authorised for the earth. When the Holy Spirit reveals something through the apostles and prophets, Heaven can no longer contain it, it must be released. However, the greatest challenge facing the Body of Christ is that Heavens are pregnant with the possibilities of God and is therefore ready to unleash from the womb of the Spirit the power, anointing and glory but the earth is not ready to receive or incubate that which Heaven has given birth to in the spirit realm. That is why in some cases, there is so much power that is released from Heaven but it never gets to be utilised effectively because people are not sensitive to the move of God. This is contrary to the will of God because Jesus declared in Mathew 18:18 that, *"Whatever we bind on earth shall be bound in heaven and whatever we release on earth shall be released in Heaven"*. This means as far as God is concerned, Heaven and earth are supposed to function in synchronisation, in order to release the blessings of God. It is God's ultimate plan that Heaven and earth work together as one and not as separate entities. If you understand the law of release, you will know when to ask and when your blessing has arrived after praying for it. The danger is that so many believers are praying and praying but they never get to know when their prayers have been answered or when their blessings have been released. The truth is that *release* and *reception* takes place concurrently. In other words, blessings are received from Heaven the instant they are released into the natural realm. Contrary to how the lukewarm church has portrayed, you don't release the blessings or power of God today and then wait for tomorrow in order to see the results. Instead, you must procure the blessings at that very time when you release them. With this understanding, you certainly realise that blessings manifests at the point of release, hence there is no need for waiting and procrastination.

The Law of Response

The law of release is suchThe law of response is such a powerful divine principle that precedes the law of release because in prophetic language, you can only respond to something that has been released. Do you remember when God declared in Jeremiah 33:3 that, *"Call unto me and I will answer thee and show you great and mighty things which you knewest not"*. This is the essence of the *law of response*. This law gives a practical guide on how to respond to Miracle money when administered from Heaven. It states that in order to harness Miracle money from the supernatural realm and precipitates it into the natural realm; you must be in a position to respond accordingly when you sense its presence in the atmosphere. In other words, your spirit must be in an upper room position to respond to what God is appropriating in the spirit realm. Whenever the presence of God shows up, there are always three types of people who would usually respond in a particular way under normal circumstances. Firstly, there are those who are *spectators*, and have no clue of what God is doing in the spirit realm, hence they don't take any notice of His presence. Secondly, there are those who are *resistors* and are able to sense the presence of God but they are simply resisting it because their spirit is closed. Thirdly, there are those who are *detectors* and are able to feel the presence and desire to participate in it but have no revelation of how to channel the presence or benefit from it. The word of God gives an account in Luke 5:17 of how *the power of the Lord was present to heal*. In other words, the atmosphere was charged with God's presence but nothing happened until four men took a leap of faith and lowered a bedridden man through the roof and he was the first to receive his healing. However, there are those who are *partakers*, who have received a revelation of how to respond quickly whenever they sense the presence of God. And notable is the realisation that it is this last group that always excels in matters of demonstrating the power of God. This is akin to the incident in Mark 9:20, whereby people were pressing upon Jesus but only one woman who had a flow of blood for twelve years knew the art of how to respond to the anointing and sneaked her way through to touch the hem of Jesus' garment and she instantly received her healing.

It is a typical scenario in many churches that God's presence is felt but nothing more happens. His presence is there because some people paid a price for it but now that it comes, no one knows precisely how to respond or how to act whenever confronted by the presence. The atmosphere remains charged yet no one actively participates in it. This culminates in a scenario whereby miracles, signs and wonders and transformations are delayed because people have no idea of how to respond and appropriate the blessings of God. It is wrong to find some people being spectators in the presence of God because God demands that he who comes in His presence must participate in order to reap benefits of power and blessings from it. The power of God meets every need depending on individual desire and while others are receiving deliverance, others are being healed and others receive breakthroughs and impartation of spiritual substances. Hence, the correct prayer that we should pray whenever the presence of God shows up is *"Lord, reveal the purpose of your presence"*. This is because whenever God show up, He comes for a specific purpose and what He wants to do today might be different from what He did yesterday. We therefore need to respond to the presence of God through elevated worship, prophetic declaration and proclamation of our blessings, shouting for victory, dancing and yelling in praise as well as through practical demonstration and exercise of the gifts of the spirit.

The law of expression

Knowing how to express your spirit in God's presence without shame, fear, hesitation or unbelief is such a key determinant to partaking of His glorious blessings of which Miracle money is a part. Expression in this regard entails developing a high level of *sensitivity, acknowledgment and consciousness of God's power*. Some people are not able to appropriate their blessing because they are not *sensitive* to the move of the spirit. In other words, they cannot sense or detect the presence due to the fact their spiritual senses have not yet been activated, developed or trained to operate in the spirit realm. Moreover, some people do not receive because they are not *conscious* or cannot discern God's presence. Developing one's level of consciousness through spending time in the presence of God is one such vital key to receiving or flowing in the power of God. *Acknowledgment* of the anointing or the power of God present is also a highly imperative action.

The Bible records in Mathew 20:29-34, that *when the blind man heard that Jesus was passing by, he cried out loud* and because of his high level of expression, Jesus healed him. According to the culture of the people at that time, it was a taboo for a man in his sins to cry out to a Rabai but because of his desire to reach out to God, the man expressed himself vocally until Jesus paid attention to his cry and healed him. The scripture further proclaims in Genesis 18:1, that *when Abraham saw three angels purporting to be passing by, he ran after them and invited them to come to his house* and because of his expression, he was blessed at the end. All these are physical expressions but there are also different ways of expressing one's self in the spirit and that is through praying in other tongues, laughing and singing in the spirit, dancing in the spirit, travailing in prayer, falling under the power and how one expresses himself will determine the amount of power that will flow through him

It is evident that other people try to resist or stop the flow of spiritual expressions and in the process they short circuit or deactivate the power of God. For example, the Bible records a myriad of incidents where men of God expressed themselves fully before God. For instance, David danced in the presence of the Lord until his clothes were torn, the apostles were so drunk in the spirit on the day of Pentecost to the extent that they were out of control, Saul prophesied until he tore his clothes off although this manifestation ended up being in the flesh. These were such powerful expressions that launched them into greater depths in the spirit. However, while in the presence of God, some people tend to maintain their cool and be overly conscious of their self and in the process they fail to express themselves, hence receive nothing from God. It is therefore advisable that you release yourself unreservedly in the presence of God because the extent to which your spirit is open will determine how much you can receive from God.

The Law of Connection

It is a greater truth that the blessings of God such as Miracle money flows through divine connection. Jesus declared in John 15:13-17 that, *"I am the vine and you are the braches grafted in the vive, therefore abide in me and I shall abide in you.* This implies that if you stay connected to God, His divine power will continuously flow upon your life and the opposite is true. Do you know that when the Bible says in Psalms 91:1 that *He that dwells in the secret place shall abide by the shadow of the almighty*, it actually speak of divine connection? This fruits or results of such divine connection are protection, prosperity, promotion, increase and so forth. Therefore, continuously staying in the presence of God will also ensure that you draw from the source of power. However, the power does not only flow when you are connected to God but when you are connected to those upon whom the Lord has made an investment of His power. Our blessings and destiny are closely related with those to whom God has connected you. God will connect you to specific people, hence we must be a wise discerner of relationships. It is through relationships that we capture the mantles and blessings upon those whom God has connected us. On the other hand, if you disconnect yourself from a spiritual covering, you lose the anointing because one would have been cut off from the atmosphere, association and influence, in the same way a branch is cut off from a tree. However, some divine relationships are under heavy attack because whenever God connects us to someone, Satan will try to destroy the relationship because he knows that if we never make such a connection, our purpose will never be completed. Therefore, if you want to launch into greater depths of the miraculous, connect yourself to a source of power and miracles, signs and wonders will follow you.

The law of connection also implies being at the right place, at the right time, doing the right thing. The law of connection entails connecting yourself to two fundamental sources of power, that is, *connection to God* and *connection to His word*. Connecting one's self to the word of God is tantamount to connecting yourself to God because He has placed His word above His name. Hence, you are guaranteed of *kratos power* that is leased from the pages of the Bible straight into your spirit when you meditate on the word of God. Do you remember that the Bible declares in Psalms 1:1-6, that *blessed is a man who walks not in the counsel of the ungodly, nor stand in the seat of the scornful but his delight is in the law of the Lord and upon it he meditates day and night. He shall be like a tree planted by many rivers, whatever he does prospers.* Do you notice that prosperity is conditional; in other words it is dependent on the extent to which you mediate on the word of God? This is the essence of *connection*. The above scripture unveils the reality that prosperity depends on the extent to which one is connected to the word of God.

The Law of Divine Transitivity

It is worth exploring the divine truth that there is an original blue print of everything that exist in the spiritual realm. Likewise, there is an original blue print of money in the realm of the spirit. During manifestation, it is this money that is transferred from the spirit realm into the natural realm. That is why it is important that you secure a divine revelation of money as a spiritual substance. This is because Miracle money is transferred from the realm of the spirit into visible manifestation in the realm of the natural. Understanding Miracle money as a spiritual substance will help you secure an in depth revelation behind the mechanics of how it operates, originates, manifests and transferred from the spirit realm into the physical realm. In order to tap into the grace of manifesting Miracle money in the natural realm, it is important that you understand the principles of operating in the glory realm because it is the realm of glory that produces Miracle money since everything that exist, including humans were given birth to in the glory realm. In the glory realm, things are not made but created. That is why transition from the realm of the anointing into the realm of glory is an imperative action in these end times. To be precise, Miracle money grace is manifested when a minister is operating in the territories of the glory realm. Therefore, if you want to get to the depths of practically demonstrating Miracle money, you must tread on deeper territories of the glory realm and Miracle money will unreservedly stream in your direction.

The Law of Manifestation (Action and Reaction)

It is worth highlighting the divine truth that spiritual things work through demonstration. You can never know that you have received the grace to demonstrate Miracle money until you command it into manifestation. Therefore, in this season, every opportunity you get, you should boldly and fearlessly commanded angel tellers to release Miracle money by calling it forth into visible and tangible manifestation in the natural realm. You need to develop a significant degree of sensitivity to angel tellers because they are the ones whom God has entrusted with the mandate to dispatch and propagate Miracle money to the extreme ends of the world. The divine orchestration of the Miracle money grace is from God but its transportation is the responsibility of angels. It is therefore important that you be highly sensitive to the movement and work of angels so that you can command them to release Miracle money whenever it is needed in the natural realm. As you command Miracle money into manifestation, in the invisible realm, angels will move swiftly and place Miracle money into bags, wallets, pockets and other unexpected places. Some of the money is supernaturally sent via the banking and electronic system so that it reflects in their cell phone as a new bank balance. On that note, determine right now to manifest a 100-fold blessing of God in your life for the purpose of bringing glory to His name. Your definite goal, coupled with your commitment to increase your finance will cause a miracle that will dazzle the minds of onlookers.

The law of Divine Purpose

It is important that you understand God's mind and purpose concerning the divine orchestration of Miracle money in this end time season. This grace is not for self-enrichment or selfish gain for which ministers to build an empire for themselves. Instead, its sole purpose is to draw multitudes of people to God for the salvation of their souls. Jesus said *no one can come to the father unless He draws him*. Miracle money is an end time reservation grace which God is using to draw millions across the globe to Christ. Miracle money is not an end in itself but a means to an end. The end is that billions of souls across the globe can come to the knowledge of Christ and be saved. Therefore, whenever this grace is publicly demonstrated, it must lead to an avalanche of millions of souls streaming into the Kingdom. If ever you want to demonstrate Miracle money but you don't have a passion for the lost souls or to expand the Kingdom, then you might never be a partaker of this grace. The ultimate purpose is to reveal God's glory and love for His people, hence the masses must not only see you in the picture but God at the centre of Miracle money demonstrations. In order to understand the reason behind the supernatural manifestation of Miracle money, ask yourself this question: Why did God send manna for the children of Israel in the wilderness? It's because there is a specific purpose He wanted to accomplish? He wanted them to see that He cares for them as their father and would always provide anything they need in the physical realm. It's not because of drought that God rained down manna. If it was so, then how many drought seasons have this world gone through since time memorial and did the masses receive manna in all these times? No! So, this shows that God wanted the people to realise His presence and the love He has for them so that their faith could be strengthened in Him and so that they could depend not on man but on God.

Spiritual Laws And Principles That Provoke Miracle Money

THE SEVEN-FOLD DIVINE PRINCIPLES OF THE GLORY REALM WHICH CAN PROVOKE THE RAIN OF MIRACLE MONEY INTO MANIFESTATION IN THE NATURAL REALM

PROPHETIC DECLARATION

In the glory realm, things happen the instant they are declared.

There is a new prophetic dimension in the glory whereby things are coming to pass as they are being said. In the glory realm, there is no procrastination, or delays because time is inconsequential. It is for this reason that Miracle money appears in the physical realm the instant it is commended to. When God declared in an atmosphere of glory, *let there be light*, light came forth instantly. He didnt have to wait. Instead, results came forth as words were declared. In the glory realm, there is no waiting because waiting is a process in time, of which we have dominion over time; we operate outside the time dimension because we were given birth to in the eternal realm which falls outside our time dimension. The reason why some believers experience delays in their finances and manifestation of Miracle money is because of the absence of glory. The less you are filled with the glory, the longer it takes for you to cause Miracle money to manifest in the natural realm.

Because we have dominion over time, in the glory realm, you can declare Miracle money and use your royal prerogative to stipulate the time frame when it must manifest, where it should appear and in what amounts it should manifest. When the Bible attests that *you shall declare a thing and it shall be established for you*, it doesn't talk about flippantly declaring empty words in any direction but it talks about declaring things while in the glory realm or in an atmosphere of glory. That's when things happen. That is why those who function in higher realms of glory don't wait for things to happen, instead, they make things happen. This is because in the glory realm, it is possible for you to be instantaneously elevated to the reality of *overnight success*, whereby prayers are being answered even before you start praying. Let's look closely at how Ezekiel functioned on the prophetic glory:

So, I prophesied as I was commanded and as I prophesied, there was a noise, and suddenly a rattling and the bones came together bone to bone (Ezekiel 37:7)

The instant Ezekiel prophesied, the noise began and the miracle started the moment the prophecy commenced. This is to tell you that prophecy does not just foretell; it creates that which is being said. It is the tool that brings it to pass. Confessing what you want God to do is different from declaring what He is saying right now while the glory is present. Both Elijah and Elisha walked and lived in the prophetic glory realm and when they spoke, it caused heaven and earth, kings and nations, to react and respond. They prophesied the opening of wombs, rain and drought, provisions, resurrections, and deaths, and the list goes on.

DIVINE RESPONSE

Every created thing has sound waves and responds to sound waves spoken in the glory and Spirit of God

It is worth exploring the divine truth that when you speak words of faith directed by God in the glory realm, everything responds to your words. When you speak to Miracle money and command it to appear, it hears you and respond swiftly according to your word. The principle is that every created thing has sound waves and responds to sound waves spoken with the glory and Spirit of God. That is why Jesus spoke to a fig tree and commanded it to wither and it instantly responded because it was created with the capacity to hear and obey. Now, you understand why Jesus said we could speak to a mountain and it is possible for it to be removed (Mathew 17:20). The disciples also marvelled that *even the winds and the surging waters obey him*. The truth is that it's not only diseases that obeys and responds to our commands but the creation itself. Even Miracle money can be commanded to appear and swiftly come on feet in your direction and it will be established in the realm of the spirit. Do you notice that God told Moses to speak to the rock so that it would produce water? This is the same principle of operating in the glory that we tap to when healing the sick. Because every body part and object of creation can hear and respond, when praying and commanding broken bones to reconnect, they can hear and respond just as all created things can. Likewise, Miracle money is manifested this way. This realisation opens a whole new world of authority over creation.

In the Biblical account of creation, God spoke for the first time in recorded history in Genesis 1:3 saying, *"let there be light"* and instantly, there was light. Accordingly, everything was created with sound directing it to be a certain thing. This means that if you are in the glory of God, it is possible to redirect an object to be another created thing. If the original raw materials that created a certain object are present (Spirit), then sound can redirect the same created object into another form, especially if you are in the glory realm of God where the Spirit is hovering. The greater truth is that nothing created can be uncreated. According to the *law of thermodynamics*, things created only change form. For example, when you burn wood, it turns to ash but does not disappear completely. Although the ashes seem to dissolve, it is reduced to smaller molecules that still contain imbedded sound particles. This is to show you that one created object can turn into another created thing if directed by sound waves or commanded under the direction of the Holy Spirit.

How do you think Ezekiel was able to prophesy and speak to the bones such that they responded as a proof that they could hear and obey such that the sinews and flesh joined in and reformed? How could the flesh that was dissolved, rotten and now skeletons turn into an army? It's because nothing created is really gone even though it might have disappeared in the natural realm. It only changes form into smaller molecules and atoms we cannot see. It's just that it exists in another realm, in another form; hence, it can be brought back to its original form. Do you notice that Ezekiel even spoke to the dry bones' breath, which is the spirit such that it obeyed and returned? That is why when demonstrating Miracle money in the natural real, simply speak and command it to appear and it will be established. Imbued with this understanding, you realise that demonstrating Miracle money is certainly as easy as taking a walk through a park.

The greater truth is that creation responds to what human beings say or do. That's why the Bible says *the creation itself groans with birth pangs for the manifestation of the sons of God* (Romans 8:19, 22), meaning the earth is eagerly waiting for humanity to command it on what to do. Do you know that the Bible says money is crying out in the hands of those who use it for evil? As a believer, filled with the Spirit and inundated by the word of God, you have the authority over all creation and subjects in the natural realm, including Miracle money. In the same manner in which Jesus spoke to the billowing storms and boisterous winds of the sea, you can change weather patterns of geographical territories by speaking or commanding the winds, rain, sun (heat), and other physical phenomenon in the natural realm and they will obey you. By the same token, you can speak to financial storms to cease and command Miracle money to manifest in the natural realm and it will be done for you. For instance, when you wake up in the morning, you can command your morning and determine the exact financial conditions that you would want to see prevail in your life and neighbourhood and it shall be established.

To cement this divine truth with reference to further scriptural evidence, did you notice that the Bible says *the blood of Jesus speaks better things than that of Abel?* Do you notice in the context of the above scripture that the blood speaks? How possible is it that blood can speak? It's because it has sound waves and responds when commanded. In a similar vein, the Bible also mentions that *the blood of martyrs is crying out* (Genesis 4:10). We need to realise that all things have a voice and their sound can be carried over time to be experienced again. Are you not shocked that after more than 400 years, Elisha's bones still retained the anointing and the sound of God emanating from them such that a dead man who came into contact with Elisha's bones was raised back to life (2 Kings 13:21). This is to inspire you to get into the glory zone and speak Miracle money into visible manifestation.

CONFESSION

The realm of glory is activated by spoken words.

It is a divine truth that Miracle money is a product of a spoken word. What you speak has such a tremendous effect on everything that you do. Speech is so powerful that it is recorded that everything was created by it. Speech was one of the first ingredients that created everything else you see and the invisible things you don't see. In the beginning the Creator spoke in Genesis 1: 3, saying *"let there be light"*, and light came forth instantaneously. The truth is that when you speak over the airwaves, you are invading and taking back the space of, *"the Prince of the power of the air"*, and displacing the enemy so that God can rule over the airwaves and bring His purposes to pass. From a scientific point of view, sound waves created by speech are so small that if you were to divide the smallest particles and atoms into some of the smallest forms inside them, at their core you would find vibration waves called *quarks*. From this scientific reality, comes a spiritual truth that sound waves are embedded in everything on earth, including rocks, food, trees and everything ever created. Therefore, these sounds waves can be altered and respond to other sound waves or speech. According to the studies conducted by a Japanese Researcher Masaru Emoto, water particles and other subatomic particles actually respond to sound and even speech or words spoken to them. If this is the case, then every created thing can hear in a sense and respond in some way, as they were first created with the same core ingredients – sound and light. This understanding can revolutionise your life, including the way you pray, minister and operate in the things of God.

In the light of the above, start to speak things you want to see manifested in your life. If you are going for a job interview, say that you are going to have favour with everyone you meet, and you will be successful. If you are sick, start telling your body that it is strong and healthy and that no sickness can survive in such a healthy state. Create your day each morning by speaking what you believe will be created that you will be successful in all that you do, that you are full of energy and this will cause things to shift from the invisible realm to the visible realm and will also take you from normal to supernatural. This is what we call *commanding your morning*. When you command your morning, you give your reality divine assignments and pull success from the spiritual realm into your day. On the basis of this principle, you can also speak to Miracle money and it will obey and appear wherever you want it to.

DIVINE FREQUENCY

The glory travels through space and time.

The glory of God can be carried by invisible sound waves travelling through time and space. That is why it is possible for you to watch a miracle crusade on television that was filmed 3 months back and you receive Miracle money while watching it. It's because the glory has travelled through time and space to you. Even though you were not there when the actual crusade took place, whenever you watch it, the same glory is reactivated and you receive the same impartation of Miracle money as if you had been there 3 months ago. The glory of the meeting that took place at a particular time is frozen and reactivated the moment you watch it. So, the voice waves of the one speaking, the worship and the very atmosphere in that meeting can be contained in sound and light in the form of images and can be reactivated. That is why it is important to watch DVDs of anointed man of God because there is an impartation of Miracle money grace from these meetings frozen in time, waiting for you to receive it and release it by just pushing the play button of the DVD player.

This is the same principle by which the Bones of Elisha held a reservoir of glory and sound waves of power such that a man who was thrown into the same grave where Elisha had been buried more than four hundred years back was instantly resurrected (1 Kings 13:21). This is simply because the glory travels through space and time and in this case, it had travelled ahead more than four hundred into the future such that the same degree of resurrection glory which soaked into Elisha's body during his life time on earth was still present to raise the dead. As Elisha was now in a higher realm of glory in Heaven, his body was now the only point of contact to transmit the glory between Heaven and earth. This is what we call *Elisha glory,* when a torch of the last generation is passed to the next generation with even greater power. This is to tell you that the glory travels through time and space, which is why in in the glory realm, one can be divinely transported in the spirit dimension to other places just like the experience of Philip in Azotus. That is why multitudes of believers shall experience *divine transportation* in the spirit in the end times days.

DOMINION OVER THE TIME FACTOR

The realm of glory falls outside the time dimension in the natural realm, hence functioning in that realm grants us dominion over time.

It is worth exploring the divine truth that as believers, we have authority over time, hence we can command Miracle money to manifest in the now or at whatever time we want it to appear and it will be established in the realm of the spirit. This is because time is not one of the characteristics of God. God is not defined by time because He lives, functions and operates in the eternal realm that is outside our time dimension. Time is not an absolute because it only exists when its parameters are defined by absolutes. God set the earth in time while man was created from the eternal realm. Although man lives on earth, he doesn't operate according to earthly time because he was created in the eternal realm which falls outside the scope or domain of time. Man was never designed to function according to earthly time. It was only after the fall that the clock started ticking. Heaven is governed by the glory which is the realm of eternity where there is no time. Therefore, when we are caught up into the glory, we experience *"timelessness"*. The eternity realm is the womb from which time came. In other words, eternity existed before time. Time is the offspring of the eternal design. Time was created or set in creation after eternity on the fourth day. God set the sun to rule by day and the moon to rule by night, thereby establishing time and season. That is why we have dominion over time because we were created first in the eternal realm which is outside the time dimension of the earth.

With this understanding, when operating in the realm of glory, the key is to learn the art of how to speak from the eternal realm into the realm of time. In the gory realm, time does not exist as we consider it on earth. The only thing that can break the cycle of time is faith. Faith is a higher law than time. It is the ascent out of time into the eternal realm. For a man who knows his rights as a citizen of Heaven, time is made to serve him. Man was not designed to serve time. Time is a part of matter, not a matter of time. Faith is God's matter - the substance or material which represents elements which are made by God to serve an eternal purpose. Time was designed and created specifically for this earth. It doesn't exist outside this planet. The reality is that when people loose track of time and step into the eternal, the eternal becomes real and the supernatural becomes your normal. In this Kairos moment, God is bridging you from time into the eternal realm whereby it is naturally supernatural to perform miracles. That's when you will realise that the eternal is more real than time. The truth is that miracles are in a higher realm, without the influence of time, while our circumstances are the product of time with a beginning and an end.

DIVINE SPEED AND ACCELERATION

The realm of glory is a realm of divine speed and acceleration.

It is worth exploring the divine truth that speed and acceleration are key processes involved in the manifestation of Miracle money in the natural realm because God's work needs to be accomplished with a sense of urgency in this season. As the Body of Christ, we are about to enter a new season in Church history, a phase that goes beyond the initial Pentecostal experience. When this glory invasion is fully realised, it will usher in a supernatural acceleration of the things of God. To substantiate this truth with reference to a quintessential example, Elijah prayed and saw the first sign as small as a man's hand and the Bible says when he saw it, he gird his loins and outran King Ahab's horse which was probably the fastest and best fed horse in the country. But how possible is it that a man can outrun a horse while he is on foot? Running is a prophetic sign, symbolic of divine speed and acceleration in the realm of the spirit. That was a *dramatic prophetic gesture*. It was a prophetic action of faith, symbolic of how we should move in the spirit dimension to overtake things in the natural realm. While he was seen sprinting in the natural realm, in the spirit realm, that was actually an action of faith. When you read this portion of scripture with the eyes if flesh, you will see Elijah running in the natural realm but if you read with the eye of the spirit, you will see him flying in the spirit. This is a dimension in the spirit called *Holy Ghost transportation*. Elijah was catapulted into a higher realm of glory and divinely transported through the tidal waves of the spirit to Jezreel. Prophetically speaking, as God has already unveiled the first sign of the *glory cloud* heralding a new outpouring of glory in the realm of the spirit, now is the time to run in the dimension of the spirit. As Elijah did, pick up your loins and run so as not to miss the next move of God. Don't just casually walk towards it, but run so you don't miss it. This is the season of the *overtaking anointing*. It's time that you run ahead of everything which represents Ahab's horse in your life.

Did you know that when you are operating in the glory realm, which is outside our time dimension you can actually overtake time in the natural realm. You have two options when operating in the glory realm; it's either you stop the time until you have completed certain divine tasks as exemplified by Joshua or you can simply overtake it. When we stop the cloak, we step backwards in time but when we overtake it, we step forward. That is why the Bible concurs that in this *Kairos* moment, we have unequivocally stepped into Amos 9:13— a critical moment in which *the ploughman is overtaking the reaper and the treader of grapes him that sows a seed*. While the *Reaper* is harvesting as fast as he can, on his heels comes the *Ploughman,* who is already preparing another harvest in the soil that the reaper has just harvested. This infers that in this final chapter of human history, all of eternity is pouring into the present, causing us to accelerate forward. In other words, we have entered *the rush hour* of God, a critical moment in God's calendar in which things are moving so fast in the realm of the spirit as we are adjourning quickly towards the second coming of the Lord, Jesus Christ. The truth is that the glory is an accelerator; hence what would normally take years happens in a moment in the gory realm. Those who don't understand the operation of the glory realm are forced to wait for the date the doctor has set for them to receive their healing. This is an error because the glory realm is a realm of speed and acceleration where there is neither procrastination, postponement nor delays. If the doctor has told you to wait for six months, just defy the law of time and activate the higher law of faith; reach into the future and take your healing right now!

DIVINE REVELATION

The realm of glory is a realm of revelation.

It is worth exploring the divine truth that Miracle money is a product of revelation, which is given birth to in the deeper territories of the glory realm. The glory realm itself is also a realm of revelation. It is a realm whereby everything is known. It is beyond the realm of gifts, faith and the anointing. Figuratively speaking, common sense is to the natural man what revelation is to the man in the Glory of God. Revelation comes before manifestation and without revelation there is no acceleration of the manifestation. By the same token, without revelation, Miracle money cannot be demonstrated in the natural realm. Hypothetically speaking, you cannot get fire from water; it takes fire to set a fire in the same way it takes a certain amount of rain to cause a flood. By the same token, without a constant flow of revelation, manifestation will not tarry. *The glory realm is a realm of Revelation.* That is why there is such a thing as *the revelation glory*. This involves allowing God to speak to our spirit when we are basking in the atmosphere of His glory. It incorporates seeing things materialise before they happen and witnessing things happening while they are being spoken. In the spirit realm, unless something is revealed, it remains a mystery. The Bible concurs with the divine truth that *it is the glory of God to conceal a thing but the honour of kings to search out a matter* (Proverbs 25:2). It is important to unveil the divine truth that Miracle money is manifested through *revelation*. Unless and if you have a personal revelation of what Miracle money is, where it comes from, how it operates and manifest, it might be a daunting task for you to manifest it's results in the natural realm. I'm not talking about saying what a pastor has said or trying to do what you have seen men of God doing but I'm talking about receiving your own revelation from God concerning Miracle money. The reason why certain miracles do not happen is because people do not have a personal revelation of how to operate or flow in them. This is why God is raising a distinct calibre of believers whom He shall breed in His presence, to ignite the passion for progressive revelation in this end times.

The greater truth is that what is revelatory to the Heavens is prophetic to the earth. The distinguishing characteristic feature of the glory realm is that in Heaven, things are not learnt but they are revealed. In other words, it is not possible to study and learn the revelatory realm. It must be revealed and this explains why Paul wrote three quarters of the New Testament when in actual fact he never went to a Bible school. This is what defines the distinction between *theology* and *revelation*. While theology is a human attempt to explain God's word and His works in a reasonable and systematic way, revelation is the mind of God revealed to our spirits and is received by spiritually seeing, hearing and perceiving. This is knowledge beyond mere memorisation of scriptures but spiritual perception or nuggets of spiritual truths and divine insights emanating directly from the Throne Room of Heaven. It is the mind of God revealed so that mankind could exercise dominion over time, space and matter. Notable in this reagrd is the realisation that it is possible to learn the operation of the prophetic realm, but not the revelatory realm. There is a world of difference between the *revelatory* and the *prophetic experience*. They are governed by different rules, as the one originates from the Throne of Glory, and the other originates from this fallen atmosphere. The truth is that Heaven operates in present tense, while the earth has different time zones or tenses. Here, we have the past, present and future perfect tense. If anything comes to the earth from the Heavens, it has to fit into one of these three tenses in order to remain in the earth and manifest in these three dimensional realms. It has come into the earth, leave the realm of eternity from where it came and penetrate the realm of time. For this to happen, it must be framed, or proclaimed by the words of our mouth. Then it remains in our time zone, and will manifest to us in the natural realm. In view of the above, it is therefore scripturally evident that revelation is such an indispensable necessity to unlocking the supernatural doors to abundance. Without revelation, Miracle money remains a mystery and God's people remain trapped in a morass of debilitating poverty.

DIVINE ORCHESTRATION

The glory realm is the birthplace for all creation; everything was created from the realm of glory.

It is a divine truth that Miracle money is a product of God's glory as it originates in the glory realm. Before the beginning began, God existed. He always was eternal. Before the beginning, there was nowhere for Him to come from. This is why He had to create *"the beginning"*. While the majority of believers seem to subscribe to this divine truth, some folks erroneously believe that God created the earth out of nothing and that everything came out of the blue, out of the invisible matter. No! That is not the correct picture because everything He created was already in Him. So, when He spoke, and said *let there be light,* light proceeded from within the depths of His being into manifestation in the natural realm. That is why with an indwelling presence of the Holy Spirit, everything you will ever need in life is in you. Therefore, we follow the same pattern which God used to speak things from within our being into existence. Isn't it amazing that God created all things out of himself? As He called, *light be,* light came forth from the depth of His being into existence. When God said, *Let there be light,* what came forth was the voice of the almighty penetrating the vastness of His perception in the eternal realm as He spoke into existence that which He had already created within His being. The very essence of His thought life was thrust into existence, and seen when He spoke. Thoughts became words, words became objective reality. All He had to do was to call out of Himself those things which were a part of His glory and they responded. The sound of His voice preceded the visible manifestation of each creative work. In this final chapter of human history, the lion of the tribe of Judah is therefore roaring again, unleashing the sound of heaven on earth through the end time generation. It could therefore be deduced that everything that you will ever need in this life, be it miracles, finances, healings, prosperity, is available in the glory realm. The glory realm is a spiritual reserviour that inhabits the riches in Christ glory which Paul spoke about in Ephesians. It is your birth right to tread in the deepest territories of the glory realm, hence you should tap into the atmosphere of glory to speak anything that you want to see happen in this world and it shall be established for you.

In view of the above, it is worth exploring the divine truth that the Glory realm is the realm of our birth; it's where we were born into the glory. That's were our true identity and origin is. We were created in the realm of glory. We are from there. Our origin is in the glory, in the Heavenly realm. By the same token, Miracle money also originates from the same realm. Heaven is the only place in eternity that is named, and yet, Heaven is created. Heaven is the Capital of the Eternal Realm that is why it is a city. To elucidate more on this divine truth, the Bible speaks of *three* Heavens. The *first Heaven* is the atmosphere around the earth. The *second Heaven* is the atmosphere where Lucifer and his fallen angels were assigned to exist, between the third Heaven and the earth. The *third Heaven* is where we find God's throne room. This is where the Glory of God dwells. This is where we originated. This atmosphere is where we long to be, because it is where we came from. Therefore, when we get hungry for the presence of God, we are actually homesick for the atmosphere He created us in.

Have you ever asked God to take you back in time through the spirit dimension to an epic era before conception when you were a created spirit before His throne? Only in that realm would you fully comprehend that you were created in the *Throne Room* of Heaven. The reality is that when we are born again, God places His glory in our spirit so that we receive the divine *"breath of life"* and His spiritual DNA. God's DNA contains His glory as His son Jesus. Before being born again, we had Adam's sinful DNA, but now we have God's sanctified DNA hence, we can always carry the glory of God wherever we go. However, the greatest challenge facing us as believers is that we are more comfortable talking about the anointing, instead of manifesting the glory, which is denotes our birth place in the spirit realm. We have already been in this realm before. We were created there. Now, we must learn how to access it once again, and re-enter its atmosphere. That is why Paul uses the phrase *"Whom He foreknew"* to show that we have known this glory realm before. We have functioned and operated in it before the foundations of the earth. Now, we are just replaying the tap in which we have featured as actors before and acting like a man trampling on his own footsteps where he had walked before.

CHAPTER FIVE

A DIVINE REVELATION OF HIGHER LAWS OF FINANCIAL PROSPERITY

What Divine Principles Can We Take Advantage of In Order To Rain Down Miracle Money from Heaven?

In order to have an in-depth understanding of the dynamics of Miracle money, it is imperative that you secure a revelation of the higher laws of finance because Miracle money is accessed not based on what you have done but on the grace of God. In our endeavour to pursue the end time financial prosperity agenda and amass humungous financial wealth from Heaven, it is vital that we introspect ourselves and relook into our theology to see from a different light if there is something relating to godly prosperity that we cannot see clearly. Amongst these things which should be re-looked into is what I call *higher laws of finance*. Apparently, dozens of preachers and ministers of the gospel have always customarily over emphasized the *law of sowing and reaping* above all other laws as a prime law by which God prospers His people. In some cases the survival of pastors depends on the message they preach, hence there is a tendency to over emphasise certain portions of scripture especially where money is concerned. To the extreme end of the scale, some even rant and rave about sowing and reaping yet their congregants continue to be entraped in a morass of dibilitating poverty. It is a typical scenario in some charismatic cycles to find Christians who sow and then claim a hundred fold increase in return to what they would have sown in hope that whatever they sow would bring forth a bumper harvest, yet there are other *higher laws of finance* which believers could apply in order to reap the same bumper harvest quickly and bountifully. It is worth exploring the divine truth that Miracle money is not a product of sowing and reaping. In other words, you don't have to sow in order to reap Miracle money. Instead, it is based on higher laws of finance which places a recipient in a position of favour, to receive from God even without doing anything to reciprocate His gesture of love. Millions of believers in the Body of Christ are rigorously engaged in sowing and reaping in the hope of becoming millionaires but the sober truth is: How many of them are Millionaires? Very few! Why? Because there is more to prosperity than just sowing and reaping, which is a basic, entry level law in the realm of God's prosperity. Three higher laws of finance seem to surface with regard to the practical demonstration of Miracle money in this last season shortly before the Master comes back for the Grand Finale of the earth. And these are, *the law of reaping where you did not sow, the law of buying without money and the law of loosing and appropriating money.*

THE LAW OF REAPING WHERE YOU DID NOT SOW

One striking reality is that as I assiduously examined the scriptures and analytically looked at all the laws of finance which have been brought forth and overemphasized by modern day preachers, God began to show me something from a different light. There is a higher law of finance than what preachers have over emphasized and this is *the law of reaping where you did not sow*. Notable is the realisation that in the realm of God, there are *greater truths* and *lesser truths*. By the same token, there are *higher laws* and *lesser laws* of finance. Althaugh hailed as a universal key to every financial breakthrough in the realm of the spirit, the law of sowing and reaping is a lesser law while the divine concept of *reaping where you did not sow* is a higher law in the realm of God's financial prosperity. Taking into account the nature of the end time season in which we have been ushered as per God's calendar, we no longer just rely only on the law of sowing and reaping as a key determinant for our financial prosperity. If God were to wait for the church to reap what we sow, it would take a considerable length of time for the church to reap everything He wants us to reap before the Lord Jesus Christ comes back. Even if it's a hundred fold harvest, the church will not be able to reap all that which Jesus wants us to experience or be blessed with before His second coming. If God were to rely just on what we sow, the church of Jesus Christ may never reach the fullness of what God wants us to receive. Notable is the fact that if we only reap what we sow, there is a sense in which it is limited to our own works. Therefore, there has to be a higher law of finance that comes forth like a booster, which God has provided to expedite His divine plans and purpose in this end time season which marks the conclusion of His eternal plan on earth.

It is for this reason that in this end time season, God is propagating the grace for Miracle Money so as to speed up His divine plans and purpose concerning financial prosperity and provision. The release of Miracle Money is therefore what I call *a practical demonstration of signs and wonders in the arena of our finances*. It is unequivocally evident that God uses Miracle money for His children to catch up where they have lacked behind financially. So, Miracle money is a catalyst that speed up the rate at which finances are supernaturally dispatched in the natural realm to expedite God's purpose. Prophetically speaking, in this season of Miracle money, the Lord shall accelerate you to your divine destiny, the gravity of faith shall propel you into the future and the power of the Spirit shall catapult you to highest realms of Glory whereby you shall amass humongous financial wealth from Heaven like a farmer sent out to the field for a bumper harvest. What could have taken you months of sowing and reaping will be manifested in a flip of a moment; what could have taken you years of toiling and labouring to accomplish, you will achieve it in few minutes; and what could have taken you years of studying and researching to figure out, will be revealed in a twinkling of an eye. This is to tell you that speed and acceleration are twin processes behind the manifestation of our financial breakthrough in this critical season. It should come to no surprise that your life is programmed to move progressively in one direction, upward and forward only. There is no reverse gear to your walk of faith with God. There is neither a bus stop, parking lot nor road block in your journey into the spirit dimension. Pertaining to the pursuit of His end time financial prosperity agenda, the Lord once said that,

> *"I desire to do signs and wonders in the finances of every one of My children, because they've been so far behind. The only way I can really bring them up in their finances before Jesus comes is to do miracles, signs and wonders in their finances." God said, "I'm going to do a quick work in order to get the money back into the hands of My children. I'm going to show signs and wonders in the arena of finances, because My people have been lagging behind for too long. Those who will take Me at My Word, I'm going to do a quick work in their finances."*

This is to tell you how expedient it is to be catapulted into the realm of Kingdom millionaires to fulfil God's plan in this end time season. As far as God is concerned, miracles, signs, and wonders are the only means for believers to catch up to where He has always wanted them to be in terms of their financial prosperity. Therefore, He will do whatever it takes to ensure that they are brought to that realm of plenty. In other words, in the same way God took Paul and Silas out of prison with speed and haste (Acts 16:16-40), He is going to do some things *"immediately"* and *"suddenly"* in people's lives to provide a supernatural escape from poverty and lack into a realm of super abundance. Owing to lack of revelation, many people have always thought that signs and wonders are only about lame people walking again, the blind receiving their sight, deaf ears being opened and the dead being raised but God wants to perform signs and wonders in people's *finances* too. In other words, in this season, we don't have enough time left for us to go the old confession route. Certainly, we have to maintain our faith and our confession but in this end time season, God is going to add a *booster* to our confession so that we can experience a torrent of miracles, signs, and wonders in our finances. God said, "I will do a *quick* work with their money so that they will know that it is of Me. Philosophically speaking, if you could think of the speed of a jet plane flying overhead, that is how fast things are going to happen in many people's finances. And if you could think of the number of stars in the sky on a clear night, that is how much money He's going to pour on the members of the Body of Christ who steadfastly hold on to this divine revelation. However, the power to create miracles, signs and wonders in your finances will not be activated until you learn to depend totally on God's Word. More so, your faith has to be unhindered by religious beliefs and misconstrued traditions of the past that you have perhaps been holding on to.

It is imperative that in order to receive a humongous financial breakthrough and millions of wealth in our lives, we need to practically demonstrate signs and wonders in our finances. This is in view of the fact that as much as money is natural, on the other side of the coin, it is also spiritual. The Bible concurs with this revelation as it asserts that the *things which are seen are made out of the things which are not seen* (Hebrews 11:3). That means there is an original blue print of money in all currencies of this world in the realm of the spirit. Therefore, in order to release money which is a spiritual subject, we need to practically demonstrate signs and wonders in our finances so that money can come swiftly and speedily from the realm of the spirit into the realm of the natural. However, it is disheartening to note that while multitudes of Christians have tapped into the realm of demonstrating the power of God in healings, miracles and deliverance, very few hardly get to think about demonstrating signs and wonders in their finances yet this is critical in the release of our millions of wealth in this present time. It is for this reason that as part of the last wave of prosperity in this end time season, God uses Miracle money to bless His children so that it can be ingrained in their thinking that money is spiritual. Hence, in order to cause its abundant and humongous manifestation in the natural realm, signs and wonders must be demonstrated in our finances.

It is worth exploring the divine truth that speed and acceleration are crucial ingredients which characterises the move of the Spirit in this end time season. In other words, there is a heightened degree of acceleration in the realm of God's financial prosperity. The Lord showed me recently in an encounter how time is running out and eternity is rushing in. In this experience, I began to understand how in the Book of Amos, the ploughman could overtake the reaper—the eternal realm was literally overtaking time in the natural. As the Body of Christ, we are standing at the threshold of a new era—the brink of a new age. The power for acceleration is in the timeless realm of God's Glory. When the realm of the Glory of God moves into the realm of the natural, there comes a great acceleration for financial prosperity and the release of creative power to create wealth. It is vital to step into maturity—as you encounter new realms of God's supernatural financial provision. Therefore, in this end time season, seeds of destiny are ready for reaping. The Lord has shown me that we are in this time of acceleration; we have stepped into Amos 9:13—*"the ploughman will overtake the reaper."* All of eternity is pouring into the present causing us to accelerate forward. Seeds that have been sown in the past, seeds of destiny, are full-grown and ready for reaping. As the realm of eternity is meshed with the present, we are witnessing a culmination of events—loose ends are being tied up before the return of Christ. Things that would normally take ten years to happen will only take ten months—even ten weeks. There is a rapid maturity taking place in the Body of Christ as the cloud of His presence descends and blankets us corporately. This season is not simply coming—it is here!

Therefore, in this critical season, God has reserved this truth and understanding that it is not by works but by grace of God that we will be able to enter into the realm of supernatural financial prosperity that God wants us to step into. In this season, you don't just reap what you sow but you reap what Jesus sowed. It is on the basis of this revelation that many believers shall reap humungous wealth from Heaven and be elevated into the realm of Kingdom millionaires even without sowing anything. Therefore, in this season, God is saying to us,

A Divine Revelation of Higher Laws of Financial Prosperity

"Come up higher in your finances there is a higher law of finance you can tap into.

Contrary to how dozens of preachers have stigmatised it, sowing and reaping is an entry level, training phase or elementary truth in the realm of God's financial prosperity and abundance. The greater truth is that all those things which we have learnt in sowing and reaping are just an epitome of God' training ground for us so that upon maturity, we can progress or migrate to God's higher laws of financial prosperity. God wants to elevate and awaken us to a higher law, which is learning to reap not what we sow but what Jesus sowed. This is such a powerful revelation which if understood across the Body of Christ, shall unreservedly release the superabundance that God has determined for you in this end time season. The question you are probably asking yourself is: *But what did Jesus sow?* He sowed His entire being and whole life -- everything that He had, everything that He represented when He came here to earth, He laid it at the cross as a seed and sowed for us. Therefore, one of the notable blessings of the finished works of Christ is that it has now ushered us into a realm of superabundance and thus, put a definite halt to a life of untold hardship, fruitless toils and bitter experiences. And if every believer could get this spiritual reality engrained in their thinking that Jesus freely sowed for us to reap bountifully, then practically demonstrating millions in Miracle money will be a walk through a park.

To cement this revelation with reference to scriptural evidence, in Deuteronomy 6:10, it is strikingly interesting to note what God said to the children of Israel just before they went into the land of Canaan.

God promised to give them cities which they did not built, wells which they did not dig, and vine yards which they did not plant.

It is evident on the basis of the above mentioned scriptural evidence that obviously the promise of the land of Canaan was not reaped because of what they sow. Instead, it was reaping a promise and blessing which God had given to Abraham. If they had to reap what they sow for Israelites to enter into the land of Canaan, it would have been very meagre because most of the time they were complaining and grumbling against God. They did not know how to sow yet they were reaping and they didn't even reap what they deserved. Instead, they got everything that they obtained by the grace of God. No way could they have reaped what they sowed in such a huge expanse of Canaan. So, they reaped what Abraham sowed as they looked forward in time to the coming of the Lord Jesus Christ to earth. This divine truth is corroborated by the Apostle John's remark that *I sent you to reap that which you have not laboured: others have laboured, and you have entered into their labour* (John 4:38 (ASV). It is interesting to note that the act of reaping here is tied to Abraham, Isaac and Jacob, in what we call the *Abrahamic covenant*. When God spoke to Abraham that was way back in Genesis 12, where He said *in you shall all the families of the earth be blessed* (Genesis 22:18), it was this blessing given to Abraham which the Children of Israel later reaped without doing anything or working for it. When God said to Abraham all the families of the earth shall be blessed through you, He meant that Abraham was now being bequeathed the inheritance of the entire world which Adam lost to the devil in the playground of the Garden of Eden. In Galatians 3:13-14, Paul tells us that Jesus was hung on the cross so that all the blessings of Abraham might gravitate upon us through the Holy Spirit. Imbued with this understanding, you suddenly realise that as a seed of Abraham, the whole world is yours and that all the silver and gold, measured by the best currencies of the world, are yours to unreservedly indulge.

It is unequivocally evident that everything which Jesus sowed for us have to be reaped by the church before it is taken out by the rapture. Therefore, let's move into the *higher laws of finance* and not just depend on what we sow. However, I'm not ruling out the idea that people should give but I'm awakening believers to the divine consciousness that they are levels in which divine truths are ranked in the spirit as there are greater truths and lesser truths. I believe a hundred fold is a fantastic law but God wants to accelerate the manifestation of His blessings as we step into the higher realm of believing what Jesus has sown. Thank God for the entry level principle of sowing and reaping but due to the urgency and perspicacity with which divine tasks have to be executed in this season, you need to go further than the basics of the law of sowing and reaping and begin to declare that *I'm going to reap what Jesus sowed*. By so doing, you will be thrilled at how you shall trigger a heavy torrential downpour of God's financial rain in your life. In Galatians 3, Paul expounds on the prophecy that *Abraham will be the heir to the world* when he says *to the Seed he will give* and the word "*Seed*" has a capital letter "*S*" which denotes the person of Jesus. Subsequently, Jesus came to the world, died on the cross and fulfilled the promise such that the whole world through the precious blood of Jesus Christ now by legal spiritual transaction belong to Jesus and Satan and his cohorts have been reduced to zero and legally they have no more rights to this earth. This debunks the wayward mentality of the devil's crowd that he can give Miracle money. How can the devil give something that he doesn't even have? In Galatians 3: 8, Paul unveils the fact that *those who are of faith are blessed through their divine connection to Abraham*. The truth is that as a born again believer, you are called and separated unto the blessing of God. Therefore, you don't have to do anything to be blessed; just because you are in Christ, you are in Abraham and you are already blessed. Through the revelation that Jesus has sown for us and has paid the price for the entire world, we now reap or partake of all the blessings which Christ has brought through His precious blood, hence there is not even one single thing we need to do to reciprocate the blessing. In a sense, you don't have to sow in order to receive because Jesus has already sown for us. All other spiritual exercises such as prayer and fasting, we do them not because we want to reap what we have sown but we want to align our spirits so that we can move swiftly in the spirit dimension to get hold of what is already ours. As far as God is concerned, spiritual exercises such as fasting, prayer, giving are elementary truths or teachings of the gospel. The law of sowing and reaping was originally designed to teach us this principle. It is an elementary teaching. It works just like how we teach a child. In order to train a child, you start with the fundamentals or basics and once the child has learnt and grasped these, only then would you move to solid staff. In the same way, sowing and reaping as a spiritual law was originally designed to teach us what Jesus has done. All these laws are essential as they tell us in a little picture what God has done in a big picture but the sad thing is that many believers get stuck in the lesser and lower laws such that they don't realise that there is a higher law up there that is already been fulfilled for us. The law of sowing and reaping was a small picture of the biggest seed of what God has done. God has sown Jesus for us for He died so that we might receive all the fullness of His blessings and that is *the higher law of finance*. And when we understand that, the next question would be: *How do we tap into this higher law?*

In a practical sense, you must not just believe God based on what you are, what you have or what you can do because there is a sense in which that is tied to your own works. Instead, believe God based on what Jesus had done. Jesus has sown in an unlimited measure, hence we just to have faith to rise and take what Jesus has freely done for us. God can move us into a higher realm to receive by His grace what we cannot receive by our works. The minute we believe that we are entitled to receive from God based on what we have done, we shut ourselves against the covenant of grace. One other striking reality is that the law of sowing and reaping operates for all human beings whether they know God or not. It is as workable as the law of gravity, it affects both Christians and non–Christians. That means non-Christians who actually sow, do reap too and that explains why some of them are wealthy even if they do not know God. It is therefore not good enough for Christians to solitarily rely on a law that works for everybody because I believe that there should be a demarcation line that clearly distinguish between Christians and non-Christians. Partaking in the portion of unbelievers through sharing the same level of grace is not good enough. However, for those who have a blood covenant, there is a higher law of reaping what Jesus sowed and this is a higher law which Jesus wants to bring us into in this season that will clearly distinguish between believers from unbelievers. That is why God is populating this world with Miracle money as a mark of distinction engraved upon His chosen ones.

Now, the question is: *How does this higher law operate?* The answer is simple! By accepting and embracing everything Jesus has done for you on the cross and freely positioning yourself to receive and partake of the blessings which are legally and rightfully yours. This is done through the dynamic working of the Spirit, intimacy with God through spiritual encounters, the degree of manifestation of God's presence and deep expressions of faith. Therefore, if you want to function in the arena of God's unlimited financial prosperity, just plunge yourself into the greater depths of God's presence to access the unlimited financial blessings and you will be instantly catapulted into the realm of millionaires. According to Galatians 3:14, when you exercise faith in God, you receive it through the Spirit. Your spiritual capacity to receive or the extent to which your spirit man is developed is what determines how much of God's financial provision you can receive and not how much you have sown. It is through the Spirit of God which illuminates a revelation in your spirit and drops a spiritual substance that you are able to produce the wealth according to the grace God has for your life. Therefore, let's migrate to higher laws of finance which Paul describes as weightier matters of the Kingdom. When the whole Body of Christ catches this revelation, we will be able to believe God not just based on what we have or what we are able to sow. This is what will provoke an avalanche of the river of Miracle money, streaming copiously from the Throne Room of Heaven, to precipitate upon the masses who are connected to God's grace in the natural realm. Therefore all the **SEVEN** dimensions of supernatural financial prosperity such as *Miracle money, Wealth transfer, Supernatural Debt cancellation, Supernatural multiplication of wealth, the golden rain, Supernatural Recreation of substances and Reclamation of lost property* are not based on the law of sowing and reaping but on the higher laws of financial prosperity because you have full access to partake of their portion even without sowing anything. They are accessed based on the availability of God's grace, glory and degree of manifestation of His presence and not how much you have sown.

THE LAW OF BUYING WITHOUT MONEY

Have you ever walked into a shop and bought things without paying for them, or you were at the airport and while waiting in the queue to pay for the plane ticket, somebody else pays for you or you were in a restaurant and while waiting to pay the bill, somebody else settles it on your behalf or you were at a fuel station and while you wait to pay for your full tank, somebody interrupts you and pay the bill? If yes, then you will easily understand this divine principle of buying without money. By buying without money, I don't mean walking into a supermarket and using your faith to pay for your groceries. No! I mean being in a situation when you are expected to pay for a service rendered or a product bought, then all of a sudden, someone appears from nowhere and pays for you. This is highly attributable to the work of angels in the invisible realm in which a supernatural influence is released in the realm of the spirit that compels forces of divinity to work on your behalf. This is a higher law of finance because through it is the grace of God exhibited to its highest degree, without any reservations. There are divine arrangement of circumstances in the realm of the spirit that causes Heaven's attention to be directed towards you such that you just find yourself in a situation in which people are paying things for you, without necessarily having to ask them to. This is still Miracle money but manifesting in another form. It's Miracle money in the sense that there is a monetary value attached to what you could have paid but then by God's grace, somebody else is paying for you.

This is what Jesus described in prophetic language as *"Buying without Money"*. Jesus made a public declaration saying *"Hey there! All who are thirsty, come to the water! Are you penniless? Come anyway—buy and eat! Come, buy your drinks, buy wine and milk. Buy without money—everything's free! Why do you spend your money on junk food, your hard-earned cash on cotton candy? Listen to me, listen well: Eat only the best, fill yourself with only the finest. Pay attention, come close now, listen carefully to my life-giving, life-nourishing words* (Isaiah 55:1). Although this revelation was spoken in the context of salvation, there is a sense in which it relates to God's supernatural financial provision. It is irrefutably evident in this season of Miracle money that Jesus is re-echoing the same words which He uttered thousands of years back and He is calling men and woman to step out of the level of impossibility thinking to a realm of superabundance in which they unreservedly partake of His grace without paying anything. Do you notice the language of money which Jesus uses in the above-mentioned portion of scripture? He says, *Buy without money—everything's free!* Clearly, He is not talking about buying the anointing, power or healing here because these ones cannot be commoditized as they are rendered free of charge. Instead, He is talking about Miracle money which He is freely pouring out upon the masses who accept and embrace His saving grace in the light of His creation. Consider the rhetoric question which Jesus is asking you in this season: *Why do you spend your hard-earned cash on cotton candy?* Isn't it interesting to note that Jesus is against the idea of you spending your hard-earned money on things which you could easily obtain using Miracle money? This is to tell you how eager Jesus is to ease your burden so that you don't labor and toil from dusk till dawn for the substance of money when you can receive it supernaturally. In the realm of the spirit, a door has been wide opened and Jesus is saying, *"Come, you who do not have money, come eat and drink"*. Do you notice that in the context of this scripture, what Jesus is saying here is that He wants to give you money so that you can pay all your bills? Depending on the amount received, some recipients of Miracle Money will use it to for Kingdom expansion purposes such as building churches, conference centres, sponsoring Kingdom projects, taking care of the needy and orphans while others will use it to simply pay their bills and cover their debts. This is the extent to which Miracle money shall be widely manifested in this season. In view of the above scripture, people tend to ask a question, *"Can God give anybody money without working for it?"* Emphatically, Yes! He can because He is revealing to us His integral role as the father who cares for His children. Miracle money is given by God free of charge, even without working for it or paying for it or doing anything but it's a manifestation of God's grace as a way of showing deep love and care to His people. In this regard, an open invitation is still being made by God through the angels, calling men and women to step up in faith to freely access the grace which He has reserved for His children. Miracle money is one of those free gifts which God wants His children to partake of in these end times.

THE LAW OF RELEASING AND APPROPRIATING MONEY

It is worth exploring the divine truth that Money is not just a theoretical concept but a practical phenomenon. In your quest to becoming Kingdom Millionaires and Billionaires, you must make a practical demonstration by commanding money into existence. This is the essence of the *Law of appropriation*. The principle is that if you don't release Miracle money in the spirit realm, it remains hanging over the atmosphere. Have you ever wondered why the Bible says that *we are blessed with all spiritual blessings in the Heavenly places* yet multitudes of believers are still entangled in a morass of dibilitating poverty? It's simply because they have not yet learnt how to appropriate their blessings from the spirit realm into tangible manifestation in the natural realm. God has placed humungous blessings in the Store Houses of Heaven but it is your responsibility to approproate them by transmuting them into a tangible form in the natural realm. It is disheartening to note that multitudes of believers continues to enjoy the limited outer court of God's blessings and while some might have received *some* return on their giving and experienced *some* financial blessings, the truth is that we haven't gotten our money loosed yet as we ought. Did you know that the precipitation of Miracle money in the natural realm is a product of the binding and loosing processes that takes place in the realm of the spirit? The greater truth is that this law of appropriation is a higher law of finance which works like a double-edged-sword that dismantles the walls of lack, insufficiency and poverty while at the same time releasing abundance into our lives.

It is worth exploring the divine truth that during Miracle money demonstrations, we must loose Miracle money in the same manner in which we loose our healing. It is of paramount significance to highlight as an introductory perspective to this revelation the fact that many of the scriptures which multitudes of Christians rely on for the exercise of their healing can actually be used to loose money. To cement this revelation with reference to scriptural evidence, Jesus declared in Mathew 18:18, that, *"Verily I say unto you, whatsoever you shall bind on earth shall be bound in Heaven, and whatsoever you shall loose on earth shall be loosed in Heaven"*. Unknown to many folks, this is a higher law of finance in the sense that it authorises the instantaneous release of our finances whenever it is demonstrated in the natural realm. In the context of the above-mentioned scripture, the word "loose" means *to let go, untie, release* and *set free*. This means that through the knowledge of God's Word and His will concerning your prosperity, you can *bind* poverty and lack in your life and *loose* or *release* divine prosperity and abundance. Moreover, the word *"whatsoever"* means anything. Well, does *"anything"* include money? Certainly, it does! It doesn't make any difference what it is, whether it is healing or money or deliverance —if you loose it, Jesus said, *"I will loose it."* Do you realize what Jesus is saying? First, He is saying, in effect, "Whatever is loosed in your life is going to be loosed because *you're* doing the loosing, not Me. It's not up to Me to loose it first. *You* are to 'call the shots.' But when you loose something according to My Word, no one can stop it from being loosed"! Therefore, whether you loose hundreds, thousands, millions or billions in Miracle money into your account, the bottom line is that they shall be loosed regardless of quantity.

The other reason why this is a higher law of finance is because it enables us to operate from a higher Heavenly realm in which we are able to bind any demonic principalities responsible for the manipulation and interception of our finances from the spirit realm into the natural realm. Colloquially speaking, in the spirit realm, when you say" *I bind you devourer of my finances,"* you can literally see a string coming and tying down those devils. In a similar vein, if you say to money, *"Money cometh into my bank account now,"* because you are releasing it, you can literally see piles of paper money in all the currencies of the world raining down upon you. Moreover, in the context of our opening scripture above, Jesus said, *"I will loose it in Heaven,"* Note that He is not talking about loosing something in Heaven. Yes, Jesus is in Heaven, but He is "loosing" *from* Heaven, not *in* Heaven. He is speaking of releasing your blessing from a Heavenly realm where you are seated with Him at the right hand of God. As aforementioned, in Heaven, your blessings won't need to be loosed, because they are not bound up! No, Jesus was talking about loosing something on the earth because the money you need is already in the earthly realm although it might be in possession of wicked people. Therefore, when you release it using your Heavenly authority, it is loosed from the hands of the wicked and start to gravitate like a current, streaming in your direction. Owing to lack of revelation, some people think that when you loose money on the earth, the Lord looses money in Heaven. But, no, the Lord in Heaven looses the money which is here on the earth. The Lord is saying, "When you loose money, using your authority on the earth, I will loose the ability to cause that which you said to come to pass." It's as if the Lord is also saying, "Whatsoever you *don't* bind on the earth shall *not* be bound in Heaven. And whatsoever you *don't* loose on earth shall *not* be loosed in Heaven." In other words, He's saying, "I can't permit it unless you permit it." So we know that if *we* permit money to come to us—if we loose it—*God* will permit it to come to us. He will loose it and when God looses something, it is loosed.

Poverty, lack, debt or discontentment cannot hold us anymore, because we can exercise our covenant rights to prosper and be elevated to the realm of millionaires.

To cement this divine revelation with further scriptural evidence, the Bible records in Mathew 13:17-2, an incident whereby Jesus loosed a woman whose back had been bunt over for over eighteen years. According to the narrative, Jesus commanded, *"Woman thou art loosed from thine infirmity"*, and she was instantly loosed. Do you notice that when Jesus loosed the woman from the bondage, results were instantaneous? There was no procrastination due to unwavering faith. This is the same principle by which Miracle money is demonstrated. When you command it to appear in the natural realm, you must not expect it to appear after hours of prayer but immediately after you command it into manifestation. One striking reality is that according to Jesus, this woman was a daughter of Abraham who had a covenant of healing. Just as it was that woman's right to be loosed from her infirmity, it is *our* right to be loosed from poverty, lack and debt. Christ has redeemed us from the curse of the Law. He has *loosed* us from the curse of the Law. *Poverty* is a curse just as *sickness* is a curse. And *prosperity* is a blessing just as *healing* is a blessing. Just as we have been legally loosed from poverty, we can make certain demands on our covenant and command prosperity—and that includes Miracle money—to come our way. When we say, *"Money, thou art loosed!"* we are boldly testifying and witnessing to the fact that debt, discontentment, discouragement, and lack cannot hold us anymore, because we know our covenant rights and we are using our mouth, not just in words but in power and in much assurance of faith, to appropriate the money we need in the natural realm.

It must therefore be ingrained in your thinking that every time you use the term, *"Money, thou art loosed!"* you'll see with the eyes of faith, Miracle money raining down upon you because you've taken authority over money. You see, you have to *command* money to come to you. You have to make demands on money. The greater truth is that you can't just *wish* it would come; that will never work. You have to use the same authority Jesus used when He said to that woman, *"Woman, thou art loosed from thine infirmity."* In Luke 13, even though Jesus was talking about this woman's healing in connection with the covenant, we know we can apply what He said to other areas, too, such as finances, because our covenant includes more than healing. I want you to understand that if you take your place in Christ and do the things God wants you to do concerning money, it has no other choice except to obey you. It has to be loosed if you command it to. However, you must understand that in some instances, Miracle money might not manifest itself in a direct financial form but indirectly through the deposit of air time into people's cell phones, resuscitation of old equipment, electric gargets or cars without having a mechanic to fix them as well as driving cars without spending money on fuel. During ministerial sessions, the power of God can go beyond the church walls such that it touches and resuscitates malfunctioning possessions of congregates such as cars, electric gargets, animals, pets and anything that belongs to them even in their absence. This is an indirect manifestation of Miracle money because the money that believers could have used to repair these gargets is now used to advance the gospel.

The greater truth is that the key to provoking an avalanche of Miracle money is worship. A heightened degree of Praise and worship can break the chains of financial bondage of poverty, lack or debt and launch us into the depths of financial prosperity and catapult us into the realm of millionaires. To cement this revelation with scriptural evidence, the Bible further records an incident in Acts 16 whereby Paul and Silas had been beaten and thrown in prison for preaching the Gospel:

> *"And when they had laid many stripes upon them, they cast them into prison, charging the jailer to keep them safely, Who, having received such a charge, thrust them into the inner prison, and made their feet fast in the stocks. And at midnight Paul and Silas prayed, and sang praises unto God: and the prisoners heard them. And suddenly there was a great earthquake, so that the foundations of the prison were shaken: and immediately all the doors were opened, and every one's bands were loosed.*

There is a great revelation gleaned in this narrative. Some people have been experiencing "midnight" in their finances, but Jesus have come to bring them daylight. Do you know what I mean by *"midnight"*? I mean, it's dark in the arena of your finances. You love God, attend church and walk in love toward others yet it's dark in your finances. You need an opening somewhere for light to come in on your situation. Miracle money is the solution to that darkness in the arena of finances, which is a product of praise and worship. That's what can happen for you, too, when you pray and sing praises to God. Notice something else about that verse. It says, *"...Suddenly there was a great earthquake and immediately all the doors were opened, and every one's bands were loosed."* God knows how to turn things around for you *suddenly* and cause things to *immediately* become better for you! By the same token, in your finances, you could read that verse this way: *"Suddenly, there was a great earthquake, so that the foundations of debt, distress, discontentment, lack, and poverty were shaken: and immediately all the doors were opened, and everyone's bands were loosed."* God wants to shake the foundation of your money problem and open doors of opportunity for you to have plenty! There's no lock strong enough to lock what Jesus has loosed! There's no rope or chain strong enough to hold back what He's loosed. I tell you, the devil does not have a big enough rope to hold you back and keep you broke!

Moreover, the Bible gives an account of Lazarus in John 11:14 who had died and was four days buried in the grave until Jesus stepped on the scene and turned around the situation. When Jesus came, He commanded, "Lazarus, *come forth!*" Then notice what happened: *And he that was dead came forth, bound hand and foot with grave clothes: and his face was bound about with a napkin. Jesus said unto them, loose him, and let him go.* Note that Lazarus had been in the grave for four days. His sister Martha said to Jesus, "Lord, he stinks by now", but that didn't stop Jesus. In the context of this revelation, our "dead," stinky financial condition is not going to stop Him, either! Jesus has already called us to come forth. When He redeemed us by fulfilling God's great plan of redemption, He called us forth out of darkness and into His light. He called us forth out of poverty and into His riches. But many of us are still bound. We still have on those old grave clothes with that napkin on our face where prosperity is concerned. We haven't seen the truth as we ought. We haven't been able to walk in the light of prosperity as we ought. The way we're going to get ourselves untied and get our money untied is by taking hold of the truth by faith and by *commanding* money to be loosed unto us. We can't "try it and see if it works." And we can't wish money were loosed unto us. No, we have to say, *"Money, thou art loosed!"* and witness a torrential down pour of Miracle money flooding every area where there is lack and insufficiency in our lives, glory to Jesus!

CHAPTER SIX

THE DIVINE SECRETS OF HOW TO PRACTICALLY DEMONSTRATE MIRACLE MONEY FROM THE SPIRIT REALM INTO VISIBLE MANIFESTATION IN THE NATURAL REALM

What Divine Precepts Do I Need to Take Cognisance of In Order to Release Miracle Money?

Speak to money as if it hears you and it will obey and stream in your direction

It must be expressly understood that because you are Abraham's seed, you are under the covenant of an endless and perennial stream flow of God's blessings, hence you are wholly exempted from the calamities of life and its misfortunes such as poverty, lack and debt. By virtue of your covenant of exemption, you can therefore attract only good things to yourself while at the same time repelling anything that does not work for your own good. That means poverty or lack can no longer have a grip on you. This revelation is substantiated with scriptural evidence in Matthew 13:17-21 in which Jesus loosed a woman whose back had been bent over for over 18 years. When Jesus confronted her, He commanded, *"Woman thou art loosed from thine infirmity,"* and she was instantly healed. Notable in this narrative is the realisation that, according to Jesus, this woman was a daughter of Abraham, which implies that she had a covenant of healing. However, owing to ignorance and the lack of revelation of God's word, she was entraped in such a debilitating situation despite the fact that she was a daughter of Abraham, with full divine rights and privileges of prosperity and healing. It is a typical scenario in the Body of Christ today that many people have allowed poverty, lack and sickness to rule their lives even though they are operating under the covenant of prosperity.

Allegorically speaking, just as it was that woman's covenant right to be healed from her infirmity, it is also your right to be released from poverty, lack and debt. This is because Christ has redeemed and set you free from the curse of the Law. The greater truth is that *poverty* is a curse just as *sickness* is a curse while on the other hand *prosperity* is a blessing just as *healing* is a blessing. Therefore, just as you have been legally freed from poverty, you can make divine legitimate demands on your covenant and command Miracle money to come your way. In other words, you should speak directly to money and command it to stream in your direction and it shall be established in the realm of the spirit.

> *In a practical sense, when you say, "Money, or millions, be thou released," you are boldly testifying and witnessing to the fact that poverty, lack, debt, discontent, discouragement or any other form of despondency can no longer hold you.*

Instead, you are taking advantage of your covenant rights and you are using your mouth, not just in words but in power and in much assurance of faith, to place a demand on what is rightfully and legally yours, to appropriate the money you need from the Heavenly realm. And that's where you belong as a child of God—*above only and not beneath* (Deuteronomy 28:13).

There is a principle in the realm of the spirit that everything created by God has sound waves, hears and responds when you speak to it. Likewise, money has sound waves and can here and obey you when you command it to gravitate in a specific direction. It is for this reason that during Miracle money demonstrations, you should speak to money in the same way you speak to a human being, and command it to come and you will be thrilled at how it will speedily stream in your direction without much effort. When you step out in faith and utter the authoritative command, *"Millions in Miracle money, be thou released,"* you will literally see, with the eyes of faith, Miracle money coming to you because in the spirit realm, you would have taken authority over money. The greater truth is that you have to *command* money to come to you. You can't just hope that because you are born again, then money will automatically come your way. You have to speak to it and instruct it to gravitate in your direction. In other words, you have to make authoritative demands on money and not beggarly requests as is the norm in the Christian fraternity today. The greater truth is that you cannot just *wish* money will come to you; that will never work. Instead, you have to use the same authority Jesus used when He said to that woman, *"Woman, thou art loosed from thine infirmity,"* and you will witness an unprecedented avalanche of Miracle money supernaturally streaming in your direction. In Luke 13, even though Jesus was talking about this woman's healing in connection with the covenant, you can also apply what He said to other areas too, such as finances, because your covenant includes more than healing. It comes as a divine package of which Miracle money is a part. The bottom line is that if you take your place in Christ and do the things God wants you to do concerning Kingdom Finance, money has to obey you. It has to be released to you if you command it to be released. This means that becoming a Kingdom Millionaire should never be an issue in this season of Miracle money.

Demonstrate unwavering faith by commanding Miracle Money into manifestation in the physical realm

It must be expressly understood that without faith, it is impossible to demonstrate Miracle money because faith is the only bridge between the spiritual and physical. Faith is like an invisible hand or forces that breakthrough into the spirit realm to get hold on Miracle money and then comes down to manifest it in a form that is visible in the natural realm. That means without faith, one cannot demonstrate Miracle money because faith is a vehicle by which Miracle money is transported from the spirit into the natural realm. The Bible concurs in Ephesians 1:3 that *we are blessed with all spiritual blessings in the Heavenly places* but faith is that commanding force that will propel these blessings from their location or disposition in the spirit to their displacement in the physical realm. Faith is undeniably a spiritual force that brings forth our blessings from the spirit realm to the natural realm. Blessings are released in the spirit but the channel or means by which they are brought to manifestation in the natural realm is by faith. It is for this reason that God says *without faith it is impossible to please God*. By the same token, without faith it is impossible to receive from God because if you can't please God, then you can receive from Him. So, you need faith to please God and you need faith to receive Miracle money from God.

Faith is the key that brings Miracle money into the physical realm. The writer of Hebrews states that, *"Now faith is the substance of things hoped for, the evidence of things not seen"* (Hebrews 11:1). Notable in this regard is the fact that your faith brings what God has accomplished into physical reality. God gives it to you in the spirit, and then faith brings it into the physical realm. Many times you don't know God has answered your prayer because you can't perceive it in the physical realm. You have to believe something is happening beyond your five senses. If you don't believe it until you see it, you won't receive from God. The Bible says you have to believe you receive when you pray. What happens between the time you say, *"Amen"* and the time you see the answer manifested? We learn something about this when we read about the prayers of Daniel. In Daniel 9:20, Daniel is praying, and the angel Gabriel appears and tells him, *"At the beginning of thy supplications the commandment came forth, and I am come to shew thee."* In only three minutes, God answered his prayer. Gabriel said at the beginning of his prayer that God answered him, but it took three minutes for it to become visible. Sometimes it takes a little time to manifest in the physical because people's level of faith has not yet been perfected. Often, we step out of faith and stop the manifestation from coming. Owing to lack of revelation, some people say that God is making them wait to teach them something. That is not scriptural. The Bible says that the Scripture is given to teach us. We can learn through trials, but God doesn't send them to teach us. Miracle money is supposed to manifest the instant you declare it.

It is worth exploring the divine truth that demonstrating the supernatural dimension of Miracle money goes beyond mere confession. It is an expression of faith. To shade more light on this divine truth, the Bible records an incident in Luke 17:1-6 whereby the apostles asked the Lord Jesus to increase their faith following their failure to cast out a demon from a young boy. Contrary to what they expected to hear, in response, Jesus said in effect, *"You don't need more faith. You just need to use the faith you already have."* He said, *"... If you had faith as a grain of mustard seed, you would say unto this sycamore tree, be thou plucked up by the root, and be thou planted in the sea; and it should obey you."* In the context of this revelation, Jesus was not talking just about a sycamore tree. He was giving a physical illustration using objects that were probably in the vicinity of where He was at the time. What was Jesus referring to in regard to the sycamore tree? He was talking about faith's ability to create substances. He said that when you speak to something in faith, whatever you speak to must obey you. To bring this scripture into clarity of explanation, Luke 17:6 could easily read, *"If you say to money, 'Be plucked up and come over to my house,' it should obey you.* In other words, Jesus was saying, *"If you have faith just as a grain of mustard seed, you could do this and you already have that much faith"*. However, it is disheartening to note that some preachers in some circles like to talk about the size of the mustard seed yet Jesus wasn't really emphasizing the *size* of a mustard seed as much as He was emphasizing the power of faith behind the mustard seed. In other words, that mustard seed had the power within itself to cause a big mustard plant to grow, but it had to be planted in order to be effective! In other words, a seed laying on top of the ground can't get the job done. It must be put in the soil. In the same way, your faith has to be planted or spoken, and you have to continue to speak to it to get the job done. Then whatever it is you are using your faith on according to the Word must obey you. In this case, if you speak to money, it will be supernaturally manifested right in front of your eyes. Unfortunately, multitudes of people have been making positive, even Word-based confessions about money, but there's more to it than that. You have to make your confession in the spirit of faith, which believes and speaks (2 Corinthians 4:13). When you know with "much assurance" that money must obey you as the sycamore tree obeyed Jesus in Luke 17, you will begin to see results in your finances. Moreover, Paul declared in Thessalonians 1:5 that *"For our gospel came not unto you in word only...."* Note that Paul didn't say the Gospel didn't come in words, he said it didn't come in words *only*. So, when you're talking about losing money, you can't teach it or learn it in words only but you have to have the truth down in your spirit. Then it will become power unto you for whatever it is you need.

Another negative spiritual gravity that can short-circuit your ability to manifest Miracle money is unwavering faith caused by fear. To deal decisively with this syndrome, don't ever be scared of what people will say in the event that you attempt to demonstrate Miracle money and nothing happens. At least your actions of faith would have been registered as genuine faith in the realm of the spirit. Therefore, if you demonstrate Miracle money and nothing happens, that's not your problem, but God's problem. Your duty is to unwaveringly speak it forth in faith and God's duty is to manifest it in the physical realm. While you are responsible for the *"What"* part of the equation, you must leave the *"How"* part to God. This is because God cannot be put in a box. You can't instruct Him to move in a certain way just because you want to pursue your own agenda. In His sovereignty, God does what He wants to do, whenever He wants to do it and however He wants to do it. Therefore, as much as we have the privileged to demonstrate the Miracle money, this is undertaken within the confines of His will.

Always have an expectation to receive and partake of the grace for Miracle Money

The law of expectation is vital to the manifestation of Miracle money. If you want to receive or demonstrate the grace for Miracle money, you must expect it and it shall be manifested according to your expectation. If you don't expect to receive it, then you won't receive anything. Miracle money does not manifest because you prayed for it, it doesn't manifest where it is needed, instead, it manifests where it is expected. I noticed that in our meetings, people who usually partake of this grace are those who would have paid a price in terms of expecting Miracle money to manifest by rightly positioning their spirit to receive either by preparing bags or wallets where money will be transferred or by verifying their bank balances prior to the ministerial services. Such preparations are registered as actions of faith in the spirit and thus provokes an uninterrupted stream flow of Miracle money in the natural realm. The law of expectation or desire state that spiritual things are given birth to through desire. Unless and if you desire, expect or long for it, you might not have it. Expectation opens an avenue for the power and blessings of God to flow from the spirit realm ito the natural realm unperturbed. *In essence, expectation breeds manifestation.* However, it is disheartening that some people want to be casual about miracles. No one should get used to miracles. Although miracles are supposed to be daily experiences of believers, they should not be taken lightly because every miracle manifested in the natural realm counts in Heaven. Therefore, Miracle money should be a daily occurrence, common experience and order of the day in this "God moment". In the Body of Christ, believers should not only expect money when they are in a service or church gathering. Miracles should be expected outside church bars and doors as well. The reason why some people are not seeing a full display of God's miraculous power is because they have confined it behind church doors and bars. Yet in this present end time era, the anointing and glory of God has been released and has gone forth to all the ends of earth to precipitate everywhere in the streets, offices and the public arena. This is to tell you that you should expect Miracle money in your home, car, office, streets, and everywhere you go and you shall see the abundance of God being displayed in measures you have never seen before.

Dispatch Angel Tellers (angels of finances) to release Miracle Money

It is important that every time you demonstrate Miracle money, you must command angels to visibly appear on the scene and you shall be thrilled at seeing white beautiful transparent figures manifesting visibly in the natural realm. If they don't manifest visibly, they will always leave behind *angel fathers* as a sign that they had been around. This is because Miracle money grace is not independent of angelic manifestation. Instead, they work hand in glove in a similar fashion in which the Holy Spirit works with the anointing. During practical demonstration sessions, as you release angels, Miracle money is released concurrently. When you take an action of faith and declare, *"I command Miracle money into visible manifestation in the natural realm, right now,"* in the invisible arena, angels start dispatching and populating Miracle money in unexpected places without the masses even noticing. Angels are key in this kind of manifestations because they are actively involved in everything that God is doing in the invisible realm. That is why some believers are able to see angels moving in the spirit dimension to the extent of them manifesting visibly in the physical realm whenever the grace for Miracle money is demonstrated. Some angels go to the extent of physically appearing in the congregation as if they are also listening to the message being preached. In the dimension of the spirit, when a minister begins to teach God's word with revelation and power, angels are dispatched because God said, *"I watch over my word to perform it"*. In the context of this scripture, to *perform* means to back it up and release whatever is needed or to produce results of what the Word of God talks about. The question is: *How does God perform His Word?* Although He does it by His Spirit, part of it comes through the work of angels. Because of the high degree of God's glory they carry, whenever angels move into the natural realm, they carry Heavenly spiritual substances, right into our meetings. Angels stand by during ministerial sessions and listen to the Word being preached so that they are ready to release anything the minister instructs Heaven to provide under the circumstances. Therefore, once the minister says, *"Miracle money,"* angels start precipitating the money in the natural realm. In actual fact, when the Word says *whatever we release on earth shall be released in Heaven*, it speaks specifically about the ministry of angels that as believers command things into existence, angels swiftly move from the realm of the spirit to ensure that they bring whatever is required in the natural realm.

Always testify the instant Miracle Money miracle is declared

It is worth exploring the divine principle that miracles should be testified the instant they manifest in the natural realm. Anything that leaves the spirit realm and is received in the natural realm without it being acknowledged is deemed as illegitimate in Heaven. In other words, any miracle that takes place in the earthly realm and is not acknowledged or testified, is declared as an illegal supernatural act in Heaven. The principle is that all miracles or supernatural occurrences must be declared or certified the instant they take place in the natural realm. Have you ever wondered why some people received their healing and after a while they lost it? It's because certain spiritual laws were not fulfilled or perfected during its manifestation. For it to be permanent, you must testify, talk about it, and tell of the goodness of the Lord to others. Testifying about the miracle is a divine legal act that duly authorises and certifies the miracle with a stamp of God's approval, endorsing that the miracle is indeed deemed authentic by Heaven. That is why concerning believers, the Bible says *they defeated the devil by the blood of the lamb and the world of their testimony*. Why? Because testifying about something reinforces its credibility in the realm of the spirit and makes it to be established in the natural realm in accordance with the fulfilment of spiritual laws. Therefore, if you are a recipient of Miracle money, you must testify instantly so that God's glory is revealed and that the level of people's faith in God may be strengthened.

Change the spiritual atmosphere and climate by practising the presence of God

To demonstrate Miracle money in the natural realm, you must usher the presence of God on the scene to such an extent that whenever you go, you are able to change the prevailing atmosphere. In other words, you must overlay the natural atmosphere with the atmosphere of Heaven, culminating in what we call *Heaven-on-earth*. Notable is the realisation that while there is the natural atmosphere that engulfs geographical territories in the natural realm, there is also a spiritual atmosphere of Heaven on earth which prevails over specific territories. As much as the natural atmosphere has its own climate, clouds, wind, rain and other properties, the spiritual atmosphere has its own clouds which needs to be saturated before it could release the rain of Miracle money. It is when the spiritual atmosphere is activated, triggered or cloud-seeded that Miracle money is released. It is this atmosphere that lubricates the natural realm and provides a vehicle of transportation for angels to swiftly move in the natural realm. Therefore, cultivating the spiritual atmosphere means creating a *glory cloud* that upon saturation, would burst and release Miracle money. The way rain falls in the natural can be likened to how Miracle money is precipitated from the spirit realm. In the natural, for it to rain, water must evaporate into the atmosphere where it condenses and then form clouds. By the same token, our confessions of faith are spiritual seeds which we send into the spirit realm to create a *glory cloud* which upon saturation would then burst forth to release Miracle money in the natural realm.

Owing to lack of faith and revelation, at times it takes time for the spirit realm or spiritual atmosphere to be perfected so that it can manifest in the physical. The reason why some people are not able to manifest the Miracle money grace is because their faith has not yet been perfected to a level where they can make a pulling on the supernatural realm. Spending time in the presence of God is what breeds a breakthrough point in the realm of the spirit, thereby provoking the flow of Heavenly substances into the natural realm. Miracle money is a product of God's glory, hence it is in the presence of God that it gravitates like a current in the direction where the glory of God is moving. That is why the extent to which your spirit man is developed will determine how much of the Miracle money grace you can demonstrate in the natural realm. Therefore, spending time in the presence of God through praying in the Holy Ghost, meditation and other spiritual exercises is one way of ensuring that your spirit man is capacitated, trained and groomed to move in the spirit dimension and precipitate Miracle money in the natural realm.

Always be sensitive to the new move of the Holy Ghost

It is important that you be sensitive to the new move of God whenever Miracle money is demonstrated. In a similar fashion in which the *sons of Issachar had an acute understanding of what Israel ought to do at a time* (1 Chronicles 12:32), as a believer, you are expected to be sensitive to the new move of God's Spirit especially in these prophetic times. In other words, you must be catapulted into the realm of *prophetic perception*. This is a spiritual sight necessary to see what God is doing in the invisible arena and in tandem with Him, you do exactly the same in the visible realm. It incorporates the ability to see the unseen, hear the unheard and then speak the unspeakable. This means that your imagination was intended by God to be the lens through which you apprehend the realms of spiritual realities and in terms of the current times and seasons as stipulated in God's calendar, all scriptural evidence seem to align with the fact that this is indeed the most ripe season and opportune time to demonstrate Miracle money. By prophetic perception, I hear God echoing the voice of Prophet Isaiah, saying, *"Behold I'm doing a new thing"* (Isaiah 43:19). Miracle money is one of the *"new things"* which God is unveiling and unfolding from His Throne of Grace. The unveiling of the Wealth of Heaven manifested in the form of gold dust, silver stones, diamonds and other precious stones is an ample evidence of this divine truth. Notable is the realisation that it is very dangerous for a man to be left at the same bus stop yet God has already moved forward and is doing something new. Philosophically speaking, Miracle money grace is like a pool of Bethsaida. Those who are sensitive to the new move of God and plunge into the depths of this grace with a sense of urgency, shall reap a bumper harvest. You must be therefore be rightly positioned in the spirit dimension to partake of this *new thing* called Miracle money which God is unfolding from the Throne Room. This is the new manna which God is currently pouring out over the Body of Christ as a way of unveiling His love for His creation in the arena of supernatural financial provision. This season marks the beginning of the greatest financial revival ever witnessed in the history of mankind. This is what I call *the last wave of financial prosperity* which is currently sweeping across the Body of Christ in this end time season. Hence, as a believer living in this critical time, you have no other business to pursue except to plunge into the pool of Miracle money.

Always acknowledge the source of Miracle money grace

There is a divine principle that in the realm of the spirit, blessings and spiritual substances flow through acknowledgement of the source of provision. The ministry of angels is also activated through acknowledgement of their presence. Likewise, the current of Miracle money also flows through acknowledgement, hence will always gravitate towards those who acknowledge its source of provision. Acknowledgement is a way of re-enforcing the supremacy of spiritual subjects in terms of the legal authority they have to dispatch God's blessings in the natural realm. Great men of God in our time, some of which have been labelled *the pioneers of Miracle money*, for being at the frontline of the Miracle money revival, seem to attest to the truth that if you want to see a greater manifestation of Miracle money, you must acknowledge its source. In other words, you must give credit where you got it from. Acknowledgment means developing a consciousness of God's miraculous provision and understanding of His divine principles of provision by observing Heavenly protocol. The greater truth is that every spiritual blessing regardless of the gravity or viscosity of its manifestation, is connected to a source. As believers, we are the seed of Abraham because we are connected to Abraham by faith, hence all the blessings of Abraham are gravitating towards us. Likewise, Miracle money is connected to God by grace, hence it flows directly from the Throne Room of Heaven to precipitate upon the masses who are recipients of the out-workings of God's grace in the natural realm. Therefore, it is advisable that believers should seek more of the *Blesser* than the *blessing* because many at times people run after Miracle money yet they forget the hand behind it's divine orchestration in the realm of the spirit. It's akin to what Jesus said to same of His so called, "followers": *You don't follow Me because you love Me but because of the bread and fish.* Although your motive of going to places of worship at first glance might be to receive Miracle money, once you have received it, your focus must be diverted to worship and adoration of the Father. Jesus said *No one comes to the Father unless He draws him.* In this current season, it is evident that God is using divergent divine strategies to draw His own people to Him. To some, He uses healing, while to others He uses Miracle money so that they can come to Him. However, once they have come, it is important that they be trained in the matters of the Word so that their faith is established in God.

Develop a relentless passion to win the lost souls

In order to demonstrate the viscosity of Miracle money to a heightened degree, you must have a passion to see the lost saved. The good thing is that unlike other miracles, Miracle money manifestation is so spectacular, thrilling and enthralling to such an extent that it draws the attention of unbelievers on the scene. It is through the manifestation of Miracle money that even the crowd of the cynical, sceptical and critical get to see the power of God at work, hence it becomes easy for them to turn to Christ for the salvation of their souls. The miracle itself boggles the mind, dazzle the minds of the sceptics, thereby debunking any myths and misconception people might have about God. Gone are the days when people used to talk about God as if He is an invisible God who is far away from His people. The day has arrived that God wants to manifest Himself visibly in the natural realm, hence He will do anything to make people feel His tangible and visible presence. In this end times, He wants to reveal more of His grace and love so that people may believe and be saved because the time for the second coming of Jesus Christ is imminent. This is in view of the truth that the number one business of God in these critical times is soul wining. It is the key agenda in the Kingdom. It forms part of the winning strategy of the *Board of Heaven*. It is the ultimate purpose for miracles, signs and wonders. Therefore, Miracle money is not an end in itself but a means to an end. The end is that the masses may get to know the truth of the gospel so that they can receive eternity in their spirit. God does not just want you to receive Miracle money and after that proceeded to hell. That is why any demonstration of Miracle money in the natural realm which is not accompanied by the salvation of souls is deemed as worthless in Heaven. It's actually a waste of Heavenly resources, so to speak. That is why it is important to channel it in the right direction such that unbelievers see the saving grace of God and His love for humanity so that they can be saved.

Practically demonstrate the grace for Miracle Money in the natural realm

It is worth highlighting the fact that there ought to be a paradigm shift in the way Miracle money is demonstrated in this end time season. The Miracle money grace is not ideally designed to be an inexplicable phenomenon that is only secretly displayed behind church doors but an open ministry just like healing and deliverance. It must be practically demonstrated live in the streets, market places and the public arena in order for it to be revealed to the masses. In one of my powerful books titled, *"The Realm of Power To Raise The Dead"* in which I decoded the divinely coded mysteries on resurrection, I hinted that in order for you to raise the dead, you must practically pray for someone who has died because the dead are not going to leave the mortuary and come to your living room. By the same token, in order for you to see Miracle money being demonstrated in the natural realm, you must practically command it into manifestation. This is the essence of *the law of manifestation*. The Bible says *the earth waited in earnest expectation for the revealing of the sons of God*. As a son of God, the world is waiting for you to demonstrate Miracle money. The *"world"* denotes your sphere of contact, the masses in the community in which you live. That means if you don't demonstrate Miracle money in your life and in the life of others, it remains a mystery while you also remain hidden. Therefore, practically demonstrating the Miracle money grace is a way of accentuating an avenue for the glory of God to be revealed on the scene. As a believer, you are called to exhibit or display the glory of God. It is disheartening to note that in the present times across the Body of Christ, multitudes of people are too theoretical and theological, hence they never practically tap into the viscosity of demonstrating the power of God. For example, many talk about faith but they never talk faith. By the same token, many are talking about Miracle money but they are not talking the language of how to demonstrate it in a tangible and visible way. It is not enough just to have a theoretical or theological understanding of this divine phenomenon. Talking about Miracle money, no matter how eloquent you are, is not going to provoke its manifestation in the natural realm. Peaching about it either, will not make much of a difference. The truth is that for it to manifest tangibly and visibly in the natural realm, it must be practically demonstrated. That is why even the spirit realm itself needs to be activated through demonstrations. Therefore, you need to grow beyond *logos* into a realm where you are able to practically apply *rhema* in a particular situation. When *logos* becomes *rhema*, that's when we see mighty demonstrations of God's power.

Point every manifestation of Miracle money to the love of Christ

The manifestation of Miracle money denotes the unrelenting and unquestionable love which Jesus has for His people. Because money is something that has value and is highly esteemed in the world, no one can give money to anybody He doesn't love. Therefore, the demonstration of Miracle money is a sign that God is also concerned about the physical needs of His people. He wants to show them that He loves them, which is the greatest gift any human being can ever receive. Do you know why love is said to be the 7th dimension of the supernatural realm? It's because it is the highest and most powerful energy force in the universe. That is why God went to the extent of sending His only begotten son, Jesus Christ into this word to die for all our sins. This completely debunks the religious mind-set that all God wants from a human being is worship because He already has superfluous angelic worship in Heaven. Instead, God wants to show love, mercy and goodness to His own creation who bores His very image and divine inscription as a creator. It is worth admonishing in this regard that a man of God must not be glorified or seen as if he is the one who divinely orchestrates Miracle money. Instead, you should point every Miracle money manifestation to the love of Christ. As a believer, it must be ingrained in your thinking that you are just used as a vehicle or pipeline to channel Miracle money into manifestation for the inhabitants of the natural realm to unreservedly partake of God's unlimited grace. Have you not forgotten how God gave a stern warning that flesh and blood shall not glory in His presence and that God will not share His glory with man? This should alert those who are toying with the anointing and playing with Miracle money as if its chaff under the influence of wind. The truth is that behind every Miracle money manifestation is the hand of God, hence every miracle must be attributable to Him in praise, honour and worship. As a matter of fact, every demonstration of Miracle money must lead the masses into a session of deep and unfathomable worship. It must not just be for entertainment or enticing crowds. God is in a serious business of expediting His purpose, hence the Miracle money grace must never be taken for granted under whatever circumstances. That is why humility, obedience and understanding God's purpose are keys to unlocking greater manifestations of Miracle money in the physical realm.

Understand your position of son-ship and authority in the Kingdom

As a believer, you must walk with the divine consciousness that you are an heir to the Throne of God and a co-heir with Christ. Demonstrating Miracle money is not for those who seem to have somehow attained a stratospheric pinnacle of enlightenment in matters of the spirit. It is not an exclusive preserve for pastors and church leaders only because demonstrating power is not a pastoral mandate. Instead, demonstrating Miracle money is your divine legitimate birth right and an irrevocable inheritance bequeathed upon you as a son of God. The Bible also makes it explicitly clear that by divine protocol, you are a *King* and a *Priest* in the Kingdom of God. Therefore, you don't have beg for Miracle money to appear because begging is not a language that spiritual subjects understand. Nor is it part of the vocabulary of Heaven. Instead, you must step into your position of authority as a son of God, to manifest that which legally belongs to you. Moses begged to see the glory of God but now the glory of God is domiciled in your spirit such that you should speak money from within the depths of your being into manifestation in the physical realm As a believer operating in the New Testament dispensation, you should be more conscious of your legal rights and privileges in Christ so that you can walk in the fullness of what Christ has freely made available for you in the capacity of a co-heir. It is through this co-ownership that you are entitled to command things in the realm of the spirit to manifest in the natural realm on behalf of the Kingdom. That means you are in partnership with Christ to disseminate the Miracle money grace to the nations. As you work with Christ and His angels, this grace is manifested in its intensity. Therefore when you step up in faith to command

Miracle money to appear, understand that you are not just speaking from the earthly realm but you are commanding money from God's Throne where you are seated in Christ at the right hand of God. Therefore, when you speak from that realm, angels don't hear your voice per see but the voice of Jesus speaking through your vocal codes such that they will swiftly respond to dispatch Miracle money as if it is Jesus Himself instructing them to. The Bible speaks of *the riches in Christ glory*. Unknown to many people, Miracle money is one of the riches in Christ which God has reserved for you as a believer, to walk in before the foundation of this world. Therefore, you must not be afraid of demonstrating this grace, whether you are a farmer, teacher, engineer or vendor, you must demonstrate Miracle money so that God's glory is revealed in your sphere of contact.

Get rid of any misconstrued Christian traditional teachings that can short-circuit or deactivate your ability to partake in the Miracle Money grace

It is disheartening to note that it's not only the devil's crowd of unbelievers who speak ill of Miracle money but ill-informed believers in some denominational cycles as well. While some believers have been elevated to the realm of demonstrating Miracle money grace, others have gravitated to a lower plain of life in which they criticise, demonise and derail its manifestation. This is attributable to misconstrued traditional teachings which have been engraved in the minds of believers for ages, one of which is the notion that God cannot rain Miracle money from Heaven. Believers must therefore be circumspect not to put God in a box because He is bigger than the world. If God moved in a certain way yesterday, it does not necessarily mean that He is going to move in the same way today. Unfortunately, those believers who have joined the crowd of the critics and sceptics, because they are customarily acclimatised or familiar to a certain formula or pattern in which God moved in the past, will not partake of it. In I kings, when a man refused to believe the report from Heaven concerning the latest economic revival which God was ushering at that time, he was told that he will only see it but shall not partake of it. Some believers are so sceptical about Miracle money manifestations because they are more conscious of the devil than God, hence whenever God does something great, they are always suspicious that it might be the devil. Christians must be more Christ-conscious than devil-conscious. As far as Christ is concerned, devils and demons do not exist in our world; they are far inferior for us to be bothered or worried about. Philosophically speaking, in the world of lions, termites and other insects do not exist. The lions rule over elephants, buffalos and other animals in the jungle. By the same token, in the realm of God, only God is what matters; the devil is just a nonentity, hence Christians must not focus more on him but on God. Miracle money is a pure gift flowing directly from God's Throne Room, hence cannot be counterfeit by the devil. The other burning issue which have played a major role in terms of deactivating and short-circuiting believers' power to demonstrate Miracle money is that of denominationalism. The fact that your pastor does not believe in Miracle money does not mean that you should follow suit. It might be possible that he doesn't have a revelation of the dynamics of this divine phenomenon. Therefore, you should not allow yourself to be limited by the lack of revelation and ignorance of other people. You can distinguish yourself as a pioneer of Miracle money and be the first in your church, community or city to demonstrate Miracle money like a soldier sent out to war for a massacre. As a matter of fact, your yardstick, benchmark and standard of operating in matters of the spirit is not your pastor, but Jesus. For example, Jesus commanded us saying, *"Go, heal the sick, cast out devils and raise the dead,"* but the question is: How many pastors have obeyed this command by raising the dead in our generation? The fact that the previous generation has gravitated below the standard which God has set for the church doesn't necessarily mean the current generation should follow suit. On that note, let's step up in faith and demonstrate the Miracle money grace, to the glory of God.

DIVINE PRINCIPLES OF HOW TO MAKE A FINANCIAL WITHDRAWAL FROM THE BANK OF HEAVEN

Based primarily on the fundamental principles of God's word, supplemented by my own individual peculiarity and supernatural encounters through practical demonstrations of Miracle money, the following are revelational guidelines of how one could follow suit and apply Biblical principles of faith to withdraw millions of money from the Heaven's Spiritual Bank, even when there is no cent in your physical bank account. The dawning of this global move is what I call a *Revolution of Miracle Money*. However, my solemn intent is not to create a doctrine on this subject but to birth forth by revelation, the practical guidelines which believers in the Body of Christ across the world could apply in order to command Miracle money into visible manifestation, for the global propagation and furtherance of the gospel of our Lord Jesus Christ.

Have a written plan or vision of the finances you need from God

In order to freely make a withdrawal from the Heavenly Bank account, you must decide on the exact amount you need from God (James 1:5-8). Be exact and single-minded without wavering. Make a list your needs, debts and desires and put all your plans in writing according to (Habakkuk 2:2). Having all your financial plans and demands written down will help channel your faith in a specific direction to reap alarming results of supernatural financial abundance. The greatest challenge which is attributable to multitudes of believers not being able to command their millions into visible and tangible manifestation in the natural realm is the issue of being aimless in their declarations. Don't just say, *"I command money into my bank account"*. Instead, be resolute and specify the exact amount which you want to deposit into your account and which account you want the money to be deposited into and it shall be established according to your word. This is because the forces of divinity works *according to what you say* and this is a key spiritual principle in demonstrating Miracle money (Mark 11:23). You must be precise, concise and specific about what you want God to do for you. Specificity is such a fundamental principle in the spirit realm which increases the likelihood of physical manifestation because you must be able to see the money in the spirit with the eyes of faith and as you see it, it is manifested in the physical realm in the exact quantities in which you would have seen it in the spirit.

Place a demand on the Heaven's unlimited supplies by faith to appropriate what is rightfully yours

Faith is a key that unlocks Heavens' Storehouses to release humongous wealth in every currency of the world. It is a breeding ground or a warehouse for an inventory of Miracle money testimonies in the natural realm. Faith is what culminates in a factory of signs and wonders in which it is naturally supernatural to demonstrate Miracle money. The Bible declares that *God calls things that are not as though they were*. Therefore, release the God Kind of faith in you by commanding any amount of money to appear wherever you want it. Command the amount you want to have, where you want it and in whatever quantities you want it to appear. In the realm of the spirit, something becomes yours only when you claim it and is manifested in the natural realm when you proclaim it. Unless you declare it in the spirit realm, it is just potentially yours. Which is why faith gives us legal entrance into the spirit realm to procure our blessings, hence without faith it is virtually impossible for one to receive millions of Heaven's wealth and resources. Faith travels across both realms of existence. It moves in the spirit dimension as a rebuttal to command the millions of wealth to come forth and then it comes back into the natural to secure their visible and tangible manifestation in the physical realm. The realm of the spirit works more by yielding than trying, hence you are not trying to make Miracle money appear but rather you are simply using faith to appropriate the money which is already yours to manifest in a tangible and visible form in the natural realm.

Bind the devil and his forces of darkness

During Miracle money demonstrations, stand upon God's word in Matthew 18:18 and command Satan to take his filthy hands off your money. The Bible explicitly state that we are blessed with all blessings in the Heavenly places but why is it that some people are still poor? It's because their blessings are intercepted in the demonic realm by evil forces. Therefore, identifying where your finances have been hijacked and then commanding satanic forces to loose their hold is one such powerful key to securing a financial breakthrough in the realm of the spirit. Take note that the kind of prayer that you can make under the circumstance is a double-sword-edged declaration which involves both *binding and loosing.* As you bind the forces of darkness and the horde of demons responsible for financial loss, lack and poverty, don't forget to release your millions of wealth into your account because it is this spiritual act that will cause your millions to visibly manifest in your bank account. Although you have bound him, the devil will not deposit your money into the account. However as you bind, cast and burn him, he will loose it but it will remain hanging over your head until you release it into a specific account.

Discharge the angels to swiftly bring forth the money intro manifestation in the physical realm

According to Hebrews 1:4, *angels are ministering spirits* which are responsible for getting the money from the spirit realm into the natural realm, thereby committing it into your hands. Kenneth Hagin testifies that He received the revelation of faith for finances and learnt how to release his faith in that area to appropriate getting his needs met. The Lord said to him, *"Don't pray about money like you have been. Whatever you need, claim it in Jesus' Name. And then you say, 'Satan, take your hands off my money.' And then say, 'Go, ministering spirits, and cause the money to come"*. This is the exact formula or pattern which believers across the globe should apply to generate alarming results of financial abundance. It must be understood that contrary to what a multitude of believers in some Christian cycles believe, the work and ministry of angels is not automatic. It has to be activated. Your angels are always waiting on standby and according to spiritual laws that govern their operations, they will do virtually nothing until you command them to go and get your millions. In order for you to get the anointing, you must develop a high level of sensitivity to the Holy Spirit. By the same token, in order to receive Miracle money, you must develop a high level of sensitivity to angel tellers. In the same way the Holy Ghost rubs or imparts the anointing upon a vessel, angel tellers imparts or precipitates Miracle money upon those appointed to partake of it by the grace of God.

Release and appropriate the Miracle money you need

The Bible declares in Mark 11:24 that *when you pray, believe that you have received*. It does say that pray first and then after that wait for an answer. Contrary to how some believers have portrayed, during the exercise of faith, we don't speak faith and then after that wait for the results to manifest later in the natural realm. Instead, exercising faith and receiving Miracle money takes place concurrently. This is different from how the natural realm operates. According to natural laws, you start by asking first and then you receive. But according to the laws of faith, while you are asking, you are also receiving as the same time. This is very important in the formula of faith. It is not only binding and releasing that will place your millions of wealth into your account but what completes the faith process is when you receive. As a matter of fact, the reason behind our exercise of faith is to receive something at the end. If it happens that you exercise your faith but then you didn't see the results of your faith, it means that you did not receive anything. This is a challenge facing many believers in the Body of Christ today. Some of them pray and exercise their faith but they never get to know whether their prayers were answered or not. Some, by the time a response is sent from

Heaven, they have already moved on and busy praying for something else, hence they are not in a position to receive. To receive means that you must be rightly positioned in the spirit realm. In other words, your spirit man must be enlarged, capacitated and well developed to create room for you to receive. This is because the amount of financial blessings which a man can receive from God is directly proportional to the size of his spirit. The larger the spiritual capacity, the greater the ability to receive and accommodate the blessing.

Continually praise and exalt God for the manifestation

During Miracle money manifestations, it is important that you start by praising God as if you physically have the money in your hands. According to Psalm 34:1, your praise is the evidence of your faith and your receiving. Walking in this divine consciousness is what will cause your millions to break forth into physical manifestation either into your bank account or anywhere you deem necessary for it to manifest. The greatest obstacle to seeing a demonstration of the supernatural power of God in the arena of wealth is that the spiritual atmosphere does not exist for the glory of His presence to manifest. You therefore need to invite a spiritual atmosphere of praise and worship so that the glory of God may release miracles of supernatural provision. Praise is an exuberant, clamorous, enthusiastic expression directed to the Father so that His sovereign presence and blessing can manifest. Praise is what provokes a downpour and torrent of heavy financial rain from Heaven upon the masses, hence if ever you want to see your millions manifesting speedily, just acquaint yourself more with God through praise and worship and you shall be elevated instantaneously into the realm of God's supernatural provision. You will be easily catapulted into an arena in which it is naturally supernatural to demonstrate Miracle money and waking up in the morning to find money stacked in your bags, wallets and pockets is the order of the day.

Give a testimony to ascribe all the glory to God.

As aforementioned, in the realm of the spirit, miracles should be declared the minute they happen, otherwise they will be declared illegitimate in Heaven. If you receive Miracle money and you don't testify about it, you might loose it. That is why you hear people confessing regrettably that they received a lot of money into their bank accounts and kept quiet but then after few days, the money disappeared again. Speaking of saints, the Bible says in Revelations 12:11 that *they defeated the devil by the blood and the word of their testimony.* This implies that a testimony reinforces victory of demonic powers that twist and manipulates our finances, thereby rendering them useless. Notable is the realisation that some miracles especially those involving millions of money from Heaven are not about you. Instead, they are about God manifesting His glory to mankind, hence you need to create a platform for God to receive all the glory in the same way He received glory through the resurrection of Lazarus from the dead. Miracle money demonetisations should always be followed by a catalogue of testimonies in which the masses give evidence of the factory of signs and wonders which God is unfolding in the arena of supernatural financial provision.

A QUINTESSENTIAL MODEL OF A PRACTICAL DEMONSTRATION OF MIRACLE MONEY IN THE NATURAL REALM

It is important to highlight in this regard that any born again believer who is filled with the Holy Spirit and inundated in the depths of God's Word, is eligible to express the God kind of faith by commanding Miracle money into physical, visible and tangible manifestation in the natural realm. It is your legal right and divine birth right as a son of God to release God's creative power in you by commanding any amount which you want to manifest in a visible or tangible form. You only need to be elevated into a supernatural realm or dimension whereby you catch the revelation that as much as we have money in the natural realm, the original blue print of money is in the spirit, hence you can transmute that substance of money into a visible form in the natural realm.

While reminiscing fresh divine memories of God's supernatural provision into my mind, I still remember the first day I made a supernatural withdrawal of heaven's wealth in the form of miracle money from an ATM. I initially inserted my bank card into the ATM Machine and to my disappointment, I received a receipt indicating that I did not have any money. In other words, I did not have even a cent in my bank account but an overdraft. But being determined to change my status quo, I then released my faith by inserting the card back into the ATM and this time I supernaturally released the money into my bank card and then commanded the ATM in the Name of Jesus Christ to produce Four Thousand Rands which I urgently needed. Instantly I heard the sound of the ATM machine rolling paper notes indicating that money was being processed and as the machine ejected the full amount I grabbed it with both hands and started declaring miracle money and shouting praises to God.

To my amazement, the results were instantaneous and I needed not to wait or delay to see its manifestation. If I had commanded a Million Rand to be deposited into my account, that could have been the case according to my word. Remember, Jesus said you shall have whatever you say, so, use Mark 11:24 as a formula of faith to command Millions in Miracle money into your accounts and you shall be thrilled at the instantaneous results of what the Word of God talks about in this season, Glory to Jesus!

PRACTICAL GUIDELINES AND PRINCIPLES OF HOW TO PRACTICALLY DEMONSTRATE AND FLOW IN THE REALM OF MIRACLE MONEY

Expression of unwavering faith during Miracle money demonstrations:

It is important that you believe God for everything that He says in His word without any wavering of faith or doubt. Have the audacity of faith to declare that Miracle money appears supernaturally and it shall be established in the realm of the spirit. It is important that you deal with any trace of fear since it is a reverse gear of faith. *Faith comes by hearing the word of God but Fear comes by hearing the word of the devil.* The devil operates in the realm of senses but God operates beyond senses. Faith and fear cannot co-exist. Faith and fear are antonymous because fear is inverted faith. To invert something means to reverse the position, order or condition thereof. In other words, fear means you simply believe more in what you don't want to happen versus what you actually want to happen. While faith is the evidence of unseen realities, fear is the evidence of doubt. Fear is also a product of ignorance because you tend to fear what you don't know. That is why in your exercise of faith for Miracle money, it is imperative that you get rid of any misconstrued traditional teachings that are contrary to the doctrine of prosperity. If you can reframe from these, then it shall be easy for you to unreservedly manifest Miracle money in the natural realm.

Understanding of God's divine Purpose with regard to the dispatch of Miracle money:

It must be expressly understood that the purpose of manifesting Miracle money is not to show off, enrich ourselves or to become a glamour driven spendaholic. Instead, it is designed to usher the glory of God on the scene so that we can help connect people's faith to God. Therefore, you must understand that the sole purpose of Miracle money is to give God all the glory by winning millions of souls, strengthening people's faith to depend on God's supernatural provision and for the furtherance of the gospel. Moreover, understanding God's divinely orchestrated financial plans and purpose with regard to the manifestation of Miracle money will help you view all things from God's perspective and thus operate within the confines of His will to expand the Kingdom through propagating the gospel of the Lord Jesus Christ to all the nations of the world. That is why the Bible says in Proverbs 4:7 that *in all your getting get understanding* because once you understand spiritual laws and principles of financial prosperity, the manifestation of Miracle money shall come forth speedily.

Acknowledgment of the source of provision where Miracle money is concerned:

As aforementioned, in all your spiritual endeavours to manifest Miracle money, always acknowledge that God is the source of provision, hence all the glory should not be attributable to the wisdom of any man but solely to God, for no flesh shall glory in His presence. Men of God, who have been labelled as the pioneer of Miracle money testify that the secret to moving in greater dimensions of manifestation of miracle money is to acknowledge where you got it from. However, even when you have received the grace to manifest supernatural money through impartation from a man of God, you still need to acknowledge its source. Acknowledgement is a way of recognising heavenly protocol thereby provoking a perennial outburst of God's supernatural provision upon humanity. In other words, it moves the hand of God and compels all Heavenly forces to work on behalf of you. It brings Heaven and earth into perfect harmony or synchronisation according to God's will. Acknowledgement is such a powerful spiritual force law and principle that declares Miracle money legitimate and gets Heaven to ordain it in the natural realm. Any miracle that is not declared or acknowledged the instant it takes place is declared illegitimate in Heaven.

Sensitivity to angelic operations during Miracle money demonstrations:

It is highly imperative in your endeavour to demonstrate Miracle money that you need to develop a high level of spiritual sensitivity, vigilance and consciousness of the activities of *finance angels* since they are the ones responsible for the dispatch of Miracle money. Without the work of angels, there is no such thing as Miracle money because they are the ones whom God has entrusted with the responsibility to drive and spearhead this ministry on behalf of Heaven. Therefore, work closely with them and command them to dispatch Miracle money and it shall be exactly as you say it *for you shall declare a thing and it shall be established for you.* The substance of Miracle money is created from the words we speak, hence speaking or confessing God's word gives angels spiritual material to work with in order to bring forth the required supernatural provision. Failure to engage angels might result in loss of humongous wealth and unnecessary delays in the dispatch of millions of wealth from Heaven. The *Angel of precious stones* works in conjunction with the *Angel of finances* to supernaturally manifest the wealth of Heaven on earth. The angel of precious stones rains down gold dust, silver and diamonds stones, jewels and supernatural oil while the angel of finances propagates Miracle money in all currencies into the bank accounts, wallets, bags, houses and hands of believers as per need. The presence of Angel's feathers during the manifestation of Miracle money is ample evidence that they are the engines behind the manifestation of this golden phenomenon.

Practical demonstration of Signs and Wonders in the arena of finances:

Whenever we talk about demonstration of God's power, very few people would expect power to be displayed in the realm of finances. In most cases, they tend to confine signs and wonders to matters of healing and deliverance and this is the reason why they are excelling in those areas but still lagging behind financially. It must be understood that the manifestation Miracle money is an evidence of a practical display of God's power in the supernatural realm. God's power manifested in the arena of prosperity in this case is called *wealth* but the spiritual energy or force that brings forth that wealth into manifestation is called the *financial anointing*. It is a fact that money cannot resist the anointing since it gravitates or naturally flows in the direction where the anointing is flowing. Therefore, as a money magnet, be practical and command Miracle money to manifest and God will see to it that He performs His word. Notable is the realisation that there is a difference between praying about money and commanding money to manifest in the physical realm. While praying has its own place praying in the face of Miracle money demonstration is a sign of whamming and whimpering if the Word authorises action. Therefore, don't just pray about money, speak to it, command and move things in the spirit realm by the words of your mouth. It is the financial anointing that would enable you to command Miracle money into physical manifestation and also to cause angels to move swiftly in the spirit dimension to execute God's divine financial plans.

Relentless persuit of Heaven's agenda of salvation of billions of souls across the globe:

As aforementioned, the fundamental purpose of Miracle money is not necessarily to make people wealthy as tempting as it might sound. Instead, its sole purpose is for souls across the globe to be saved in millions. The manifestation of Miracle money is therefore a divinely orchestrated strategy to strengthen people's faith in God so that they can believe in His son Jesus Christ for the salvation of their souls. Therefore, as people's faith level is stirred up following the manifestation of uncommon money, create an opportunity for the unbelievers to be saved. Therefore, make it a habit to lead the masses to Christ every time miracles of this nature are performed. Due to its visibility and tangibility, Miracle money is one such convincing miracle whose manifestation cannot be easily refuted or discredited by any scepticism, hence it presents an opportunity where even the worst sinners can turn their hearts to Christ and be saved.

Committment to the furtherance of the gospel to the extreme ends of the world:

If you happen to be a millionaire though Miracle money, understand that this wealth is meant to be strictly used for the establishment of the Kingdom's end time visions and plans and divine projects. It is not for personal use, hence must never be used under whatsoever circumstances to pursue selfish interests. There is an intricate connection between *millions of money* and *millions of souls* in that millions of money are supernaturally dispatched by Heaven in this season to bring forth millions of souls into the Kingdom. Advancing the Kingdom means taking the gospel to newer and hostile territories around the world, sponsoring Kingdom visions, building churches, feeding the needy and orphans, spearheading global outreach programmes, intervention at global levels to save the afflicted, building Christian universities, cities and towns as well as acquiring property and investment for other Kingdom purposes. This is what believers in the extreme ends of the world will be able to accomplish in the Kingdom through massive Miracle money demonstrations, glory to Jesus!

CHAPTER SEVEN

THE ROLE OF ANGELS IN THE MANIFESTATION OF MIRACLE MONEY

It is worth highlighting that angles play a key and integral role in the manifestation of Miracle money. Without the direct, active involvement of angels, Miracle money would not be manifested in the natural realm. Angles are the ones whom God has entrusted with the responsibility to despatch or propagate Miracle money to earth so as to expedite His end time purpose and divinely orchestrated Kingdom plans. Debunking the myths and misconceptions which have held the masses in ignorance for ages, this teaching breathes life into the nuts and bolts of angelic activity, ushering believers into the greener pastures of God's supernatural provision. Believers are therefore admonished to be circumspect, vigilant and sensitive to the work of angels in order to unreservedly partake of this abundant grace. It is for this reason that Paul cautioned believers in Ephesus not to forget to entertain strangers for some entertained angels unaware. Sensitivity to angelic operations means acknowledging the work of angels, cooperating with their presence and provoking their manifestation in a similar fashion in which Abraham's engaged two angels when he saw them purporting to be passing by (Genesis 19:9). Therefore, if ever you want to abundantly partake of this grace, it is of paramount importance that you actively engage angels in the process. With regard to the ministry of angels, Paul asks a rhetoric question that: *Are they not ministering spirits sent forth to minister to those who will inherit salvation?* In the context of the above scripture, the Greek word for "*sent forth*" is *apostelo*, which is the same word that is used to describe an apostle, the sent one. That means, angels are sent forth from Heaven on a divine commission to propagate Miracle money to the extreme ends of the world. Be that as it may, it's not every angel that will give you Miracle money. because angels perform different functions and diverse assignments. The types of angels involved in the dispatch of Miracle money are called *Angel Tellers* or *Angel of finances*. These work in the Finance Department in Heaven and are mandated to process and facilitate any divine monetary transactions in the same way bank tellers process funds in the natural realm.

It is worth exploring the divine revelation that within the same angelic kind, are *Angelic Finance Directors*, who are high ranking angelic beings that serve in the *Board of Heaven* and make high decisions with regard to the authorisation and propagation of Miracle money; others are *Angel tellers* responsible for the smooth processing of financial transactions in the realm of the spirit while others are *Warring Angels* that provide security for Miracle money to be safely dispatched into the natural realm without any demonic interception. Therefore, whenever you find Miracle money supernaturally deposited in any unexpected territory, either in your wallet, pocket, hand bag or house, it's because these angels would have been actively involved in the invisible realm to make *Angelic deposits*. Notable is the realisation that two groups of angels seem to be striding at the frontline of the Miracle money revival. The *Angel of precious stones* works in conjunction with the *Angel of finances* to supernaturally manifest the wealth of Heaven on earth. The angel of precious stones rains down gold dust, silver and diamonds stones, jewels and supernatural oil while the angel of finances propagates Miracle money in all currencies into the bank accounts, wallets, bags, houses and hands of believers as per need. The presence of Angel's feathers floating in the air or resting on the floor of buildings where Miracle money would have been practically demonstrated, is ample evidence that these angels are the engines behind the manifestation of this golden phenomenon.

Angels play a key role in making Angelic deposits

In the realm of God's prosperity, angel tellers regulates the economy of the Kingdom of God and are actively involved in the invisible realm by supernaturally depositing money in the bank accounts of believers. Hence, there is in the realm of prosperity such a thing as an *angelic deposit*. In the light of this revelation, believers must therefore be awakened to the reality that money is spiritual and as much as it is widely used in the natural realm, the original blue print of it is in Heaven, hence angels have control and access to distribute and deposit money supernaturally. Angelic deposits is therefore one of the ways through which God distributes millions of wealth in this end time dispensation. The greatest challenge is that lack of revelation and ignorance is what robs people of their right to fully partake or participate in the supernatural manifestation of the blessings of God because you cannot walk into what has not been revealed to you.

The major challenge facing the Body of Christ today besides issues of conflict of faith is lack of understanding of God's system of governance and financial provision. According to God's system of governance, He has placed the money in the spirit realm under the close supervision of angels. The problem is that many believers are crying out to God for financial breakthrough but they don't know where the real money is. It's like someone crying out to the President of a country for help to withdraw money from his bank account but then runs the risk of not receiving any help at all. Although the President owns the country, the money might not be directly in his hands but committed to the Reserve Bank under the close supervision of the Governor. This is typical of the way of governance in God's Kingdom. As it is the natural, so it is in the Kingdom of God. The greater truth is that the money is in the realm of the spirit governed and committed into the hands of angels of finances, hence we need to rigorously engage angels in order for us to become recipients of Miracle money. Knowing where the money is and in whose hands the wealth of the Kingdom has been committed is key to determining your financial breakthrough. In most cases the person who deposits the money might not necessarily be the owner of the money but a messenger sent to deposit it. Knowing how to get the money from God's hand is therefore an imperative action. It must be understood that God will not modify His laws to accommodate your ignorance. Instead, He has established spiritual laws and set in place a system by which He governs the whole universe, hence it's up to you to know His system of governance so that you can operate accordingly or function within the confines of God's will to appropriate any blessing you need. Developing a high level of sensitivity to angelic presence and knowing how to recognise and commission angels to go and gather your blessings is such a key to the ultimate manifestation of Miracle money.

Angels impart spiritual substances upon believers, of which Miracle money is a part

One of the key functions or roles played by angels in God's financial prosperity plan is through impartation of spiritual substances in the natural realm. Do you remember the incident at the Pool of Bethsaida, whereby an angel had to stir the waters of the pool such that a sick person who happened to be the first to step into the pool, received their healing? What do you think the angel was doing by stiring the waters? He was imparting the glory of God into the waters such that the ordinary water was turned into miracle healing water, highly charged with the power of God. This is what we call an *angelic impartation*. It is on the basis of this divine principle that some modern day ministers have orchestrated what we call *Miracle Healing Water*. In some instances, besides impartation of power, anointing and the glory, some of these spiritual substances which angels impart upon the congregation during ministerial sessions is actually real *money*. The truth is that as much as angels do impart the glory upon human vessels, they can also impart money into your spirit and your duty is to learn how to tap into the realm of prosperity to practically apply God's spiritual laws and principles to draw millions of wealth from your spirit into visible manifestation in the natural realm. Mind you, your spirit is the first point of contact with either angels or the Holy Spirit. Hence, during ministerial sessions, God touches your spirit first before touching the people that you are ministering to. Therefore, you need to understand that the blessings of God are first imparted in to your spirit before they could manifest in the physical realm. Contrary to what many folks presume, the blessings of God don't just fall like apples falling from an apple tree. In most cases, your blessings are not located in the realm of the spirit but they are in you. So many people are ignorant of the system of God's provision such that they always cry out to God for blessings yet their blessings were long released from His hands and imparted into their spirit but just because they operate so much in the realm of the flesh, they are oblivious or unconscious of the presence of those blessings in them. That is why from this minute forth, you should change the content and direction of your prayer. Rather than praying, "Lord, give me a blessing", let your prayer be:

"Lord, open my eyes to see the blessing that you have already imparted in me and give me the revelation and wisdom to withdraw from the blessings that are in my spirit".

As aforementioned, God touches your spirit first before He could touch your soul and body. Whenever someone gets healed in the body, it is because healing would have started first in the spirit and then assimilated into the soul and ultimately filtered into the body to birth forth a manifestation in the natural realm. Although you see the results of manifestation of healing in the body, the truth is that it would have started in the spirit. Spiritual manifestations such as shaking and falling under the power are a visible sign of the out flow of blessings of God from the spirit of a man into his body. Knowing how to convert the blessings of God from your spirit into visible manifestation in the natural realm is therefore highly imperative. When the Bible declares in Ephesian 1:3 that *we are blessed with all spiritual blessings in the Heavenly places*, it is talking about *the blessings of God in their raw, crude, undiluted and original state* but the refined and processed blessings of God are in your spirit. During impartation, there is a transfer of blessings from their location or disposition in the Heavenly places into your spirit and then from your spirit into the physical world through confession and prophetic declaration. This is what I call *a chain of manifestation of blessings*. For your blessings to manifest in the physical realm, they need to pass first through your spirit and mingle with faith in your spirit and then released forth from your spirit into the physical realm through prophetic declaration. There is a spiritual reaction that takes place in your spirit as the imparted blessings of God mingle with your faith and word of God in your spirit, to produce the results of what it talks about. This is a pattern or model of how blessing or millions are given birth to in the realm of the spirit. This is why faith is such a vital element in the transfer of our blessings because without faith, our blessings would not manifest in the physical because faith is that force that would draw the blessings of God in your spirit and cause them to manifest in the physical realm.

Angels activate the financial blessings by birthing forth the visions of God into remembrance to fulfil God's purpose

The reality is that during their season of visitation and manifestation, angels breathe visions and impart revelations on people's minds, to awaken them to the pursuit of the visions of God. Angels renders assistance for man to bring forth the vision of God regarding financial wealth to come to pass. At times the fallen nature of man is such that his mental faculties need to be activated to enable him to dream big and see the impossible becoming possible. In most cases, our visions of God and dreams of becoming millionaires gets clouded by impediments of unbelief, human nature and natural limitations in the realm of senses such that we don't see our visions as clearly as we should. Angels therefore help develop the visions of God in your spirit and translate them into dreams of impossibilities. That is why you can sense or detect the presence of angels through godly thoughts of impossibilities. At times when you dream or think of you becoming a great Kingdom millionaire, it's because angels were standing by you in the spirit realm and breathing godly thoughts right into your mind. At times, angels radiate God's glory on us so that as we shine forth, we receive favour in all spheres of human endeavour. There are also *Resurrection angels* who operate according to God's times and seasons and are actively involved in resurrecting every dream or forgotten vision man has to fulfil in God's purpose. These bring forth remembrance of God's vision so that man cannot deviate from God's plan. There is a limit to which man can deviate from God's purpose, hence angels intervene for their sake to bring everything vision to come to pass.

Angels breaks the rod of wickedness centred on our financial blessings and opens financial doors to bring forth abundant manifestations in the physical realm

---

In view of the role angels play in the realm of God's financial prosperity, you need to be awakened to the spiritual reality that at times the blessings of God are released from Heaven but then due to a heightened degree of evil and spiritual wickedness in the high places, those blessings are intercepted in the demonic realm and in some cases they are wickedly manipulated, twisted, exchanged, transacted and converted into another use other than the purpose for which they were initially released. Moreover, some financial blessings are stolen, devoured, hijacked and in some cases transacted to people who were not initially supposed to partake of them. In Daniel 12:13, the revelation of how the demonic principality called the prince of Persia intercepted an angel who was sent from Heaven to deliver an end time revelation to Daniel, is an acid test of gross wickedness which takes place in the spirit world. You can imagine how many believers across the world are crying out to God because their blessings have been intercepted in the demonic realm. That is why God says in Malachi 3:10 that through paying tithes, He will rebuke the devourer of our blessings because there are demons who specialises in devouring or scavenging on the blessings of believers in the spirit realm. Therefore, under these circumstances, where our wealth and blessings have been intercepted by the demonic realm or where there are obstacles and hindrances to our financial breakthrough in the spirit, it is warring angels that breaks forth to open closed doors, reinstate us to our original position of blessings and thrash the demonic powers responsible for their manipulation. In Joshua 5:13; 6:27, *an angel with a sword went forward to bring the walls of Jericho down and to make Israel loot the wealth of the city*. In 2 Kings 6:16, when Elisha was surrounded by an army of Syrian soldiers, the minute he said, *"Slew them Lord"*, the angels of the Lord destroyed all Assyrian soldiers in a flip of a moment. Angels wait for you to speak a word so that they will act on it and in the absence of any spoken word angels are restricted by spiritual laws to act on our behalf. That is why it is important to engage them if ever you desire to see the manifestation of millions of Heaven's wealth in your lives.

Angels spearhead or implements God's Wealth Transfer Programme by stirring the heart of those with finances to brings them to you for Kingdom expansion purposes

In the realm of God's prosperity, there is what is called *God's Wealth Transfer Plan*. This is a major characteristic feature of the end time dispensation that involves transferring wealth, resources, property and financial assets from the hands of unbelievers to believers for Kingdom expansion purposes. The Bible says in Proverb 13:22 that *God shall take the wealth from the wicked to the righteous*. As per God's calendar, the season of restructuring, reformation and *redistribution of wealth* has come and God is accomplishing this programme through the work of *angel tellers*. It is angels who are sent to initiate, implement and monitor the smooth flow of transaction and transfer of wealth between the two parties. By reason of this spiritual law, there are a lot of economic and financial transactions that are taking place in the invisible realm in favour of believers although the process cannot be instantaneous but a smooth transition. This is the reason why God said in Judges 1:1-2:5, that *He would not drive out the Hivites and Ammonites from the land of Canaan in one day because their wickedness was not yet complete*. In some extreme cases, God might not directly snatch the wealth out of the hands of the wicked but He might do so indirectly by causing unbelievers to give millions in wealth to finance His visions, ministries and programmes of the Kingdom, without even them understanding why they are doing it.

Prophetically speaking, this end time dispensation shall witness a wave of millions of wealth being blown over the Body of Christ by the south wind and this shall culminate in the rise of multitudes of Kingdom millionaires across the globe. The people, who shall own the best places of the world, control its economic and political systems, regulate its monetary and wealthy structures are Christians. There are angels that sit in the invisible realm in the committees of EU, World Bank and Reserve Bank, to enforce decisions to transfer the funds in the realm of spirit in favour of believers. Angels have an influence over how money is created, circulated and used, hence they play such a strategic role in this end time wealth transfer process. While for ages, the wealth of the world has been in the hands of unbelievers, evidenced by the multitude of unbelieving millionaires, God is initiating a wealth transfer process that will see a drastic transition in wealth from the hands of unbelievers to the children of God. Imagine the impact that such change will have on the Body of Christ. However, it is quite important that believers live within the context of God's will through a life of consecration so that they could qualify for this wealth transfer because God will not take the wealth from unbelievers and give it to disobedient, sinful and lukewarm believers. He is not prepared to defeat the ends of justice by violating His spiritual laws and principles in the light of His creation. In the first place the reason why He is transferring wealth from unbelievers is because of their sins of disobedience, hence it would not make any spiritual sense for Him to take wealth from sinners and give it to another bunch of believing sinners. This is the reason why Israelites did not qualify to enter Canaan although God had initially promised to give it to them. On that note, believers must therefore learn to live in total consecration, righteousness, humility and obedience to the Word at all times in order to qualify to amass alarming wealth from Heaven in this season.

Angels are involved in the supervision of Kingdom finance and wealth distribution through Angelic financial meetings and gatherings in Heaven

It must be understood that not only do angels worship in Heaven as some folks have erroneously presumed. On the contrary, there are a myriad of duties, assignments and financial projects committed into the hands of angels by God, one of which is to handle the aspects of Kingdom prosperity. At a high level, high ranking angels who serve in the *Board of Heaven*, hold occasional spiritual gatherings to decide on the fate of humanity and how Heaven's wealth will be distributed amongst unbelievers on earth. Ministering angels gather in Heavenly meetings to deliberate on key financial matters of the Kingdom. It is through such occasional gatherings and deliberations that finances are released in the spirit and the angels are sent to cause them to manifest in the physical realm. In accordance with the will of God, the names of people who are meant to be entrusted with the wealth of the Kingdom are short listed, called and brought forth as in the case of boardroom nominations. New Visions, spiritual programmes and ministries are then given birth to in the spirit during such angelic discussions, conferences and meetings. This is largely the work of ministering or financial angels who serve in Heaven's finance department and are chiefly responsible for processing financial transactions, financial requisitions, making angelic deposits and transfers, and making sure that every godly vision is financed adequately.

When God gave me this revelation, my spirit was carried through the waves of the air and I saw in the spirit a book being opened with the names of people that the *Board of Heaven* had chosen to finance the Kingdom's end time plans, visions, ministries and spiritual programmes. As I peeped into the book, I was ecstatic to see that my name was also written in the book, amongst thousands other names. Millions of wealth measurable in money, gold, platinum and the top world currencies were allocated for each name for the accomplishment of God's divine plans and purpose. I also noticed the inscription of three words popping up and inscribed by God's own handwriting and these were *Grace, Mercy* and *Destiny*. And I heard the voice of the angel saying, *"This work has to be accomplished with a sense of urgency in this very hour".*

Angels bring about a physical manifestation of wealth in the natural realm

As aforementioned, the Bible unveils in Ephesian 1:3, that we are blessed with all in the Heavenly places. But why is it that many believers don't see the manifestation of the blessings of God in their lives? This is because there are two principles involved in the release of God's financial blessings, No 1. *Placement of spiritual blessings in the spirit realm,* No 2. *Manifestation of God's blessings in the physical realm.* After the release of blessings in Heaven, angels are then sent to cause them to visibly manifest in the natural realm. For example, in Genesis 25:29-34, Jacob had a birth right to God's blessings. He was the first choice in election, he had a calling and was of a lineage that would bring forth the Messiah to the world, but it took an angel to come down from Heaven to wrestle with him and bless him. The act of *wrestling* was a divine impartation to align him to the purpose of God. Angels will do whatever it takes to ensure that the financial blessings and millions of Heaven's wealth are manifested in the physical realm. Angels embark of special spiritual education programmes whereby they enlighten individuals though the glory of God and awaken them to know when the financial blessings of the Lord have been released, how to use them and for what purpose. On the basis of this revelation, developing a high level of sensitivity to angels through acknowledgement, interaction and cooperation, are such vital keys that could unlock a stream flow of millions of Heaven's wealth upon your life. As a matter of fact, angels are God's creatures that have been sent to help you receive and manifest your millions of wealth, hence should never be neglected under whatever circumstances.

CHAPTER EIGHT

A DIVINE PROPHETIC REVELATION OF GOD'S END-TIME KINGDOM FINANCIAL PROSPERITY PLAN

How Do I Qualify To Receive Millions In Miracle Money From God In This Season?

It is worth mentioning that if you aspire to become a recipient of millions in Miracle money in this present era, it is very important that you fully understand what God's plan and purpose are for your life and the whole world and the reason why God has ordained you to become a Kingdom Millionaire or Billionaire. Understanding God's divinely orchestrated financial plans and purpose will help you to operate within the confines of His will to expand the Kingdom by propagating the Gospel of the Lord Jesus Christ to all the nations of the world. From a Kingdom financial perspective, while the Gospel of the Lord Jesus Christ is rendered free of charge, the means to take it to the nations of the world requires a heightened degree of financial sacrifice. The spiritually driven campaign to reach out to save millions of lost souls across the globe requires finances. In this end-time dispensation, there is so much that needs to be accomplished in the Kingdom in terms of church growth and expansion, global vision bearing, apostolic and prophetic revivals, ministry establishment, broadcasting of spiritual programmes, proliferation of God's special end-time projects and divine assignments, all of which uncompromisingly require huge financial resources. In view of these needs, God uses His system of provision to dispatch or distribute millions in Heaven's wealth and financial resources to vision bearers, Kingdom carriers and financiers of the Kingdom so that they can establish and expand His Kingdom on behalf of humanity. This is why David proclaims in Psalms 112:3,

"Wealth and riches shall be in His house: and righteousness endures for ever."

In view of the above, there is what in the realm of God's prosperity is called *an End-Time Kingdom Financial Prosperity Plan*. This financial prosperity plan is orchestrated by God and propagated by the angels as a blue print of how finances will be distributed across a broad spectrum of Christian faith around the world for the purpose of spreading the Gospel of the Lord Jesus Christ and the subsequent fulfilment of God's plans, vision and purpose. In essence, it is an aggregate of all universal submissions that have been made to Heaven by believers across the globe through prayer requests and petitions on matters relating to financing Kingdom visions, ministries, churches and spiritual programmes. In view of the times and seasons, as stipulated in God's calendar, it should be explicitly understood that, while financial prosperity might not have been at the top of the Kingdom agenda throughout past generations, it has now become a priority and an imperative action, taking into account the nature of the dispensation and the season into which we have just been ushered. Therefore, God is calling on men and woman of vision to distinguish themselves by stepping out of the crowd and availing themselves to be used as candidates to transfer millions in Heaven's wealth to the nations of the world. God has located you by grace and brought you to the Kingdom at such a time as this to represent the Kingdom in all financial matters. You are, therefore, not a Kingdom Millionaire by accident.

THE KINGDOM END-TIME FINANCIAL PROSPERITY PARADIGM

Prophetically speaking, the generation of Christians that God is raising today as candidates for carrying out his divine plans and purposes on earth is completely different from those who lived in past generations. In view of the times and seasons, there is a paradigm shift that is taking place in the realm of the Spirit, from a season of ordinary Christianity to the rise of a generation of Kingdom-minded people who will impact the world for Christ in every sphere of human endeavour through regulating the economic and financial systems of the world, owning banks and estates and running the economies of the nations. I'm talking about the rise of a Joseph generation, an army of Kingdom wealth owners and purpose-driven individuals; a Daniel generation, a Kingdom-oriented people who will impact the world through godly leadership, governance and spiritual influence. When God expressed His heartfelt dissatisfaction in Ezekiel 22:30, proclaiming that, "*I looked for a man amongst men who could stand in the gap but there was none,*" it does not necessarily mean that there was no man who was praying or giving or going to church or serving Him. Instead, it means that there was no one who had a vision, relentless passion, burning desire and insatiable appetite to pursue the agenda of the Kingdom with God's heartbeat. In other words, there was none who had a prophetic perception to view or consider all things from God's perspective.

This is a typical scenario in the Body of Christ even today. In this generation, God is still looking for people whom He can entrust with the wealth of the Kingdom to finance or promote His end-time agenda on behalf of the Kingdom. It is for this reason that the Bible attests: *For the eyes of the Lord run to and fro throughout the whole earth, to show Himself strong in the behalf of them whose heart is perfect toward him* (2 Chronicles 16:9): The phrase, "*To show Himself strong*" means to bestow, grant or extend His covenant wealth. God's consuming passion and determination are to locate His covenant people by grace and unreservedly bless them. It is undying devotion that propels Him bless us with everything that He is and with everything that He has. God is, therefore, looking for a Kingdom purpose-driven people of selflessness, self-sacrificing and altruistic uprightness; a Kingdom-minded people who have died to selfish pleasures, worldly desires and the pursuit of individualistic gain so that He can grant them millions in Heaven's wealth and resources. However, the greatest problem that we face in the Body of Christ today is that, while many people make themselves available to be used by God, they don't want to develop an intrinsic drive or passion to carry the cross of Jesus Christ sacrificially. On the contrary, they just want to live in the realm of ordinary Christianity; hence, they are reluctant to launch into the greater depths and heights of God's supernatural provision. In view of the above, believers must be aware that, taking into account the nature of the dispensation we have been ushered into, the days of ordinary Christianity are over, as God is calling and raising men and women with a vision and a purpose to step out of the crowd, out of the world and expand His Kingdom on earth. It is a greater truth that God uses men to handle the affairs of men. If He were to handle the affairs of men Himself, He would do it extremely quickly and accomplish it within a twinkling of an eye. It would even lose the essence of its purpose because in God there is no future, past or present; everything is already completed.

It suffices to say that there are certain teachings, traditions and experiences that believers have been exposed to that need to be given divine correction. The problem is that so many people are living in the future, instead of the present. They keep saying that God is going to bless them, God is going to prosper them, God is going to make them millionaires and in the process they ignorantly keep pushing their blessings forward and delaying the manifestation of the fullness of their wealth in the natural realm. Contrary to what they believe to be true, this is not an exercise of faith but of hope because hope is in the future but faith is in the now. As far as God is concerned, He has already done it because He lives in the realm of eternity and is not bound by time, distance, space or matter. The greater truth is that we are not going to be millionaires but we are millionaires already; it's only that we have to walk in the consciousness of that reality to produce supernatural manifestations. Tactically speaking, we have been through this way before, just like a man walking on top of his own footprints where he had previously stepped before. By faith, God breaks the law of time and takes us into the future and shows everything completed and then comes back to the present to show us how to walk in the way He has shown us into the future. This was revealed to Paul: he had already seen his future, his destiny, his crown in eternity and coming back to the present he declared in Romans 8:18, *that our present sufferings are not worth comparing to the glory we shall receive in Christ.* In other words, his spirit had travelled into the future to behold what God had in store for him and then came back to the natural to live for what he had seen.

In light of the above, it suffices to reiterate the prophetic assertion that we are living in a season where planting and harvesting are taking place at the same time. According to natural law, if you plant a seed, it takes time before you can harvest it, but as a new creation we are no longer living according to natural law but according to supernatural law, which states that as you plant the seed you will immediately see a harvest. The transcending, superseding and overruling law of faith prevails in all circumstances and breaks the law of time to cause us to walk in the manifestation of our millions in the now. This is, therefore, a season of rapid promotion, rapid growth, rapid increase and rapid results; hence, our millions in wealth are at hand.

UNVEILING GOD'S PROPHETIC END-TIME PROSPERITY AGENDA

Prophetically speaking, a mega shift is taking place in the realm of the Spirit as God is restoring and elevating the Church to its rightful place and position of original prosperity and superabundance. In the context of Kingdom millionaire hood, God's end-time prophetic agenda is unveiled in Isaiah 2:2-3 where He declares that,

A Divine Prophetic Revelation of God's End Time Prosperity Plan

It shall come to pass in the last days, that the mountain of the LORD'S house shall be established in the top of the mountains, and shall be exalted above the hills; and all nations shall flow unto it. And many people shall go and say, "Come ye, and let us go up to the mountain of the LORD, to the house of the God of Jacob; and he will teach us of his ways, and we will walk in his paths: for out of Zion shall go forth the word of the LORD from Jerusalem."

This is evidently God's end–time prophetic agenda for the Church. This implies that the Church of Jesus Christ is programmed for the top of the mountain; forward and upward only. It's an exalted, flourishing and prosperous Church. It is strikingly interesting to note that in these end times, the Church shall be a voice in this end-time, dictating the pace of things to the world. In other words, the Church will teach the world how to make money and produce results in every sphere of human endeavour. Since the world's economic system has dismally failed, as multitudes are entangled in a morass of debilitating poverty, the world will inevitably look to the Church for an ultimate solution. This is why the Bible declares: *He will teach us of his ways, and we will walk in his paths: for out of Zion shall go forth the law, and the word of the LORD from Jerusalem* (Isaiah 2:2-3). This speaks of an enviable role that the Church will play in these end times and this is God's plan for you as a believer. Since the Church is not a building where believers gather on a Sunday but the pulsating nature of Christ manifested in humanity, your enviable place in destiny is at the top of the mountain, exalted above every situation.

Prophetically speaking, the world is going to depend on the Church for its survival. The world will come to the Church to learn how to prosper and live in financial freedom. Hence, biblical principles of economics will be the solution to the financial woes of the world. As the economic policies of the nations of the world have disappointingly failed the masses, the world will have no alternative but to turn to the Church for help and an ultimate solution. However, the world will only turn to a church that has results to show, a church that is doing well and prospering, not a beggarly church. Ideally, the Church of Jesus is meant to be a problem-solving church, an asset and not a liability to the world. It is ordained to function as the custodian of God's power and, since every problem answers to the power of God, it takes power to solve problems. The good news is that you are the Church and have a place in God's end-time prosperity agenda. In other words, you are the one who is going to show the world how to prosper. You are a solution to this world, not a problem, an answer to the woes of the world as you truly walk in the reality of God's plan and purpose for your life to become a Kingdom Millionaire.

A DIVINE REVELATION OF HEAVEN'S END-TIME FINANCIAL WEALTH RESERVOIR

The Spiritual Bank of Heaven

It is a greater truth unknown to many believers that a vast deposit of reserves of riches has been freely made available for believers in the Bank of Heaven. This is the oldest bank in existence and it dates way back to a period before the creation of mankind. It operates outside time, matter and space; hence, it is not subject to how the worldly economy operates. Unlike earthly banks, it is as unshakable and steadfast as the triune God who founded it. Its doors are never closed day or night to a child of God, and as for a run on it nothing would please the Heavenly Father more than to have a daily, hourly, moment-by-moment demand for its treasures. According to Ephesians 3:8, God has placed a deposit for us in Christ of riches that can be drawn on according to our need and our desire. God has put in our possession His own promises, given in the name of our Saviour, which we may claim at any time and to any limit by an act of appropriating faith.

The Bible declares in Ephesians 1:3: *Blessed be the God and Father of our Lord Jesus Christ, who hath blessed us with all spiritual blessings in Heavenly places in Christ.* The word "spiritual" designates the character of the blessings bestowed. It speaks of Heaven's financial reserves, which are abundantly available at your call. However, although this wealth is initially available in spiritual form, it can transmute itself into the physical realm. In other words, through the power of faith, placing a demand, appropriation and being catapulted into confession, it can be translated from the realm of the Spirit into manifestation in the natural realm. When Paul proclaims that,

"We are blessed with all spiritual blessings in the Heavenly places,"

In this cryptic sentence, he opens the door into the Epistle to Ephesians, and gives us a glimpse of what awaits us. It is the key to this house of spiritual treasures. Paul could not wait to unfold these riches gradually, so he places, as it were, a nugget of gold in our hands at the threshold, a sign of what we will find within the Epistle.

In view of the above scriptural reference, it is evident that the wealth of a believer as reserved in Heaven's store house or Spiritual Bank is royal, munificent and unlosable; altogether sufficient to meet the requirements to overcome his moral and spiritual delinquency and bankruptcy, and wholly adequate for even the greatest trial, financial, physical, mental or spiritual. The availability of this huge wealth in Heaven was revealed to David, who proclaimed in Psalms 36:7-9 (Amplified Version), *"How precious is Your steadfast love, O God! The children of men take refuge and put their trust under the shadow of Your wings. They relish and feast on the abundance of Your own house; and You cause them to drink of the stream of Your pleasures. For with You is the fountain of life."* This implies that there is a wealth storage system or *Spiritual Bank in Heaven*, which is a reservoir that contains wealth in the form of money in every currency under Heaven. This money is always readily available to be dispatched or distributed by angels to earth as occasion demands to fulfil God's purposes. However, it has to be claimed by residents of the earth so that it can be dispatched. In the event that it is not claimed, it remains in Heaven's store house, underutilised and untapped. This is why the Bible declares in James 1:17 that *every good gift and every perfect gift is from above, and cometh down from the Father of lights, with whom is no variableness, neither shadow of turning.* This is God's system of governance regarding the dispatch of Heaven's wealth and resources. Now, you can imagine the millions in wealth that have remained largely untapped by Christians up to today.

As stated earlier, the Bible attests to the divine truth that we are blessed with all spiritual blessings in the Heavenly places. There are two vital aspects to be clarified in this scripture. First, these blessings are in spirit form and not in natural form. Second, their location is in the spirit realm and not in the physical realm. This implies that converting these blessings from a spiritual form into a physical form and also transferring their location from the spirit realm to a natural location require faith because faith travels across both realms of existence. The question is: How is Heaven's wealth transferred from the spiritual realm into the physical realm. This is made possible through meditation and visualisation because in the spirit realm, unless you see something, you cannot have it. Other means include prophetic declarations, appropriation of blessings by placing a demand and commanding faith. However, in this season, the Miracle money anointing is the most common strategy which Heaven is using to transfer money from the spirit realm into visible and tangible manifestation in the physical.

A DIVINE REVELATION OF THE END-TIME FINANCIAL ANOINTING

The Miracle Money Anointing

It is worth exploring the divine truth that in this end-time dispensation, uncommon millionaires are going to emerge in the Body of Christ than ever before. However, it is important to note that the ability to manifest Heaven's wealth and resources in the natural requires the *Miracle Money anointing*. It has been noted that while the Body of Christ relies heavily on *confession,* for the supernatural manifestation of the abundance of Heavenly resources, confession is not bringing the finances in like it should be. So, there must be a missing ingredient that we can add to our confession that will cause money to come to us as God intended, which is the *Miracle Money anointing*. The Bible proclaims that it is God who gives *the power to make wealth* (Deuteronomy 8:18; Proverbs 16:22; Genesis 24:35; Psalms 37:21-22) and this power to create wealth is the *Miracle Money anointing*. Wealth is the anointing manifested in the area of finances. Notice the word *"power"* in this verse. You see, the Lord is not going to give you wealth unscrupulously. Instead, He gives you *power* to get wealth, through His Word and His financial plan. He's not going to give you wealth because He's already provided you with wealth in His redemptive plan. There is no limit to the things God wants you to have in life, but you have to take hold of the *power* He gives (the anointing) to obtain them. You must therefore understand that one becomes a Kingdom Millionaire or Billionaire as a result of having received an impartation of the *Miracle Money anointing*, which is God's *super* abundance added to our *natural* situation. Philosophically speaking, *money is like a current; it is either flowing to you or flowing away from you*. This is why it is called "currency". The Miracle money anointing is therefore, the only divine or spiritual substance that can attract money in the realm of the natural so that it can flow in your direction.

> *Money cannot resist the anointing; it naturally flows where the anointing is flowing. Hence, there is such a thing as the anointing for prosperity and the anointing for finances.*

On the basis of the above revelation, it is evident that the only thing which attracts or magnetises money in the Spirit is the *Miracle Money anointing*. This is why some people have the ability to attract money while others repel money. The difference between these people is in the *Miracle Money anointing*. It is worth mentioning that different types of people are involved in the pursuit of money: *there are those who create it, there are those who manage it and then there are those who spend it*. As a believer, in your journey to becoming a Kingdom Millionaire or Billionaire, you must not find yourself in the company of those who are toiling from dusk till dawn searching, jostling and hustling for money. Your divine and sole mandate as a believer is to manifest the newly emerging financial patterns of God in a global revival and to provide believers with the financial resources to break every chain of financial bondage and consequently step into an entirely new dimension of financial freedom. Therefore, your responsibility is to learn how to attract and magnetise money so that you can use it to advance Kingdom plans and purposes; the best way to do this is through the *Miracle Money anointing*. It is the financial anointing that enables you to command Miracle money into physical manifestation and also causes angel tellers to move swiftly in the spirit dimension to expedite God's financial plan on earth. God is ready to pour out this great financial wealth or anointing on every believer just as He did to Abraham, Isaac and Jacob, the Israelites, Solomon and many other believers in the past generations.

Pertaining to the release of the financial anointing, God declared in Isaiah 45:3, "*I will give you the treasures of darkness and the hidden riches of secret places.*" In the context of this scripture, the word "darkness" does not necessarily refer to something evil but rather to something that is hidden, unseen, unexplored, reserved, stored, and not yet brought to light. These are deep secrets of God in the arena of financial prosperity that the world has not discovered yet. In essence, the hidden treasure is the huge financial wealth of Heaven, which can only be excavated by the financial anointing because the anointing is one of the spiritual substances that are used as a lubricant to move the financial blessings of God from Heaven to earth so that people can be wealthy and prosperous and can fulfil their divine purpose. However, God doesn't want us to be taken by surprise at His divine outpouring of financial wealth and resources; hence, He declares in Amos 3:7 that *He will do absolutely nothing unless He reveals the secrets to His servants*. In the context of the above scripture, this implies that Heaven's great wealth is no longer a mystery or a hidden treasure because God is unveiling it to believers so that they can use it to take the life-changing, gracious Gospel of the Lord Jesus Christ to the extreme ends of the world. Moreover, the Bible speaks of deep secrets of God, which He has unveiled to us by the Holy Spirit (John 16:4-15). These deep secrets are actually Heaven's financial wealth, which the Holy Spirit has unveiled to us by the Holy Spirit. This is indeed a great season of exploration and discovery in the realm of the spirit, of the millions in wealth that has been laid up for generations.

Prophetically speaking, there is coming *a season of an unprecedented financial outpouring* and an avalanche of millions in wealth for believers who understand God's timing and direction during these days. There is an unusual anointing that is being released from the Heavens in this end-time season specifically for the purpose of accomplishing God's end-time divine purpose. The practical demonstration of this *Miracle Money anointing* is what will culminate in a wide-spread church planting and the global propagation of the Gospel of Jesus Christ. People whom the world had side-lined or alienated through its monetary system and who never thought they could be millionaires will rise up with such amazing wealth and financial power as the world has never seen before and these people will establish Kingdom property, Kingdom banks and Kingdom investment holdings and will spearhead a Kingdom monetary system that will work in favour of the Gospel of Christ Jesus. Even in the midst of the world's projected global financial crisis, these people will dominate the world's monetary systems to advance the Gospel.

However, despite the fact that God has released the *Miracle Money anointing*, there are still some believers across the broad spectrum of Christian faith who experience financial demands during challenging times and try to figure out how to supply their own need. Under pressure, they forget to factor in the key element that would completely alter their financial condition, the *Miracle Money anointing*. As a consequence, a large number of believers have not been able to experience a manifestation of the wealth of Heaven and are struggling financially because their financial blessings have been intercepted, manipulated and twisted in the spirit realm by spiritual forces of evil and wickedness. However, it only takes the *Miracle Money anointing* to break demonic forces so that great financial wealth may be released to the masses. This is the reason why the prophet Isaiah declared in Isaiah 10:27, *"It shall come to pass in that day, that his burden shall be taken away from off thy shoulder and his yoke from off thy neck, and the yoke shall be destroyed because of the anointing."* In the context of this revelation, the "burden" refers to a heavy load carried with great financial difficulty; i.e. to be weighed down with debt, poverty or lack. The "yoke" refers to an agency of oppression, slavery and servitude and is a symbol of subjection, defeat and humiliation, which a multitude of Christians are exposed to as a result of lack. The key, solution or answer to all these predicaments is the *Miracle Money anointing*. The *Miracle Money anointing* is God's provision poured over, smeared on and rubbed into our financial lives. It is the burden-removing, yoke-destroying power of God. It is the power of God that removes the burden of lack and destroys the yoke of debt. It is God's "super" abundance added to our "natural" situation. The anointing will make a way where there is no way, accelerate the increase of your store houses, wipe out outstanding debts and reveal the wisdom you need to thrive and not just survive in these harsh economic times. It is when you have taken a drink from the cup of God's new financial anointing that millions in money and wealth will flow in your direction.

CHAPTER NINE

THE PRACTICAL DEMONSTRATIONS OF MIRACLE MONEY IN THE NATURAL REALM

It must be understood that Miracle money is not just a theoretical concept but a practical one. As a matter of fact, you tend to understand it in depth the more you practically demonstrate it than when you are just talking about it. I never fully understood Miracle money until the day I practically demonstrated it in the natural realm. Understanding it from a practical perspective helps to solidify your faith in God and increases your appetite, perennial hunger and unquenchable thirst to reach out to others. This grace can be demonstrated by anyone who is born again, spirit filled and Word enlightened, to step up in faith and make a pulling on the supernatural and cause it to manifest in a tangible and visible form in the natural realm. Did you know that the original blueprint of everything that exist in the spirit ream can be manifested in a visible way in the natural realm? Angels can manifest in a visible form just like human beings on earth. The anointing can manifest in a tangible form as a rain of liquid water. By the same token, Miracle money can manifest as a tangible liquid substance in the natural realm. Although a greater part of this publication has been devoted towards the unveiling of revelation knowledge, this last section of the book is a practical snap shot that deals with how Miracle money can be practically demonstrated in the natural realm. It is therefore important that you pay meticulous attention to what you say, how you say it and when you have to say it during Miracle money demonstrations in the physical realm.

HOW TO EXERCISE YOUR FAITH FOR A MILLION DOLLARS

Father, in the Name of Jesus, I boldly present myself before the Throne of Grace, according to your word (Hebrews 4:16) and I unreservedly commit every aspect of my being into thy hands. I am grateful that according to your grace and riches in Christ glory, you have made me a Kingdom Millionaire, worthy to partake of the overflow of abundant and endless riches of your supernatural provision. I therefore confess that I am a seed of Abraham (Galatians 3:29) hence I am legally entitled to place a demand on all the riches available in the Heaven Storehouses.

I stand firmly and grounded upon your word and according to John 16:23 (AMP), Jesus said, "I assure you, most solemnly I tell you, that My Father will grant you whatever you ask in My Name." Lord, Jesus, You said in Mark 11:24 (AMP), that "Whatever you ask for in prayer, believe (trust and be confident) that it is granted to you, and you will [get it]." Your Word further attests in Luke 6:38 that, "Give, and it shall be given unto you; a good measure, pressed down, shaken together, and running over, shall men give unto your bosom." In accordance to Your Word, I have therefore sown a seed in order to set this spiritual law in motion.

I therefore submit this request in the Name of Jesus and according to John 16:23 (AMP), I duly appropriate and lay claim of my Heavenly grant of *one million dollar* now. According to your word in Mark 11:24 (AMP), I am confident that whatever I ask in prayer, it is granted to me. I therefore believe I have received my grant of *one million dollar* in Jesus' Name. I declare and decree that it be known this day, both in the realm of the spirit and the natural that I have received a Heavenly grant in the amount of *one million dollar* from Heaven. I therefore proclaim and pronounce that I am a Kingdom Millionaire as a recipient of Heaven's uncommon wealth in Jesus Name.

According to Matthew 18:18, I bind and cast out Satan and all his forces of darkness, and render null and void every evil scheme designed against my finances. I quench every demonic arrow directed against my finances. I therefore declare and decree that they will be unable to operate or hinder my grant in Jesus Name. Accordingly, I release my millions worth of money in the realm of the spirit into my bank account and I command it to manifest into a tangible and visible form in the physical realm right now.

According to Hebrews 1:13 and 14, I dispatch and release the angels of God and charge them to go forth to the North, East, West, South and every dimension to cause my grant of Millions of dollars to manifest in the physical realm and land into my hands. I believe I have received now. Thank you Lord for your boundless supernatural provision, in the Name of Jesus.

Lord, I ascribe unto thee all the Glory, Honour and Power due your Name.
Amen!

HOW TO MAKE A FINANCIAL WITHDRAWAL FROM THE RESERVE BANK OF HEAVEN

The Bible proclaims in 2 Corinthians 4:18 that the realm of the natural is a shadow, fore taste and an exact representation of the spiritual realm. As much as there are bank accounts in the natural realm, there are also bank accounts in Heaven. According to Matthew 6:19-21, these accounts are not subject to theft, ruin, corruption or harsh economic conditions of any kind. This implies that contrary to the accounts that we have in the natural, heavenly accounts are more secure, credible and eternal. For example in Luke 12:33, Jesus spoke about a treasure in Heaven that fails not. However, the greatest challenge that we have is that multitudes of believers in the

Body of Christ have not been able to partake of the millions of wealth that is available in the Spiritual Bank of Heaven because they do not realize they already have an account in Heaven. Paul unveils the reality of this spiritual accounting transactions. According to the Epistles, the Philippians had established an account in Heaven because Paul says in Verse 15 (GOS) that, *"No church but yours went into partnership and opened an account with us."* They opened their account by giving. For clarity of purpose, let's look at how different versions of the Bible expresses this divine reality (AMP): *Not that I seek or am eager for [your] gift, but I do seek and am eager for the fruit which increases to your credit [the harvest of blessing that is accumulating to your account]."* CON: *I seek fruit which accrues to your account.* TCNT: *I am anxious to see abundant returns placed to your account.* MOF: *I am anxious for the interest that accumulates to your divine account.* NASB: *I seek for the profit which increases to your account.* NJB: *What I value most is the interest that is mounting up in your account.* Spiritually speaking, you get to open the Heavenly account by being born again, you make a deposit by either giving to the work of ministry or to the poor and you make a withdrawal by releasing your faith in the word of God.

More specifically, there are two main ways of withdrawing money from the Bank of Heaven. It's either you make a deposit into the Heavenly account by faithfully tithing and sowing a seed and then release your faith to make a withdrawal from the same Heavenly bank account or you can simply tap into the realm of faith to command a supernatural withdrawal as occasion demands. In the natural realm, whenever you need a lump sum of money, you have to go to the bank, take out your card, enter your pin and type the amount you want and then collect the money. As it is in the natural so it is in the spirit. Your Faith is your account number, the blood of Jesus is your secret pin and your daily limit is the size of your vision. In this season of financial abundance, you can withdraw any amount of money that you need from the Heavenly account and it will supernaturally appear in your bank account or whichever area you command it to appear in.

PRACTICAL APPLICATION OF HOW TO MAKE A FINANCIAL WITHDRAWAL FROM THE RESERVE BANK OF HEAVEN

Father, in the Name of Jesus, I stand in the apostolic and prophetic office, with the authority invested upon me from above, I declare and decree that I am a Kingdom millionaire. I therefore make a withdrawal of one million rand from my Heavenly bank account. By faith, I command and release this amount to manifest in the physical realm into my bank account right now. I proclaim and pronounce that I have this money in my account and I am withdrawing it right now. I believe I receive my million rand in Jesus Name.

Satan, I take authority over you and by the blood of Jesus Christ, I bind your operation now and render you helpless. I command you to loose your hands off my finances in Jesus Name. I therefore render null and void every demonic operation directed against my finances in Jesus Name.

Angels, I disperse and discharge you to go forth and cause this amount to manifest in the physical realm right now. I therefore believe and confess that I have received the money into my account in Jesus Name.

Father, I praise Your Name for meeting my needs according to Your riches in Christ glory in the Name of Jesus. I dully ascribe unto thee all glory, honour and power due your name. Thank you, Your Majesty. In the name of Jesus Christ.

Amen!

HOW TO EXERCISE YOUR FAITH FOR PROPERTY OR MATERIAL POSSESSIONS

Firstly you need to catch the divine revelation of dominion and authority in order to excel in the realm or dimension of financial prosperity. You must therefore have a solid and profound understanding that divine prosperity and abundance belong to you now. In your capacity as born-again believer, you have the same authority over the earth that Adam had in the Garden of Eden. The Bible records in Genesis 1:28 (AMP) that *"God blessed them (Adam & Eve) and said to them, be fruitful, multiply, and fill the earth, and subdue it [using all its vast resources]."*

Therefore be convinced beyond any shadow doubt that every material thing came from the earth's vast resources. For example, every piece of lumber, brick, glass, concrete, mortar or steel originated from the earth. As a matter of fact, there is nothing in the makeup of a car, house or business that did not come from the earth's resources. You therefore have the divine legitimate right to take authority over any material property be it a mansion, car, land or business and receive it as yours in the Name of Jesus.

However in your exercise of faith it is important what you say, how you say it and when you say it. As stipulated by *the success formula*, the first step is to find out what God's Word says about your financial situation. Then speak that Word in faith, believing for the desired result. Then meditate upon it until the Word becomes greater on the inside than the lack on the outside. Then, fearlessly act on what you see in the Word, knowing that no word from God is void or without power. The result is that you will make your way prosperous. It is also important that as part of the mediation and visualisation process that you get an image inside of you of living in a nice big house. Get a vision of having a house with nice landscaping and pretty flowers everywhere and once this image has been fully established and embedded in your spirit, it shall break forth into visible and tangible manifestation in the natural realm.

HOW TO EXERCISE YOUR FAITH FOR A BUSINESS OR INVESTMENT

Father, in the Name of Jesus, I stand in the Apostolic and Prophetic Office. With all the power and authority invested upon me from above, I take charge over the business, the resources and the finances I require to set up a business. I take my place as a Kingdom Millionaire and I take dominion over that which I need, the start-up capital, the land, venue and the equipment. By the power of the Holy Ghost, I command you to come in my direction right now in Jesus' Name.

Father your Word says in 2 Corinthians 8:9 that Jesus was made poor so that through His poverty, I might be rich. Your word further says that you have given me all things that pertain to life and godliness (2 Peter 1:3). Your word further says that you supply all my needs according to the riches in Christ glory (Philippians 4:19). I therefore stand upon your living word and I declare that I am rich and own business property. My business is thriving and flourishing like foliage. I am abundantly and exuberantly making profits. I declare that money in millions and billions is coming on feet in my direction in Jesus name.

I therefore stand upon your word and I release my business. I believe that i have received it in the name of Jesus. I declare that my business is flourishing like foliage and it shall not incur any loss in Jesus Name.

Angels, I discharge and release you to go and bring customers to my business in multitudes in Jesus Name. I command you to gather every resource, equipment and money I will need to run my business. I command you to bring forth people who will help me establish my business in Jesus Name.

I declare that I have a title deed to my new business in Jesus Name. I thank you Lord for your hand of provision. Unto to you, be the Glory, Honour and Power, forever and ever.   **Amen!**

HOW TO EXERCISE YOUR FAITH FOR A HOUSE OR A MANSION

Heavenly Father, in the Name of Jesus, I take authority over my house and the money I need to purchase it. I command you to come to me now. I take my place in the spirit dimension and I take dominion over all resources, tools and equipment, property which I need for my house. I command it to come in Jesus' Name.

Father, Your word says in Proverbs 24:3-4 that "Through wisdom is a house build and by understanding, it is established; And by knowledge shall the chambers be filled with all precious and pleasant riches." Your word further declares in Proverbs 15:6 that "In the house of the righteous is much treasure. "Your word further proclaims in (Proverbs 12:7) that "The house of the righteous shall stand." I therefore stand deeply rooted upon your word and I release my house and believe that I have received it in the name of Jesus.

Angels, I command you to go to the North, East, West, South and every direction to cause it to come forth from the spirit realm into physical manifestation in Jesus Name.

I declare that I have a title deed to my new house in Jesus Name. I thank you Lord for your hand of provision. Unto thee be the Glory, Honour and Power, forever and ever.

Amen!

HOW TO EXERCISE YOUR FAITH FOR A CAR OR A PRIVATE JET

Heavenly Father, in the Name of Jesus, I take authority over the car (BMW), the Private Jet and the money I need to purchase it. I command you to come to me. I take my place as a Kingdom Priest and King and I take dominion over that which I need for my car and Private Jet to manifest in the physical realm. I command it to come now in Jesus' Name.

Lord, your word says in 2 Peter 1:3 that God has given me all things which pertain to life and godliness and I confess that you have freely given me my car and my Private Jet in Jesus Name. Your word further says that the Lord supplies all my needs according to the riches in Christ glory (Philippians 4:19) and I thank you that my car and Private jet is supplied in Jesus Name. I therefore stand grounded and rooted upon your word and I release my car and Private Jet and believe that I have received it in the name of Jesus. I command it to move from the spirit realm into the physical realm. I thank you that I have my car and its keys in Jesus name

Angels, I command you to go to the garage and cause it to come forth into manifestation in the physical realm. I command you to drive it from the spirit realm into physical manifestation in Jesus Name. I declare that I have a title deed to my new car in Jesus Name. I thank you Lord for your hand of provision. Unto thee be the Glory, Honour and Power, forever and ever.

Amen!

PRAYER FOR IMPARTATION OF THE MIRACLE MONEY ANOINTING

Heavenly Father, in the name of Jesus Christ, I thank You for the depth of revelations of Your word encapsulated in this publication. I believe Your word and embrace these revelations for my season. I place a demand on the economy of Heaven (Reserve Bank of Heaven) for the release of Millions in Miracle money in the natural realm, to expedite Your purpose. I therefore, receive an impartation of the Miracle money anointing into my spirit, right now. By faith, I believe that I have received Miracle money grace and now I'm rightly positioned and ready to propagate the world with the Miracle money anointing. I believe that I have been catapulted into the realm of practically demonstrating Miracle money in the natural realm, for Your glory. I therefore, declare and decree that everywhere I go, Miracle money will supernaturally appear in people's bags, wallets, pockets, bank accounts and unexpected territories in Jesus name. I proclaim and pronounce that I'm a money magnet that attracts the wealth of Heaven, hence everywhere I go, Miracle money in the best currencies of the world will stream in my direction. Therefore, I take responsibility for propagating the Miracle money grace to the furthest extremes of the world, to accomplish Your divine plans and purpose in this generation. I declare and decree that I have been enlisted in God's prosperity agenda in this season. I have been singled out to be a recipient of Wealth transfer, hence I'm in line to receive thousands and millions in Miracle Money in this season. Therefore, as I step into the realm of the undefinable, uncharted and unrecorded miracles, signs and wonders in this season, I declare and decree that I'm striding at the frontline of a Miracle money revival, to launch the world into an arena of divine exploits. By the mandate of Heaven, I officially announce the expiry date of debt, poverty and untold hardship over my life and that of the masses and declare and decree that as the torrential downpour of the heavy rain of Miracle Money is precipitating directly from the Throne Room of Heaven to the extreme ends of the world, every outstanding debt is cancelled in Jesus name. I therefore, unleash and release the angel tellers on standby to swiftly and speedily respond to every demand I make at the window of faith and that all forces of divinity be postured to act on the Word I speak. I confess that the confidence of the currency of the Kingdom is backing my confessions of faith today as all Heaven's attention is directed towards me. I declare and decree that the deposits of hope that I have held in my heart are ready to be tendered in my life today. Therefore, there is no hold on the reserves of Heaven on my behalf as all the flood gates, doors and windows of Heaven are wide open over me. I confess that God is not reluctant to cash out the economy of Heaven to meet my need, hence a divine arrangement of circumstances in the realm of the spirit have been prearranged for Miracle money to unreservedly stream in my direction. Thank you, Lord, for making me such a wonder in this world by committing the Miracle money grace into my hands. I ascribe unto Thee all the glory, honour and power due to Your name.

AMEN!

PHROPHETIC ACTION:

Begin to pray in the Holy Ghost now to activate the grace to practically demonstrate Miracle money, which has already been inculcated in your spirit. I declare and decree that immediately you finish reading this book, Miracle money will invade your space and supernaturally appear in your pockets, wallet, hand bag, car, house and other unexpected places, glory to Jesus! Be vigilant and circumspect because it has already started manifesting. Now, begin to check in these unexpected places and give God all the Glory, Honour and Power due His name.

Congratulations, for you have now received the grace to practically demonstrate Miracle money, Glory to God!

PRAYER FOR SALVATION

If you have never received Jesus Christ as your Lord and Personal saviour, loudly recite the following prayer, now:

Dear Heavenly Father! I present my life before you today. I confess with my mouth that Jesus Christ is Lord and believe in my heart that He died on the cross and was raised from the dead after 3 days, for the remission of my sins. I acknowledge that I'm a sinner and ask you to forgive me for all the sins I have ever committed. Wash me with the precious blood of Jesus Christ and write my name in the Book of life. I therefore receive eternal life into my spirit right now. I declare that from henceforth, Jesus Christ is my Lord and Saviour and I proclaim His Lorship over every area of my life. Thank you Lord Jesus Christ for saving my soul. I'm now a child of God, born again, born of the Spirit of the living God.

AMEN!

Congratulations and Welcome to the family of God. You are now a brand new creation that belongs to the lineage of the blessed, the Royal priesthood, the Chosen generation and the highly favoured! Most importantly, you have now received the divine legitimate right, authority and power, to demonstrate Miracle money in the natural realm, glory to Jesus!

ABOUT THE AUTHOR

Frequency Revelator is an apostle, called by God through His grace to minister the Gospel of the Lord Jesus Christ to all the nations of the world. He is a television minister, lecturer and gifted author, whose writings are Holy Ghost breathings that unveil consistent streams of fresh revelations straight from the Throne Room of Heaven. He is the president, founder and vision bearer of Frequency Revelator Ministries (FRM), a worldwide multiracial ministry that encompasses a myriad of movements with divine visions such as Resurrection Embassy (*The Global Church*), Christ Resurrection Movement (CRM) (*a Global movement for raising the dead*), the Global Apostolic & Prophetic Network (GAP) (a *Network of apostles, prophets and fivefold ministers across the globe*), Revival For Southern Africa (REFOSA) (*a Regional power-packed vision for Southern Africa*) and the Global Destiny Publishing House (GDP) (*the Ministry's publishing company*). The primary vision of this global ministry is to propagate the resurrection power of Christ from the Throne Room of Heaven to the extreme ends of the world and to launch the world into the greater depths of the miraculous. It is for this reason that Frequency Revelator Ministries (FRM) drives divergent apostolic and prophetic ministry visions and spiritual programmes such as the Global School of Resurrection (GSR), Global Resurrection Centre (GRC), the Global Healing Centre (GHC), Global School of Miracles, Signs and Wonders (SMSW), Global School of Kingdom Millionaires (SKM), Global Campus Ministry as well as Resurrection Conferences, Seminars and Training Centres. To fulfil its global mandate of soul winning, the ministry spearheads the Heavens' Broadcasting Commission (HBC) on television, a strategic ministerial initiative that broadcasts ministry programmes via the Dead Raising Channel *(a.k.a Resurrection TV)* and other Christian Television networks around the world.

Presiding over a global network of apostolic and prophetic visions, Apostle Frequency Revelator considers universities, colleges, high schools and other centres of learning as critical in fulfilling God's purpose and reaching the world for Christ, especially in this end-time season. As a Signs and Wonders Movement, the ministry hosts training sessions at the Global School of Resurrection (GSR) which includes but not limited to, impartation and activation of the gifts of the Spirit, prophetic declaration and ministration, invocations of open visions, angelic encounters and Throne Room visitations, revelational teachings, coaching and mentorship as well as Holy Ghost ministerial training sessions on how to practically raise the dead. This global ministry is therefore characterised by a deep revelation of God's word accompanied by a practical demonstration of God's power through miracles, signs and wonders manifested in raising cripples from wheel chairs, opening the eyes of the blind, unlocking the speech of the dumb, blasting off the ears of the deaf and raising the dead, as a manifestation of the finished works of the cross by the Lord Jesus Christ. The ministry is also punctuated with a plethora of manifestations of the wealth of Heaven through miracle money, coupled with the golden rain of gold dust, silver stones, diamonds, supernatural oil and a torrent of creative miracles such as the development of the original blue print of body parts on bodily territories where they previously did not exist, germination of hair on bald heads, weight loss and gain, as well as instantaneous healings from HIV/AIDS, cancer, diabetes and every manner of sickness and disease which doctors have declared as incurable.

The author has written a collection of 21 anointed books, which include *The Realm of Power to Raise the Dead, How to become a Kingdom Millionaire, Deeper Revelations of The Anointing, Practical Demonstrations of The Anointing, How to Operate in the Realm of the Miraculous, The Realm of Glory, Unveiling the Mystery of Miracle Money, New Revelations of Faith, A Divine Revelation of the Supernatural Realm, The Prophetic Move of the Holy Spirit in the Contemporary Global Arena, The Ministry of Angels in the World Today, Kingdom Spiritual Laws and Principles, Divine Rights and Privileges of a Believer, Keys to Unlocking the Supernatural, The Prophetic Dimension, The Dynamics of God's Word, The Practice of God's Presence, Times of Refreshing and Restoration, The Power of Praying in the Throne Room, The*

About The Author

End Time Revelations of Jesus Christ and Rain of Revelations, which is a daily devotional concordance comprising a yearly record of 365 fresh revelations straight from the Throne Room of God.

Apostle Frequency Revelator resides in South Africa and he is a graduate of Fort Hare University, where his ministry took off. However, as a global minister, his ministry incorporates prophecy, deliverance and miracle healing crusades in the United Kingdom (UK), Southern Africa, India, Australia, USA, Canada and a dense network of ministry visions that covers the rest of the world. As a custodian of God's resurrection power, the apostle has been given a divine mandate from Heaven to raise a new breed of Apostles, Prophets, Pastors, Evangelists, Teachers, Kingdom Millionaires and Miracle Workers *(Dead raisers)* who shall propagate the world with the gospel of the Lord Jesus Christ and practically demonstrate His resurrection power through miracles, signs and wonders manifested in raising people from the dead, thereby launching the world in to the greater depths of the miraculous. To that effect, a conducive platform is therefore enacted for global impartation, mentorship, training and equipping ministers of the gospel for the work of ministry. Notable is the realisation that the ministry ushers a new wave of signs and wonders that catapults the Body of Christ into higher realms of glory in which precipitating the rain of Miracle Money is a common occurrence and demonstrating the viscocity of the glory of God in a visible and tangible manner is the order of the day. Having been mightily used by God at the frontline of the global Miracle Money revival, in this book, Apostle Frequency Revelator presents a practical model of how one can tap into the realm of God's supernatural provision, to practically demonstrate Miracle money, impact the nations of the world and usher an unprecedented avalanche of billions of souls into the Kingdom, Glory to Jesus! May His Name be gloried, praised and honoured forever more!

AUTHOR'S CONTACT INFORMATION:

To know more about the ministry of Apostle Frequency Revelator, his publications, revelational teachings, global seminars, ministry schools, ministry products and Global missions, contact:

Apostle Frequency Revelator

@ Resurrection Embassy

(The Global Church)

Powered by Christ Resurrection Movement (CRM)

(Contact us in the United Kingdom, South Africa, USA, Canada, Australia, India, Holland & Other nations of the world).

As a Global Vision, The Ministry of Apostle Frequency Revelator is present in all the continents of the World. You may contact us from any part of the world so that we can refer you to the Resident Ministry Pastors and Associates in respective nations. Our offices and those of the ministry's publishing company (Global Destiny Publishing House (GDP House), are ready to dispatch any books requested from any part of the world.

Email:
frequency.revelator@gmail.com

Cell phone:
0027622436745
0027797921646/ 0027785416006

Website:
www.globaldestinypublishers.co.za

About The Author

Social Media Contacts:

The Author is also accessible on Social media via Facebook, twitter, instagram, YouTube, and other latest forms of social networks, as Apostle Frequency Revelator. For direct communication with the Apostle, you may invite him on facebook and read his daily posts. You may also watch Apostle Frequency Revelator on the Dead Raising Channel a.k.a Resurrection TV and other Christian Television channels in your area.

Christian products:

You may also purchase DVDs, CDs, MP3s and possibly order all of the 21 anointed books published by Apostle Frequency Revelator, either as hard cover books or e-books. E-books are available on amazon.com, Baines & Nobles, create space, Kalahari.net and other e-book sites. You may also buy them directly from the author@ www.gdphouse.co.za via paypal. You may also request a collection of all powerful, revelational teachings by Apostle Frequency Revelator and we will promptly deliver them to you.

Ministry Networks & Partnerships:

If you want to partner with Apostle Frequency Revelator in executing this Global vision, partnership is available through divergent apostolic and prophetic ministry visions and spiritual programmes such as the Global School of Resurrection (GSR), Christ Resurrection Movement (CRM), Resurrection TV (a.k.a The Dead Raising Channel), the Global Apostolic & Prophetic Network (GAP), Global Resurrection Centre (GRC), the Global Healing Centre (GHC), Global School of Miracles, Signs and Wonders (SMSW), School of Kingdom Millionaires (SKM), Global Campus Ministry and other avenues. By partnering with Apostle Frequency Revelator, you are in a way joining hands with God's vision and thus setting yourself up for a life of increase, acceleration and superabundance.

GLOBAL MISSIONS, PARTNERSHIPS & COLLABORATIONS:

If it happens that you recieve Miracle money or you demonstrate it on behalf of others, following the reading of this book, please share your testimony with Apostle Frequency Revelator at the contacts above, so that you can strengthen other believers' faith in God all around the world. Your testimony will also be included in the next edition of this book.

If you want to invite Apostle Frequency Revelator to your church, city or community to come and spearhead Resurrection Seminars, Conferences, Dead Raising Training Sessions or conduct a Global School of Resurrection (GSR), whether in (Europe, Australia, Canada, USA, South America, Asia or Africa), you are welcome to do so.

If you want to start a Resurrection Centre or establish the Global School of Resurrection (GSR) in your church, city or community under this movement, you are also welcome to do so. We will be more than willing to send Copies of this book to whichever continent you live.

If you want your church or ministry to be part of the Christ Resurrection Movement (CRM) and join the bandwagon of raising the dead all around the world, you are welcome to be part of this Heaven-ordained commission.

About The Author

If you want more copies of this book so that you can use them in your church for seminars, teachings, conferences, cell groups and global distribution, please don't hesitate to contact Apostle Frequency Revelator so that he can send the copies to whichever continent you are. Upon completion of this book, you may also visit www.amazon.com and under the "Book Review Section," write a brief review, commenting on how this book has impacted your life. This is meant to encourage readership by other believers all around the world.

If you want to donate or give freely to advance this global vision, you may also do so via our ministry website (wwww.resurrectionembassy.org) or contact us at the details provided above. If you need a spiritual covering, impartation or mentorship for your Church or ministry as led by the Holy Spirit, you are welcome to contact us and join the league of dead-raising pastors that we are already mentoring in all continents of the world.

If you have a burning message that you would like to share with the whole world and you would want Apostle Frequency Revelator to help you turn your divine ideas and revelations into script and publish your first book, don't hesitate to contact us and submit a draft of your manuscript at the Global Destiny Publishing House (www.gdphouse.co.za). We will thoroughly polish your script and turn it into an amazing book filled with Throne Room revelations that will impact millions across the globe, glory to Jesus!

The Lord Jesus Christ is coming back soon!

Made in the USA
Lexington, KY
22 September 2017